CW01497957

Class War

A Literary History

Mark Steven

VERSO

London • New York

First published by Verso 2023
© Mark Steven 2023

All rights reserved

The moral rights of the author have been asserted

1 3 5 7 9 10 8 6 4 2

Verso
UK: 6 Meard Street, London W1F 0EG
US: 388 Atlantic Avenue, Brooklyn, NY 11217
versobooks.com

Verso is the imprint of New Left Books

ISBN-13: 978-1-83976-069-3
ISBN-13: 978-1-83976-071-6 (UK EBK)
ISBN-13: 978-1-83976-072-3 (US EBK)

British Library Cataloguing in Publication Data
A catalogue record for this book is available from the British Library

Library of Congress Cataloging-in-Publication Data
A catalog record for this book is available from the Library of Congress

Typeset by Hewer Text UK Ltd, Edinburgh
Printed and bound by CPI Group (UK) Ltd, Croydon, CR0 4YY

Class War

Ah! are there other wars, beside the wars of sword and fire?
And are there other sorrows, beside the sorrows of poverty?
And are there other joys, beside the joys of riches and ease?
And is there not one law for both the lion and the ox?
— William Blake, *Visions of the Daughters of Albion*

there are those who can tell you
how to make molotov cocktails, flamethrowers,
bombs whatever
you might be needing
find them and learn, define
your aim clearly, choose your ammo
with that in mind
— Diane di Prima, "Revolutionary Letter #7"

Contents

Acknowledgements   ix

Introduction: Class War Now   1

  1.   The Burning South   25

  2.   Army of Redressers   45

  3.   Defend the City   66

  4.   School of War   88

  5.   Towards a Red Army   107

  6.   Protracted Peoples' Wars   128

  7.   For Complete Disorder   150

  8.   The Armed Nucleus   172

  9.   Fighting after Fascism   196

10.   Army of the Wronged   218

Postscript: No War But Class War   241

Notes   251

Index   277

Acknowledgements

The idea for this book arrived in the heat of an Australian summer while boxing up the remnants of our family's quarter of the Annandale Commune, a few days before we relocated to the southwest of England. Four and a half years later, I'm writing these acknowledgements from a pub in Cornwall, where it might once again be summer, but the antipodean heat and all it comprised now feel so distant as to be unreal. Between then and now, there and here, this book and its author have accrued an immense debt of gratitude. First and foremost, thanks are due to John Merrick at Verso, who believed in this project from the start, who expertly edited the manuscript, and whose irrepressible camaraderie has been a crucial enabling force. I'm also thankful to Leo Hollis, without whose initial interventions this book would have been a very different entity. My thinking about class, war, literature, and revolution, and much of this book's historical content, has been sharpened by discussion with numerous comrades, often taking place on picket lines, during protests, in response to mobilizations, and always with an orientation towards conspiracy. At the University of Exeter, I am indebted to Chris Campbell, Beci Carver, Michael Flexer, Regenia Gagnier, Ting Guo, Aidan Power, Peter Riley, Alessia Risi, Laura Salisbury, Philip Schwyzer, Rob Turner, and Paul Young – their intelligence, militancy, and friendship has made for an exceptionally spirited milieu in which to work. At Exeter, it has been an immense privilege to teach three cohorts of brilliant students through my seminar on class war and modern literature. These multi-denominational leftists have been an ongoing source of both inspiration and edification – and are, I am sure, going to set this idyll aflame. Elsewhere, Alex Howard remains the best of friends and the most generous of readers. Andrew Brooks, Joshua Clover, Treasa De Loughry, Liam Grealy, Kristin Grogan, Helen Groth, Dominick Knowles, Coleen Lye, Astrid Lorange, Julian Murphet, Chris Nealon, Lucy Powell, and Alicia Williamson are all models of intellectual generosity and comradely support. Without my family, this book would not exist in the first place: they are the conditions of possibility for everything else. When I first started writing it, Finn couldn't recognize more than a handful of letters; he now devours books faster than I do and reads with the most gloriously mongrel of accents. Jack, who entered this world in March 2020, remains – like Karl Marx before him – interstate and stateless. Also like Marx, he is a red menace of the highest order. And Kate Montague, the best of everyone I have known, is a militant feminist whose intellect, tenacity, and belligerence will see our class to victory, or nothing else will. While your refusal to indulge anything less than an equitable division of domestic labour keeps me grounded, your sense of justice is the compass by which I measure all things: this book is for you. *Take heart, we will continue to meet with whatever life has in store for us. Take my word for it, together we will fight it out all right and we'll never forget to appreciate thankfully the tiniest bits of beauty and goodness that are left over.*

Introduction

Class War Now

Ours is the age of class war. We talk about it all the time. Barely a day goes by without class war appearing in one headline or another.

Those with most to lose sense it viscerally. In February 2019, *Le Monde diplomatique* published an article about the *gilets jaunes* titled 'France's Class Wars', announcing that 'elites have not felt such fear in half a century, and it's not the usual fear of losing an election, failing to "reform" or seeing their shares slide on the stock market, but fear of insurrection, revolt, and loss of power'.[1] Two months later, at a conference held by the Milken Institute in Beverly Hills, 4,000 well-heeled guests listened to billionaires rejoice in the free market and discuss the theme of 'driving shared prosperity'. Casting a shadow over their celebrations, however, was the spectral threat of an increasingly popular socialism. 'What's really coming is class warfare', lectured Alan Schwartz, executive chair of Guggenheim Partners. 'Throughout centuries what we've seen when the masses think the elites have too much, one of two things happens: legislation to redistribute the wealth ... or revolution to redistribute poverty'.[2]

During the summer of 2020, the convulsions of that revolution were felt in the United States, when hundreds of thousands of men and women took to the streets in collective rage against

racialized police violence. Redistribution took the form of looting. Commentators across the political spectrum identified both
the inequalities and the militancy that informed this movement,
and with that the defenders of the establishment felt fear. 'Excuse
me', wrote one, as though calling the manager in a restaurant,
'but a violent mob marauding through the streets of Chicago,
taking what they please and causing mass destruction is a classic
example of class warfare, not racial justice'.[3]

Reactionary distress follows political disturbance, codifying
social movements into enemy combatants. This is especially true
across Latin America, where open warfare is a recent memory
and mass discontent is frequently hijacked by the far right: riots
in Colombia are 'like a civil war with civilians worried for their
homes and property, and the police on one side, and on the
other side protesters . . . wanting to impose this anarchy and this
chaos in our neighbourhood'; in Chile, the state is 'at war against
a powerful and implacable enemy who doesn't respect anything
or anyone, and who's willing to use limitless violence and criminal acts'; and in Haiti, 'the streets can sometimes look like
screens from Battle Tech: Urban Warfare, with camouflage-
wearing police shooting in the direction of young men throwing
rocks, their faces covered by bandanas'.[4]

Any mention of class war suggests direct, unmediated
conflict, potentially conjuring an image of embattled pickets
facing down the mounted riot brigade. However, its popular
deployment often reaches beyond the immediacy of hurled
bricks and flaming cars to grasp at something more sedimented and systemic. Though class war appears to be experienced and enacted by individuals, it also describes the kinds
of violence that exceed individual experience. This has become
increasingly evident through the global pandemic, in which a
person's risk of infection has manifestly depended on their
position within an exploitative social hierarchy. The onset of
COVID-19 forced many into potentially fatal circumstances
– in worksites, markets, prisons, and elsewhere – for the
economic benefit of those kept safe. Within this context, access
to masks and vaccines as well as the resources with which to

shelter in place have all been hailed as expressions of an ongoing war. While politicians – like Donald Trump and Andrew Cuomo in the United States, Boris Johnson and Matt Hancock in the United Kingdom – used military rhetoric to amplify the apparent seriousness of their intent on combatting the pandemic, for many critical thinkers that kind of language marks the displacement of social antipathy into something like patriotic nostalgia.

'COVID-19 is no respecter of class', wrote the public health expert Sarah Jones, 'anyone can get sick. But some people are in more danger than others, and not just because of their biology. America exists in stratum. Each layer nestles next to the other, but they are distinct, kept apart by barriers that are difficult to breach'. All of which points to a concluding diagnosis: 'The story COVID-19 tells about America is an ugly one. There is a class war, and the rich are winning'.[5] For the political economist Grace Blakeley, the United Kingdom's economic response to the pandemic, which directed state funding to the police, the armed forces, and border control instead of social care, universal credit, and education, coheres with a singular aim: 'to wage class war on working people across the UK'.[6]

As the pandemic's economic recession accelerates the rise of insecurity and inequality across the globe, that war has extended beyond any one state and into the world-system. According to the economist and former Greek minister of finance Yanis Varoufakis, 'The European Union's response to the pandemic, including the EU recovery fund currently under deliberation, is bound to intensify this class war, and deal another blow to Europe's socioeconomic model', leaving it destabilized relative to the United States and China.[7] Elsewhere, in underdeveloped, colonial, and apartheid states, the material differential has been even more pronounced. In India, for instance, where seasonal agricultural workers depend for survival on both service work and public transport, the pandemic has been nothing short of apocalyptic. 'From the standpoint of India's working poor and her destitute masses', reads an anthropological study, 'it was as if the class war had suddenly turned nuclear'.[8]

The mobilization of state resources while human lives are sacrificed in order to protect economic accumulation in the global north is something of a rehearsal for the ongoing devastation now euphemized as climate change. And the metaphorical warfare continues. 'The war against Covid-19', writes the academic and climate activist Andreas Malm, 'could be conceived as a classical war, drawing on all the paraphernalia of patriotic pride – a nation protecting itself, as in previous moments of danger; a people sheltering behind the bulwark of the state – whereas a war against CO_2 would tend to slip out of that mould'. Locally as well as globally, at levels of cause and effect, climate change is a matter of class. Thus its combat is understood as a form of class war. 'It would be a war for the benefit of one's own and foreign others', Malm concludes. 'First of all, it would be a war for the poor'.[9]

Matthew T. Huber, author of *Climate Change as Class War*, formulates this in the language of Marxism. The fight to save the planet from ecological catastrophe is, in his account, 'a *class struggle* over relations that underpin our social and ecological relationship with nature and the climate itself: ownership and control of production'.[10] Similarly, political scientist Jodi Dean has argued that class war provides the historical backdrop against which climate change is taking place as well as the parameters within which it is to be fought. 'The class war unfolding in the context of the changing climate is an imperialist war', she writes. 'Those parts of the world most impacted by imperialist exploitation and colonialist plunder are the first to be hit by the colossal damage of rising sea levels and disrupted weather patterns. This is one of the reasons Indigenous and colonized people are leading the climate struggle from the frontlines'.[11]

While rebellious mobilizations, from the Xingu River through Standing Rock to the global climate strikes, have all been compared to class war, one of the idea's most striking invocations has emerged in response to ecocidal redlining. In September 2021, the gated community of Nordelta, built on the lush wetlands north of Buenos Aires, found itself under attack from capybaras, who destroyed manicured lawns, injured domestic pets, and caused traffic accidents. In effect, the capybaras have opposed a development that, by building out vast stretches of impervious surfaces, invites flooding and fires, the destructive consequences of which are lived by the local poor. As these semi-aquatic mammals have inspired both armed resistance from the rich locals and revolutionary graffiti from anonymous comrades, perhaps it is not surprising that the local press acknowledges them as insurgents. 'While this may at first blush seem like an infestation', concludes one article, 'it's really more like class warfare; a struggle for land justice'.[12]

* * *

Class war is happening right now. Its arena is everywhere. Its combatants are everyone. And yet, despite a collective willingness to acknowledge its existence, to invoke it instinctively or embrace it as a narrative trope, we don't really know what it is. Bertolt Brecht's 1931 adaptation of Maxim Gorky's realist novel *Mother* dramatizes the conceptual challenge. In the play, the eponymous metalworker and her comrades are taught to read. Their teacher writes three words on the chalkboard: 'hat', 'dog', 'fish'. The students are quick to protest that this is no useful vocabulary. 'We don't talk about "Hats"', insists an unnamed worker, to which the teacher retorts that no matter what they talk about they will nevertheless use the letters in 'Hat'.

> One of the Workers: But the words 'Class War' have letters in them too.
> The Teacher: Right, but you have to start with the simplest, not the hardest. 'Hat' is simple.
> Sostakovitch: 'Class War' is a lot simpler.
> The Teacher: There's no such thing as Class War. Let's be clear about that.
> Sostakovitch *standing up*: I can't learn anything from you if you think there's no class war.[13]

Class war: nothing could be simpler. Or as contested. For these metalworkers, class war is innate, an essential part of their being, and they too are an essential part of it. 'The W in "Class War"', we are later told, 'is exactly the same as the W in "Worker"'.[14] But their teacher cannot grasp this, it seems, because a life of detached curiosity has rendered him unable to think concretely and experientially, only in rules and abstractions. The semi-literate metalworkers intuit something fundamentally alien to their teacher's learning. For us, perhaps, talking of class war seems to invoke thoughts and actions and historical episodes that we don't encounter as consistently or as affectively with related narrative devices. Perhaps it connotes something more militantly combative than class struggle or class conflict. Perhaps, too, it suggests something more specific than revolution, revolt, uprising, insurgency, or insurrection, as though to imply the silent modifier 'armed'. But these categories are endlessly troubled. Class war will not be understood from intuition alone.

Revolutionary discourse will help orient our thinking. Here, class war is used less as a technical term and more as an affective catalyst, reframing actions through military concepts and rhetoric without offering so much as a program or practical strategy. That is what we encounter with Marx and Engels when, in 1848, they summarize the development of the proletariat and the bourgeoisie. So begins their famous chapter:

> The history of all hitherto existing society is the history of class struggles. Freeman and slave, patrician and plebeian, lord and serf, guild-master and journeyman, in a word, oppressor and oppressed, stood in constant opposition to one another, carried on an uninterrupted, now hidden, now open fight, a fight that each time ended, either in a revolutionary reconstitution of society at large, or in the common ruin of the contending classes.[15]

Capitalism is unique, they reason, because it has 'simplified class antagonism' by dividing the whole of society 'into two great hostile camps, into two great classes directly facing each other – Bourgeoisie and Proletariat'. By the chapter's end, the 'fight' between the classes has become so absolute that class struggle

(*Klassenkampf*) modulates into civil war (*Bürgerkrieg*) and then open revolution (*offene Revolution*): 'In depicting the most general phases of the development of the proletariat, we traced the more or less veiled civil war, raging within existing society, up to the point where that war breaks out into open revolution, and where the violent overthrow of the bourgeoisie lays the foundation for the sway of the proletariat'.[16]

The most lucid gloss on these terms is from the philosopher Étienne Balibar, for whom the 'war model' of class analysis invents 'a new concept of the political'. According to Balibar, 'the best way to understand this is to develop the text's indication concerning an oscillation between "phases" when the civil war is latent, or invisible, and other "phases" when it becomes open or visible'.[17] The work of politics is to undertake the transition from one phase to the other, from the grinding brutality of the veiled civil war to the presumably intentional, organized, and openly violent confrontation with the bourgeois and their institutions. In other words, revolution means to see the exploited class waging war against the economic regime and interstate system that maintains its exploitation and whose beneficiaries will militarily defend their advantages with everything they have. It is in this sense that militants uphold civil war as part of the revolutionary process.

For Lenin, thinking about the Paris Commune of 1871, the proletariat 'must never forget that in certain conditions the class struggle assumes the form of armed conflict and civil war; there are times when the interests of the proletariat call for ruthless extermination of its enemies in open armed clashes'.[18] Or for Mao, civil war marks the passage from contradiction to antagonism. In his view, 'the contradiction between the exploiting and the exploited classes' has persisted through slave society, feudal society, and into modern capitalism as a 'struggle' between the two; 'but it is not until the contradiction between the two classes develops to a certain stage that it assumes the form of open antagonism and develops into revolution. The same holds', he adds, 'for the transformation of peace into war in class society'.[19] Temporality, then, is one of class war's distinguishing features, and this is true of Marx and Engels as well as Lenin, Mao, and many others besides. When revolutionaries talk about class war, they tend to do so in a hybrid future-present tense: class war is coming but it's also already upon us. Battlefronts are opening up, but something else is looming on the horizon.

Ramifying complexity, class war is at once a metaphor and a statement of fact. As Trotsky once said about the militarization of labour in the service of revolution, 'this is only an analogy – but an analogy very rich in content'.[20] As metaphor or analogy, class war is used to describe the generalized struggle between those of us who must work in order to survive and those who benefit from our dispossession. 'At bottom', write the anonymous authors who call themselves the Invisible Committee, 'the rejection of war only expresses an infantile or senile refusal to recognize the existence of otherness. War is not carnage, but the logic that regulates the contact of heterogeneous powers. It is waged everywhere, in countless forms, and more often than not by peaceful means'.[21] This is the 'more or less veiled civil war', an expression of protracted class struggle.

As literal statement, class war also describes the military project of toppling states, suppressing the enemy, and abolishing capitalism. Georg Lukács invoked something along these lines while concluding his theory of class consciousness. He insisted that 'the proletariat only perfects itself by annihilating and transcending itself, by creating the classless society through the successful conclusion of its own class struggle', which, during the 1920s, had modulated into open warfare. 'The struggle for this society, in which the dictatorship of the proletariat is merely a phase', Lukács continues, 'is not just a battle waged against an external enemy, the bourgeoisie. It is equally the struggle of the proletariat against itself: against the devastating and degrading effects of the capitalist system upon its class consciousness'.[22] Such is the 'open revolution' and 'violent overthrow', the class struggle escalated into pitched battle.

Specifically: the revolutionary invocation of class war raises consciousness of the former struggle as a point of departure into the latter conflict. It seeks to recruit and to motivate comrades from a state of contradiction into acts of antagonism. It is to speak of struggle in a voice the novelist and historian of revolution China Miéville compares, in his analysis of Marx and Engels, to that of a military commander rallying the troops ahead of battle. It is, for Miéville, 'perfectly understandable that our imaginary officer insists to her soldiers that they will win, whatever private doubts she may have. And what's more, delivered well, such an inspirational claim *increases the chances that it will be the truth*'.[23] Class war means escalation. Its mood is imperative. Its tone exclamatory. Such is what we encounter in one of its clearest forms with Mark Fisher's response in 2007 to the grim resignation with which a culture of New Labour abides with Tory austerity: 'A class war is being waged, but only one side is fighting. Choose your side. Choose your weapons'.[24] The proclamation of class war is, in designations such as this, what linguists might describe as a speech act: a performative utterance that, when said, is also a kind of action – like, for instance, a formal declaration of war, which not only announces but also commences the conflict.

* * *

Despite its apparent acceptance in both popular and critical discourse, we must nevertheless be careful with this way of thinking, as the theorist of the riot Joshua Clover avers. 'Talk of class war cannot help but threaten a certain reductionism itself', he cautions. 'It does not seem, at least in the orthodox sense it has acquired, entirely adequate to the … present, when class belonging provides no less a limit than a logic for political mobilization'.[25] In that orthodox sense, class is defined by specific forms of labour and employment, thus becoming an exclusive identitarian category that renders as synonymous with white, male, industrial workers, a social entity whose species-being is derived from their increasingly scarce union jobs at the factory or in the mines. While that class has, from a social as well as revolutionary standpoint, effectively decomposed, we also know that capitalism secures ruling class power through the manipulation of gendered, racial, and ethnic prejudice – that it is what the prison abolitionist Ruth Wilson Gilmore has described as 'a death-dealing displacement of difference into hierarchies that organize relations within and between the planet's sovereign political territories'.[26] To meet that system as an enemy, at a time when the fight against exploitation necessarily comingles with the need to abolish other forms of oppression, exclusion, and injustice, our understanding of class needs to be flexible enough to include intersecting social relations without ever becoming so vague as to be meaningless.

This is not a novel suggestion. But it is one with which any militant worth their salt must reckon. For the German revolutionary Clara Zetkin, writing in 1909, sex and class were relative terms of human emancipation: 'The working-class women will never win their full emancipation in a struggle of all women without difference of class against the social monopolies of the male sex, but only in the class war of all the exploited, without difference of sex, against all who exploit, without difference of sex'.[27] Or as the feminist activist Selma James phrases it:

> Social power relations of the sexes, races, nations and generations are precisely, then, particularized forms of class relations. These power relations within the working class weaken us in the power struggle between the classes. They are the particularized forms of indirect rule, one section of the class colonizing another and through this capital imposing its own will on us all.[28]

Following this trajectory, many of today's militants embrace an expanded definition of class for practical as well as ideological purposes. 'Class', writes the Endnotes collective, 'remains the primary source of our separations – old fashioned Marxist sociology is still in many ways valid – but class belonging is today calibrated by a multitude of variables such as age, gender, geography, race, or religion that act as channels, as well as real limits, for social struggles, and make identity politics a real expression of class struggle'.[29] To insist on this is to forestall reductive definitions of the revolutionary class as identical with the working class, a collective subject that has historical associations with large-scale industry in core states, so as to affirm instead the expanded proletariat, a heterogenous population of the dispossessed.

* * *

What, then, do we really mean when we talk about class war? To answer this question, we need to clarify what class war's two constitutive nouns really mean both individually and together, in theory and in practice.

The literature on class is deep and riven by polemics, but here we can summarize two perspectives – the sociological and the historical – whose overlapping terminology will be useful. For the sociologist Erik Olin Wright, class exists in the relationship between structure and formation, between abstract vertical categories that determine social being and the concrete groupings of living humans who experience those categories. 'If class structure is defined by social relations between classes', he writes, 'class formation is defined by social relations within classes, social relations which forge collectivities engaged in struggle'. Wright's solution to the relationship between class structure and class formation is exploitation. A class is defined by its capacity to exploit or be exploited, and it is within these relations of exploitation that 'common interest' is said to originate. 'Class formation', he says, 'refers to the formation of organized collectives within that class structure on the basis of the interests shaped by that class structure'.[30]

For the historian E. P. Thompson, class is defined not by any sort of category but only by those 'as they live their own history, and, in the end, this is its only definition'.[31] In this view, class is a relationship and not a thing, an historical phenomenon as opposed to an empirical category. Class is what happens when men and women, 'as a result of common experiences (inherited or shared), feel and articulate the identity of their interests as between themselves, and as against other men whose interests are different from (and usually opposed to) theirs'. For Thompson, class formation is not determined by class structure but is the result of collective human agency as mediated by the relations of production, conditioned by capitalist expropriation and the consequent intensification of exploitation. 'The working class did not rise like the sun at an appointed time', he says. 'It was present at its own making'.[32]

Shared across both views, whose differences reside at the level of human agency, is an emphasis on 'common interest' – an undertheorized term that seems to describe those mobilizing currents that operate as something more than a reflexive action, as something other than instinct or drive, and which appear instead as collective desires born of material necessity, potentially inspiring action but without necessarily producing it.[33]

For those of us committed to revolutionary social transformation, class is not just a concept with which to interpret the world but a force to change it. Better still, class is a question to be answered, a riddle to be solved: How to mobilize, as a class formation, against the entire structure of classes? This is what Rosa Luxemburg once described, against the beating drums of national chauvinism and the opening up of an imperial war of extermination, as 'the crux of the matter, the Gordian knot of proletarian politics and its long term future', namely the need to escalate the ongoing class struggle into actual civil war. 'The proletariat does not lack for postulates, prognoses, slogans', she says. 'It lacks deeds, the capacity for effective resistance to imperialism at the decisive moment, to intervene against it during the war and to convert the old slogan "war against war" into practice'.[34] If it is in the common interest of the exploited class to extract itself from exploitation and if that can only be achieved as a class by eliminating exploitation and its enabling structures, then perhaps the foregoing explanations of class contain within themselves a revolutionary imperative.

A version of this argument, emphasizing the determinant force of common interest, is rehearsed by the political theorist Ellen Meiksins Wood, who does not wholly endorse it. 'Since the material interests of the working class cannot be satisfied within the existing framework of social relations', she writes, 'and since a pursuit of these interests will inevitably encounter the opposing interests of capital, the process of struggle will tend to expose its own limitations, spill over into the political arena, and carry the battle closer to the centers of capitalist power'.[35] But that won't do, not least because it implies rigid determination without much in the way of agency. Wood knows this. 'Concerted action by widely scattered and disparate working-class formations', she clarifies, 'even when joined by common class interests, is not something that can happen spontaneously. A united working class in this sense is certainly not "given" directly in the relations of production'.[36] To suggest that impulse equates with action, that common interests unleash organized political force, would be wishful thinking. To put it forcefully: any presumption of the capacity to act, and to act together, based on location within a class structure or even shared experience within a class formation obscures the challenge of forging those solidarities that might otherwise lead to collective transformation.

This should be uncontroversial to anyone with a practical view of movement building. Mike Davis, an undeniable expert in these matters, writes that 'increased competition for jobs (or at least the perception of such competition) has inflamed working-class resentment against the new credentialed elites and the high-tech rich, but equally it has narrowed and poisoned traditional cultures of solidarity, transforming the revolt against globalization into a virulent anti-immigrant backlash'.[37] Though it might be increasingly apparent in our era of jobless growth, this idea is hardly new. In fact, it can be found in Marx's own writing on class.

While many have lamented that the incomplete third volume of *Capital* famously ends a few paragraphs into the chapter on class, it is worth remembering that what we have of this chapter comprises a rejoinder to the notion of common interest. 'The first question to be answered', Marx writes, 'is this: What constitutes a class? – and the reply to this follows naturally from the reply to another question, namely: What makes wage-laborers, capitalists and landlords constitute the three great social classes?' Marx is swift to problematize any affirmative identity based on class survival, citing the 'infinite fragmentation of interest and rank into which the division of social labour splits laborers as well as capitalists and landlords'.[38] The point, however, is not to dismiss the actuality of class, to discount common interests based in the lived experience of material conditions, but to face the challenge head on and recognize that translating commonality into action requires some other catalyst.

Beginning with this premise, that neither class structure nor class formation is the catalytic force of mobilization, that actual revolution needs something more than the presumption of common interest, this book seeks to show that a class is forged not only through exploitation and dispossession, which irreducibly shape a commonality of experience, but also through antagonism – and that through antagonism, class is made and remade into something revolutionary.

* * *

Antagonism, in the form of material political combat, predominates in historical memory. We know it from struggles for decolonization and independence across the Caribbean and up into the Americas, throughout continental India, Africa, and Asia, as well as in Irish republicanism and the Palestinian Intifada. We have seen it in the revolutions and revolutionary armies in Russia, China, and Latin America; from the armed action of groups ranging from the Luddites and the Molly Maguires to the Red Army Faction and the Black Panthers; and with dispersed network forms like Italian autonomia, the Zapatista Army of National Liberation, and the Arab Spring. We know it from when the fight for workers' rights transforms into armed combat against the state's paramilitary guard: from the Coal Field Strikes of 1913, which became the Colorado Coalfield War and then the Ludlow Massacre, to the UK Miners' Strike of 1984, which reached its bloody apotheosis with the Battle of Orgreave. 'Pitch fucking battle now', or so the novelist David Peace has reimagined Orgreave from the standpoint of its participants. 'Ten thousand men kicking the living fuck out of each other – Like something from bloody Middle Ages. Dark Ages'.[39]

That kind of antagonism is with us today, from anti-fascist and anti-police mobilizations through ongoing battles against colonial apartheid to the blazing fires of riot that engulf the planetary terrain. 'The most realistic conclusion of this story is war', wrote the Italian communist philosopher Franco 'Bifo' Berardi, looking at the state of Europe in 2015: 'Civil war is clearly visible not only at the Southern border where corpses are floating on the sea, and at the Eastern border where Putin is deploying 40 new generation nuclear warheads, but also at the Italo-French border, at the Railway Station of Milano, and in hundreds of European cities where nationalist hatred is getting organized'. This analysis echoes Marx and Engels, and arrives at the same question posed by Luxemburg. 'Prepare for war', Berardi says, 'this is the only suggestion. But here the most difficult question pops up: how can we update the old call to turn their imperialist war into our revolutionary civil war?'[40]

The answer pursued here is that civil war is itself a social determinant, a quantifiable force of revolutionary becoming. This is a belief shared with numerous revolutionaries who have undertaken the work of building solidarity through antagonism, shaping new class formations through civil war, in situations where militant and military force enact social transformation at the level of individual psychology no less than collective identity. 'Civil war *united* working class and the peasantry, and this is a *guarantee of invincible strength*', wrote Lenin in December 1922. 'Civil war trained and tempered . . . *our best Party workers were in the army*'.[41] The philosopher and journalist Régis Debray would make a similar claim in 1967, reprising Lenin's formulation at the height of Latin America's guerrilla phase: 'Revolutionaries make revolutionary civil wars, but to an even greater extent it is revolutionary civil war that makes revolutionaries'.[42]

The American revolutionaries James and Grace Lee Boggs likewise insist that rebellion, in the forms of insurrection and revolt, is socially transformative at the level of group identities. While, in their analysis, nothing less than the complete transformation of individual and collective consciousness is the distinguishing measure between the rebellious act and the actuality of revolution – 'projecting the notion of a more human human being', they describe the revolutionary task – rebellion nevertheless manifests 'the assertion of their humanity on the part of the oppressed', forging a new sociality in opposition to the way things are:

> Rebellions inform both the oppressed and everybody else that a situation has become intolerable. They establish a form of communication among the oppressed themselves and at the same time they open the eyes and ear of the people who have been blind and deaf to the fate of their fellow citizens. Rebellions break the threads that have been holding the system together and throw into question its legitimacy and the supposed permanence of existing institutions. They shake up old values so that relations between individuals and between groups within the society are unlikely ever to be the same again. The inertia of the society has been interrupted.[43]

What is true of rebellion in the deindustrializing core is also true of decolonization in the global peripheries. According to C. L. R. James, writing on the Haitian Revolution, 'Toussaint's soldiers and generals, illiterates and ex-slaves, had been moulded by the same revolution. An army', he adds, 'is a miniature of the society which produces it'.[44] Frantz Fanon had similar things to say about the Algerian Civil War. 'Decolonization never takes place unnoticed, for it influences individuals and modifies them fundamentally', he wrote as a practicing psychiatrist and committed militant. 'It transforms spectators crushed with their inessentiality into privileged actors, with the grandiose glare of history's floodlights upon them. It brings a natural rhythm into existence, introduced by new men, and with it a new language and a new humanity'.[45]

There is ample historical evidence for such claims. 'This is the fundamental passage of modern civil war', write Michael Hardt and Antonio Negri, 'the formation of dispersed and irregular rebel forces into an army'. As they suggest via an illuminating thought experiment, that passage is as socially transformative as it is militarily practical:

The modern class wars and wars of liberation brought with them an extraordinary production of subjectivity. Imagine what happened in the Mexican countryside or in Southeast Asia or Africa when the incitement to rebellion and the formation of a people's army in a foundational, constituent war emerged from a world of misery and subjugation; imagine what profound energies this call solicited, because it is a matter of a call not simply to arms but to the construction of individual and social bodies.[46]

The salient part of Hardt and Negri's capacious argument is that civil war creates and consolidates new class formations no less than it emerges from within an extant class structure. The revolutionary army and the revolutionary class are one and the same, materially entwined in their mutual destiny.

Leaping from the historical to the speculative, this way of thinking reaches its limit with critical theorist Fredric Jameson's potentially scandalous vision of the army as utopian, and with his insistence that an army might not only end class through force but also serve as a positive model for classless society in and of itself. For Jameson – writing from a specifically American context – the armed forces constitute an instance of dual power, a state-within-the-state, with a separate culture contained within but distinct from civilian society. And while most soldiers enlist out of economic necessity, the army provides basic services – such as food, clothing, shelter, education, and medical care – without the market myths of scarcity and austerity. 'The army', he says,

is virtually the only institution in modern society whose members are obliged to associate with all kinds of people on an involuntary, non-elective basis, beginning with social class as such. This forced association, initially restricted to males, has been a useful mechanism, in the age of nationalism and the modern nation-state, for securing a certain collective unification and levelling (including the imposition of a national language).[47]

Without affirming the classlessness of any one army, a form that tends to be as xenophobic as it is misogynistic, we can nevertheless share in the belief that class is a relationship of commonality but also of antagonism, and that, in the combination of the two, class might yet provide the engine of revolutionary social transformation.

'Class war does not happen on an abstract board toting up profits and losses', the feminist philosopher Silvia Federici has reminded us, 'it needs a terrain'.[48] That the terrain of class war stretches across the globe necessitates thinking beyond the political economy of industrial labour in the global north to embrace a much wider array of geographically embedded social forms that are otherwise revolutionary. Class will therefore be understood here as one with a subaltern radicalism that faces off against colonial dispossession and military occupation, that fights against all kinds of gendered and racialized oppressions, finding its antecedent in mobilizations that first issued forth from the global south and which are now taking hold within the post-industrial, crises-ridden core of the capitalist world-system. In this way, the theory of class war can thus be reformulated as the opening up, or internationalization, of the arena of contest – an expansion of conflict, struggle, and organization not only beyond one strata of society but also beyond the nation-state while simultaneously redoubling an emphasis on the strategies and tactics of real combat fought locally. Whether consciously or not, just about every invocation of class war tends to bring with it a long history of anti-capitalist conflict and simultaneously measures itself against a post-capitalist horizon. That is one of the reasons why an account of class war is also an account of politics in the present, and why an account of class war in the present responds to a longer history while reaching toward a post-capitalist future.

* * *

This book is a literary history, but it is committed to literature as something more than a record of past events. With a textual archive comprising letters, slogans, songs, manifestoes, memoirs, and field manuals in addition to novels, poems, and other more obviously literary modes of expression, literature is to be understood here as an active participant in the revolutionary process.

To conceive of conflict at the scale of war, and to develop a potent language with which to inspire comrades to war, revolutionaries have borrowed forms and figures and concepts from literary writing, and in turn they have contributed to an arsenal of ideas and associations identifiable as class war from which future revolutionaries have drawn. In the years before the Paris Commune, for example, literary expression is said to have become newly militant. 'Prose and verse and music disappeared', recalled Louise Michel, 'because we felt so near the drama coming from the street, the true drama, the drama of humanity. The songs of the new epoch were war songs, and there was no room for anything else'.[49] Or Trotsky, in explaining his history of the Russian Revolution, insists that social transformation be understood in relation to the narrative arts. He compares his writing to the sheer amount of literary detail afforded bourgeois insularity in the novels of Marcel Proust. 'It would seem that one might, at least with equal justice, demand attention to a series of collective historic dramas which lifted hundreds of millions of human beings out of non-existence, transforming the character of nations and intruding forever into the life of all mankind'.[50] For Fanon, the native writer addressing their own people in a decolonial struggle composes 'a literature of combat', a unique narrative form that 'calls on the whole people to fight for their existence as a nation'.[51]

Taking formulations such as these as a guiding principle, the following chapters demonstrate how, within the tempest of anti-capitalist mobilization, revolutionary leaders look beyond political theory and military science to draw from literary writing in order to imagine and reimagine the significance of their actions. By asking what and how revolutionaries were reading as well as how they were writing and being written about, we learn that class war owes its viral ubiquity to its existence as a narrative concept – in the way historical events are reflected within the contested space of literature but also in the way militants have drawn inspiration from and composed literature in formulating their strategic and ideological positions.

Examples of this kind of literary thinking abound, beginning with Marx's well-known claim that he learned more from reading the novels of Balzac than from all the historians, economists, and political theorists combined. We see it in English radicals engaged with literary romance and the Communards' invention of naturalism; we see it in Lenin's affection for the novels of Tolstoy and in Mao's compositions in classical poetic verse; we see it in Huey P. Newton's engagement with carceral and slave narratives and with Assata Shakur, in hospital and under arrest, shouting lines from Claude McKay's best-known sonnet at her captors. 'I read them over and over', she says, 'until i was sure the guards had heard every word. The poems were my message to them'.[52] Indeed, we see literature in the words and deeds of countless revolutionaries, right down to Che Guevara's insistence that, in addition to the essential if instrumental rations of soap and toothpaste, the guerrilla combatant should always carry a book in their pack to read and share with other members in the band. 'These books', he says, 'can be good biographies of past heroes, histories, or economic geographies, preferably of the country, and works of general character that will serve to raise the cultural level of the soldiers and discourage the tendency toward gambling or other undesirable forms of passing the time'.[53]

While literature reminds us of flesh and blood combatants, of the lived experiences that take place under the homogenizing abstraction of common interest, of the real glory and the happiness as well as the doubts and misgivings that underwrite human struggle, revolutionaries have committed to fighting not only as a group of combatants but also as readers and writers. It is in such a way that class war emerges as a rhetorical device and narrative concept attached to real people enacting revolutionary measures before enjoying its half-life in poems, novels, and drama.

Combining historical description, political theorizing, and textual analysis, this book is intended as a guide to class war. Its chapters are written as interdependent episodes that together span over two centuries across the globe. There are, connecting these chapters, two interrelated narratives which intersect with and revise one another at exemplary moments. One narrative is told from a broadly Euro-American perspective and provisionally retains an orthodox conceptualization of class. This is a story about industrial disputes, democratic representation, and large-scale combat operations – a story that begins in England during the First Industrial Revolution, passes back through France during the Second Empire into the American Gilded Age, to finally reach something like its apotheosis in revolutionary Russia. The other narrative, which challenges and revises the first one, occurs beyond the traditional sites of capitalist industry in spaces of colonial occupation, systemic underdevelopment, and imperial resource extraction. This story has more to do with wars of decolonization, with guerrilla insurgency, and with acts of terrorism. It begins in the Caribbean and makes its way through China, Africa, and Latin America, before returning to the core of the world-system, in Europe and the United States, where combat methods and class formations that developed on the global periphery resurface on the streets and in opposition to fascist rule and the police state. Together, these chapters are not just a history but moments in history that demonstrably intercalate with one another and together form a prehistory of the present. While this book ranges across a large historical canvas, it is intended as capacious without ever claiming to be comprehensive. It does not survey the entire terrain of class war, which would be impossible within any single volume. Instead, each chapter focuses on a particular instance of class war and shows how revolutionaries in a given historical moment deploy or redeploy the idea. In short, the chapters describe key historical moments and movements that are exemplary both in themselves and because of how they are articulated elsewhere within the *longue durée* of capitalist modernity.

* * *

There are, finally, many places we could begin the story of class war. The German Peasants' War of 1524–5 provides an early iteration of the mutual determinations of class composition and civil warfare. But this conflict was doomed to failure at the level of class solidarity. The terrain on which it was fought and through which its militants were defeated was one of social fragmentation in a country divided into numerous independent, almost totally alien provinces, each subdivided into estates with their own internal factions. So Engels would later lament: 'The only possible grouping of the various troops not according to the greater or smaller singleness of their own actions, but according to the singleness of the particular adversary to whom they succumbed, is most striking proof of the degree of mutual alienation of the peasants in the various provinces'.[54]

Subsequently, the English Civil War of 1640–60 and the French Revolution of 1789 have each been described as class wars. 'The Civil War', writes the historian Christopher Hill, 'was a class war, in which the despotism of Charles I was defended by the reactionary forces of the established Church and conservative landlords'.[55] Within this telling, Oliver Cromwell stands forth as a committed militant; the Diggers and the Levellers as competing radical tendencies; and the beheading of Charles I in 1649 as an act of revolutionary justice. These claims ultimately depend on the class composition of the Roundheads' New Model Army, enabled by a statute of religious toleration and the means by which Cromwell gained popular support from the masses against a superannuated gentry. 'I had rather have a plain, russet-coated Captain', he insisted in 1643, 'that knows what he fights for, and loves what he knows, than that which you call a Gentleman and is nothing else'.[56] Of course, the introduction of a limited constitutional monarchy did not achieve the abolition of class hierarchy, but neither was it a direct continuation of feudal rule; instead, and in opposition to an older regime of property relations, the English Civil War provided the social framework for agrarian capitalism, and so helped authorize class in the sense by which we understand it today.

As a political revolution, Cromwell's victory retrenched extant hierarchies, shifting property from a system of feudal tenure into the hands of an emergent bourgeoisie, so that estates would no longer yield profits via dues but instead through enclosures, rents, and evictions. The religious visionary Gerrard Winstanley made this argument as early as 1650:

> While this Kingly power raigned in one man called Charls, all sort of people complained of oppression, both Gentrie and Common people, because their lands, inclosures, and Copie-holds were intangled, and because their Trades were destroyed by Monopolizing Patentees, and your troubles were that you could not live free from oppression in the earth: Thereupon you that were the Gentrie when you were assembled in Parliament, you called upon the poor Common People to come and help you, and cast out oppression and you that complained are helped and freed, and that top-bow is lopped off the tree of Tyrannie, and Kingly power in that one particular is cast out; but alas oppression is a great tree still, and keeps off the son of freedome from the poor Commons still, he hath many branches and great roots which must be grub'd up, before every one can sing Sions songs in peace.[57]

In gathering popular support to defeat feudalism and open the state to modern capitalism, the English Civil War prefigures the French Revolution, a conflict secretly and opportunistically fomented by a liberal bourgeoisie whose strategy was to weaponize a disenfranchised third estate against the institutions of a more conservative proprietor class.

Assessing the French Revolution, Henri de Saint-Simon's Geneva letters, published in 1803, explain the motivations of the liberal bourgeoisie for the benefit of the outgoing proprietor class, using the extended metaphor of militarily organized combat:

> They succeeded in doing what they wanted. All the institutions which from the outset they had intended to overthrow were

destroyed inevitably; in short, they won the battle and you lost it. This victory was to cost the victors dear; but you who were defeated have suffered even more. A few scientists and artists, victims of the insubordination of their army, were massacred by their own troops. From a moral point of view, they have all had to bear your apparently justified reproaches, for they were responsible for the atrocities committed against you and for the disorders of every kind which their troops were led to commit under the barbarous impulse of ignorance.[58]

Despite the impoverished status of its combatants, this conflict was settled within the propertied classes, which not only left the class system unshaken but also ensured the unfettered advancement of modern capitalism and its modes of dispossession.

By contrast to the transfer of political power from one ruling elite to another, class war moves against the very system provided by the reconstruction of German society under Luther, English society under Cromwell, and French society under Bonaparte. In other words, class war emerged from a subsequent period when hostility between the propertied and the dispossessed morphed into the latter's antagonism toward both property and dispossession. For this reason, our story begins not with the German Peasants' War, the English Civil War, or the French Revolution. Instead, it begins somewhere on the other side of the planet and in their political and economic aftermath, on the island of Saint-Domingue, soon to be reborn under its indigenous name, Haiti.

1

The Burning South

On 8 February 1802, a freed slave turned revolutionary torch-bearer, dispatched a letter to one of his lieutenant generals. The letter detailed strategy for overcoming the armed forces of colonial restoration. Its author was Toussaint Louverture, leader of the Haitian Revolution; its recipient Jean-Jacques Dessalines, commander of the revolt's western military front; and their enemy a recently arrived expeditionary force under the command of Charles Leclerc, veteran of the French Republic's Alpine and Italian campaigns and brother-in-law to Napoleon Bonaparte. The French had landed at Port-au-Prince, the former colony's capital. Their mission was to restore Saint-Domingue, what is now called Haiti, to its former status and to reinstate the system of slavery.

The letter, headed by two revolutionary watchwords – 'LIBERTY. EQUALITY.' – ordered Dessalines to burn the garrison to which the French troops had been posted. 'Endeavor', Louverture instructs his commander, 'by all the means of force and address, to set that place on fire; it is constructed entirely of wood; you have only to send into it some faithful emissaries'.[1] This would not be the first time French soldiers were met by fire on Haitian soil. Louverture's other lieutenant general, Henri Christophe, had already delivered on a similar warning, which he had put to Leclerc in writing. 'If you put in force your threats of hostility', Christophe had warned, 'I shall make the resistance which becomes a general officer; and, should the chance of war be yours, you shall not enter Cape Town till it be reduced to ashes, nay, even in the ruins will I renew the combat'.[2] Christophe is said to have led by example, setting his own house ablaze before taking an army into the island's mountainous interior.

The resulting inferno appears as a spectacular set piece throughout local accounts of the revolution, not least in *Stella*, Émeric Bergeaud's mythic retelling of the Haitian Revolution. Often described as the nation's first novel, it narrates history through the myth of Romulus and Remus, who are presented to the reader as 'collective beings' who, combined, embody the personage of decolonial insurgency. Bergeaud merges these several instances of city-burning into a single decisive gesture in which an unnamed commander rises to meet what is character- ized, almost dismissively, as an overly vague absolutist strategy. 'He was told to fight an all-out war and to defend himself with iron and flame', reads the redaction of Louverture's letter, and the rebels take this instruction at its word. Bergeaud writes:

> Standing tall, this city would be a conquest, a great prize for the enemy. It was thus necessary to burn it so that these Europeans, who were not used to the rigorous climate, would find them- selves without shelter. It was a new way of fighting. Romulus's lieutenant strictly executed the orders and set his own house aflame. The Indigènes organized a fort filled with line troops and national guardsmen a short distance away. The enemy occupied the city that had been reduced to ashes and invited their ships ashore.[3]

Bergeaud was not alone in producing this kind of account, but he was singularly sympathetic to the revolutionaries. For others, like the exiled planter Felix Carteau, such conflagrations were a 'terri- ble spectacle' that resulted in 'a rain of fire, composed of little bits of burning cane stalk that were flickering through the air. It was like a heavy snowfall, and depending on where the winds were blowing it would sweep over the harbour and the ships or over the city and the houses of the Cape'.[4] While the tropical colony was transformed into this volcanic inferno, the events became as iconic in the colonial imaginary as they were climactic in the field of combat. 'When the capital of the colony, Cap-Français, was set ablaze by Black revolutionaries', writes the historian Marlene L. Daut, 'paintings depicting the fires told tales of property destruction designed to produce more sympathy for the lost buildings than for the human beings who had been tortured and enslaved within them'.[5] One of the first French-language novels of the revolution, René Périn's 1802 *The Burning of Cap*, not only took the conflagration for its title but also saw it reimagined as an illustrated frontispiece in which the revolutionaries themselves seem to issue forth from the fires of hell.

Scorched earth: this military tactic, the unsparing destruction of everything that might otherwise be useful to the enemy, is as old as the Gallic Wars of 50 BC, during which the Gauls lured Roman armies into the ravaged countryside of the Benelux countries and France, where they would be cut off from all resources and denied the land itself. In Saint-Domingue, Louverture's call announced this tactic, but it did so in a way that might best be described as literary. Indeed, his letter combined a military command with the metaphoric language used for its narration to disclose and affirm the rebels' class identity. As though making good on apocalyptic prophesy, wherein the metaphoric inferno reveals itself as terrifyingly real, the insurgents' assault materialized their commander's rhetorical hellfire. The fire invoked the conditions that led to revolution, the composition of the revolutionary class, and the form their revolution might take. And with this passage, from struggle to conflict, from subjugation to insurrection, Louverture spoke in the language of class war:

> Do not forget, while waiting for the rainy season which will rid us of our foes, that we have no other resource than destruction and flames. Bear in mind that the soil bathed with our sweat must not furnish our enemies with the smallest aliment. Tear up the roads with shot; throw corpses and horses into all the fountains; burn and annihilate everything, in order that those who have come to reduce us to slavery may have before their eyes the image of that hell which they deserve.[6]

Destruction and flames are as much the unconditional rejection of colonial rule and slave labour as they are a call to annihilate the bodies and resources of the colonists, slaveholders, and their allies. To describe the battlefield as 'soil bathed with our sweat' is simultaneously the mark of a military tactician who knows the value of resources and an expression of class consciousness, an address of convocation to one's formerly enslaved comrades who had been forced to work the land and who are now summoned to action by the language of collective opposition: 'our foes', 'our enemies', us and them. In overcoming our immiseration, these words suggest, we shall remake the world into the hell they forced upon us. The command is for the rebels to be absolute and unsparing, to secure justice through the obliteration of every last thing. It is this localized act of warfare that unites a people as a class and simultaneously achieves the status of revolutionary gesture.

Two years later, on 8 April 1804, the revolution met its bloody apotheosis in the liquidation of all remaining white occupiers. This command was given by Dessalines, who had first joined the slave rebellion of the northern plain in 1791 and who had, after Louverture's capture by the French in June 1802, led the rebel slaves to victory over the colonial army. Similar to Louverture, who had died one year earlier in a French prison, Dessalines insisted in 1804 that under his command the rebels were to turn carnage back against its source – that brutal actions are the justice of a brutalized people. 'We have rendered to these true cannibals', he reflects, 'war for war, crime for crime, outrage for outrage; yes, I have saved my country; I have avenged America'. These words, as with Louverture's, attain their frisson by virtue of their articulation amid an organized massacre. A whole theory of violence could be extracted from the adjective 'true', which discriminates between a social system that grows out of human immiseration and the bloody means by which that system meets its reckoning – in short, it signs the difference between an ongoing struggle and the decisiveness of war. Addressing the 'mutilated victims of the cupidity of white Frenchmen' – those 'insatiate blood suckers', that 'sacrilegious horde' – Dessalines insists that Haiti will only achieve its 'regeneration' through 'exterminating these blood-thirsty tygers'.[7]

Christophe, who was made king of Haiti in 1811, shared these thoughts. After Dessalines was crowned emperor in October 1804, several generals plotted to seize power, ambushing and assassinating Dessalines at the entrance to Port-au-Prince. While Alexandre Pétion, who had commanded the rebels to victory alongside Dessalines, proclaimed himself president of a republic, Christophe, who had also been promoted to general under Louverture, broke away and took control of the island's north, establishing a separatist government that would, by 1811, capture the southern republic and establish a constitutional monarchy with himself as king. He proclaimed Haitian sovereignty in terms that would echo Dessalines, describing 'a nation which has suffered cruel persecution, and which, by its energy, its perseverance, its valor, and its prowess, has succeeded in acquiring, by the sword, liberty and independence'.[8] For the revolution's political leaders and military commanders, freedom and sovereignty were not granted by concession or realized through any sort of sanctioned democratic process; they were claimed in acts of warfare committed against colonial rule by an avenging slave class. And, for the duration of this revolutionary period, new class formations were forged and reforged in the fires of war.

* * *

'Of the three great revolutions that began in the final decades of the eighteenth century' the philosopher Peter Hallward has written, 'American, French and Haitian – only the third forced the unconditional application of the principle that inspired each one: affirmation of the natural, inalienable rights of all human beings'.[9] Even if the actions were singular, the ideas and rhetoric employed by Louverture, Dessalines, and Christophe were shared. Specifically, we can trace their affinities with revolutionary France. In *The Social Contract*, Jean-Jacques Rousseau had famously theorized the constitutive tension underlying civil society as the continuum between a state of war and a state predicated on slavery. 'The victor having', he would summarize this imperial position, 'the right of killing the vanquished, the latter can buy back his life at the price of his liberty; and this convention is the more legitimate because it is to the advantage of both parties'. Countering this state form, predicated as it is on the assumption that the supersession of war justifies slavery, Rousseau writes that 'this convention, so far from destroying the state of war, presupposes its continuance'.[10] Or, as he explains in *Discourse on Inequality*, 'the conqueror and the conquered peoples always remained in a state of war with each other, unless the nation, returned to complete freedom, should voluntarily choose the conqueror as its leader'. In other words: slavery perpetuates the 'state of war' because any society founded on the denial of liberty cannot sustain 'any other law than that of the stronger'.[11] This – for Rousseau – is the very origin of human inequality, from which modern class society devolves. Despite Rousseau having never foretold insurgency and insurrection as answers to inequality, his philosophy both inspired the French Revolution and provided a founding ideology that would guide the Haitian rebels. 'From whatever aspect we regard the question', he would insist, 'the right of slavery is null and void, not only as being illegitimate, but also because it is absurd and meaningless'. He then summarized this egalitarian dictate in language that would pre-empt the oppositional grammar of countless revolutionary slogans: 'The words *slavery* and *right* contradict each other; they are mutually exclusive'.[12]

And yet, slavery and its abolition revealed a limit to the liberal imagination, of which Rousseau was a leading figure. For this tradition, slavery served as a dominant trope; it was raised metaphorically to be contrasted with its opposite, freedom, which was affirmed as the inalienable paragon of enlightened humanity. This metaphor took root in political rhetoric at the same time that the actual practice of slavery was subsidizing the apparent freedoms to be had in Europe, 'to the point', writes the intellectual historian Susan Buck-Morss, 'that by the mid-eighteenth century it came to underwrite the entire economic system of the West, paradoxically facilitating the global spread of the very Enlightenment ideals that were in such fundamental contradiction to it'.[13] Whereas the French Revolution's values were affirmed as a set of ideals exclusive to race and nation, in Haiti those same values were fought for and won in the field of combat and against such constitutive logics of exclusion. In the confluence of word and deed, the Haitian Revolution embodies the French Revolution's radical fulfilment, affirming the core values of *liberté*, *égalité*, and *fraternité* while simultaneously challenging the emergent bourgeoisie, a social grouping which was by now the most powerful economic force in France, and whose wealth derived from enclosure, slave trade, and colonial plunder.

* * *

It was then neither the geopolitical setting nor the espousal of revolutionary ideals that separated the revolution in Haiti from those that came before. It was that this revolution took egalitarian principles literally and pursued them absolutely, in direct opposition to the social order and economic logic of the day. Haiti thus marked, for the Martinican poet Aimé Césaire, the transformation of 'formal rights into real rights', an act of material commitment to philosophical ideals about what constitutes humanity. 'When Toussaint Louverture came on the scene', he writes, 'it was to take the Declaration of the Rights of Man at its word; it was to show that there is no pariah race; that there is no marginal country; that there can be no excepted peoples. It was to incarnate and particularize a principle; that is to say, to vivify it'.[14]

While Louverture borrowed from the thinkers of the French Revolution, including Rousseau, the echoes we hear of Rousseau in Haiti were recombined with revolutionary republicanism's most blood-hungry slogans. 'Man will never be free until the last king is strangled with the entrails of the last priest', reads the standard paraphrase of Diderot's most influential poem, 'Les Éleuthéromanes', which was popularized during the French Revolution. 'I permit them to call me a drinker of blood!' declaimed Danton, the leading French revolutionary. 'Let us drink the blood of the enemies of humanity, but let Europe at last be free! And it is for you to create this liberty: the world is waiting upon your courage'. 'To punish the oppressors of humanity is clemency', claimed Robespierre, 'to forgive them is cruelty'. And often attributed to Saint-Just, a call that reverberates with the mutinous cries of the slave ship: 'The vessel of the Revolution can arrive in port only on a sea reddened with torrents of blood'.[15] Yet between these figures, on the one hand Danton, Robespierre, and Saint-Just, and Louverture, Dessalines, and Christophe on the other, we see some important differences.

While the French Revolution and its Terror were violent, that violence was never on the scale its architects had threatened, and neither was it constitutive of solidarity in the comprehensive ways we see here. In part, this was because the delivery of their promises was always more political than social, decapitating figureheads and reordering the state without enacting wider societal transformation, and doing so at the exclusion from 'human rights' of a racialized underclass forced to labour elsewhere, in the colonies. By way of contrast, Louverture and his comrades appropriated the formulations of the French Revolution and refashioned them into a bayonet used for the repudiation of empire. Appealing to the words of Rousseau, Robespierre, Danton, and Saint-Just, as well as their forebears Raynal, Mirabeau, and Diderot, the insurgents devised a language with which to demand and defend the universal freedom of all humans, irrespective of skin colour or place of origin. They also formulated a revolutionary idea of class as a collective being defined by the combative means of its liberation whose realization necessitates total demolition of the standing social order. And it was on the site of this demolition that an egalitarian organization of society might develop. What makes Louverture's letter as well as Dessalines's and Christophe's proclamations different from those of their republican kin, despite the shared aggression, is that their violence was not just a mode of attack; it was foundational to their collective being, their commonality as a class.

* * *

Situating the Haitian Revolution and its leaders within their social contexts clarifies that this conflict is also a matter of class as well as why, in Haiti, the practice of class solidarity would be understood in relation to military capacity. Starting in the 1730s, the Greater Antilles – Jamaica, Cuba, and Hispaniola – were converted by French and British colonizers into an archipelago of sugar-cane plantations. Saint-Domingue was the western half of Hispaniola, while the island's eastern half was Spanish Santo Domingo. Within a decade of occupation, the French colony of Saint-Domingue and the British colony of Jamaica were supplying the overwhelming majority of the global north's sugar. And of all the colonies, Saint-Domingue was the most profitable, with 600 hundred ships conveying sugar from there to Bordeaux every year. By 1789, it produced 60 percent of the world's coffee and 40 percent of the sugar imported by France and Britain. Given the sheer quantity of human labour required for sugar production, the colonists imported an enormous workforce made up of African slaves. As the historian of slavery Robin Blackburn writes, 'with some 465,000 slaves St Domingue was the largest and most productive slave colony in the Caribbean in 1789, it had served as a privateer base throughout the century without ever itself suffering invasion. The colony's 30,000 whites and 28,000 or more free people of color were organized and armed to defend slavery'.[16] Haiti was, as though literalizing Rousseau's philosophy of inequality, a slave state on perpetual war footing.

In Haiti, the imperial economy shaped a racialized caste system made up of three distinct groupings: white colonists, subdivided into aristocratic plantation owners at the top, above the overseers, day-labourers, merchants, and artisans; free persons of colour or of mixed ancestry, who often served in the army or as administrators; and slaves of mostly African descent. In addition to these three castes, large groups of runaway slaves inhabited the hillside woods and jungles, and often conducted raids on the sugar and coffee plantations. As Blackburn writes, 'clamped on top of the slave economy, there was a complex of interests, formed by the intersecting fields of force of a colonial and mercantile system, an aristocratic political order, a racial caste hierarchy, and a highly unequal distribution of private property within both the white and free colored population'.[17] With slaves outnumbering the other castes six to one, even those intellectual architects of the French Revolution recognized the potential for mutiny, characterizing it as inevitable as natural disaster. For Mirabeau in 1789, the French inhabitants of Saint-Domingue 'slept at the foot of Vesuvius'.[18] For Raynal, likewise, the Caribbean in 1780 was always showing signs of 'the impending storm'.[19]

These intimations of the coming catastrophe were confirmed on the night of 21 August 1791, when thousands of slaves attended a voodoo ceremony under the cover of a tropical cyclone. With the omens of thunder and lightning at their back, the slaves rose as insurgents and burnt the plantations. Within ten days, they had taken control of the entire northern province. By the end of 1791, the revolt had become an insurrection: the number of self-freed slaves who joined reached some 100,000. Within the next two months, as the violence escalated, the insurgents killed 4,000 whites and burnt or destroyed 180 sugar plantations as well as hundreds of coffee and indigo plantations. In this movement, the slave caste was reborn as the class that the great historian of the revolution C. L. R. James describes as 'closer to a modern proletariat than any group of workers in existence at the time'.[20]

But the sheer size of the slave population was not enough to ensure its revolutionary success or even its mobilization through something like common interest. With a life expectancy of the indentured labourers on arrival of only seven to ten years, plantation crews were replenished by new purchases, who would often arrive speaking different dialects, obviating class cohesion in all but shared suffering and a common enemy. For this reason, culture becomes a weapon of its own, a medium for class consciousness, through which militancy would spread across a regional and then international network of communication made up of newspapers, broadsides, and word of mouth. Within this network, the practical as well as ideological contradictions between French liberalism and Haitian militancy generate the kinds of brutal irony that historians have come to relish, apparent nowhere more acutely than in moments when loyalist soldiers were conscripted to quash a revolution founded on the very ideology to which they allegedly subscribed.

For the historian Julius S. Scott, while royalists and colonists staged protests, burning books and effigies, 'discussions of the French Revolution and its ideology had literally burst into the open by the middle of 1793', and would serve as an ideological force brought into the insurgency. 'And in societies split decisively along class and race lines, public demonstrations sponsored by local elites was something of a two-edged sword. If they intimidated and promoted conformity, these appeals to public channels also highlighted and underscored vividly the firm challenge which the French Revolution posed to the slavocracy'.[21] In one well-documented episode, during the siege of the Crête-à-Pierrot fort, the French troops approached only to hear their enemy singing 'La Marseillaise'. Back in France, a battalion of young recruits from La Rochelle was ordered to unstitch the embroidered slogan from their flag and uniforms before departure to Saint-Domingue; it read 'Live Free or Die'. According to Scott, 'the general assembled the troops and explained to them the danger which such words posed "in a land where all property is based on the enslavement of Negroes, who, if they adopted this slogan themselves, would be driven to massacre their masters and the army which is crossing the sea to bring peace and law to the colony"'.[22] Anecdotes like this abound, and in them we should recognize the contradiction between a liberal and a militant politics as well as the catalytic power of the words and ideas of revolution as they find their way along economic currents between the global north and south. On an island where property was synonymous with enslavement, these words could only be interpreted as a call to annihilate the colonial ruling classes and the system to which they belong.

* * *

During the 1790s, one form presented itself as uniquely well matched to the task and context of revolutionary catalysis: the slogan. The French Revolution spoke in the language of slogans and – while those slogans invoked slavery as metaphor – this kind of literary micro-narrative was also taken up and repurposed as literal by the insurgents of Saint-Domingue. 'Toussaint had the advantage of liberty and equality', reflected James, 'the slogans of the revolution. They were great weapons in the age of slaves, but weapons must be used and he used them with a fencer's finesse and skill'.[23] This description has its origins in etymology, with 'slogan' deriving from the Gaelic *sluagh-ghairm*, or, literally, 'army-cry'.

As though making good on this derivation, militants understand that slogans are the narrative form of the revolutionary act. Looking ahead, we see the militant theorization of the slogan in the Russian Revolution of 1917. Lenin, in response to the superannuation of old slogans by new social formations, would emphasize the need for urgency and adaptation: 'Every particular slogan must be deduced from the totality of specific features of a definite political situation'.[24] Stalin would subsequently clarify this as Lenin's 'cardinal thesis' on revolutionary propaganda, insisting that slogans will only be effective if they speak to and mobilize class formations, 'if they indicate the correct plan of disposition of the revolutionary forces on the front of the class struggle, if they help to bring the masses to the front of the struggle for the victory of the revolution, to the front of the struggle for the seizure of power by the new class'.[25]

The revolutionary slogan, at the levels of medium and content, is one of class war's prevailing literary forms. Such is what we encounter in Louverture's inaugural public proclamation on 29 August 1793. 'Equality cannot exist without liberty', read its final words, echoing Rousseau. 'And for liberty to exist, we must have unity'.[26] In a kind of radical auxesis, which renders the operative slogans of the French Revolution in order of contingency while replacing fraternity with unity, we sense the beginnings of a thought that would become manifest four years later, on the other side of conflict, when class solidarity would result not from some pre-existing fraternity but from armed militancy.

* * *

While Louverture emulated and promoted the slogans of the French Revolution, the slaves simultaneously developed a collective identity comprising voodoo and obeah, syncretic forms of religious and spiritual practice, which would infuse military strategy by way of cultural institution. In James's account, the African lineage is one means by which a class is called to action by a voice that expresses its interests in terms of political principles. During the early days of the uprising, the insurgents' assault tactics were matched to their cultural identity as much as to an untested combat capacity. Describing the insurrectionary choreography of 1792, James provides us with a sketch of the revolution's African character, which marks the confluence of class and war in a system of racial capitalism, wherein regional, subcultural, and dialectical differences are transcoded into unified militancy:

> The insurgents had developed a method of attack based on their overwhelming numerical superiority. They did not rush forward in mass formation like fanatics. They placed them selves in groups, choosing wooded spots in such a way as to envelop their enemy, seeking to crush him by weight of numbers. They carried out these preliminary maneuvers in dead silence, while their priests (the black ones) chanted the wanga, and the women and children sang and danced in a frenzy. When these had reached the necessary height of excitement the fighters attacked. If they met with resistance they retired without exhausting themselves, but at the slightest hesitation in the defense they became extremely bold and, rushing up to the cannon, swarmed all over their opponents.[27]

Deploying a kind of strategic essentialism, this combat operation weaponized commonality in subjugation, unifying the enslaved into a devastatingly effective guerrilla assault force. Binding the collectively dispossessed, utilizing their numerical superiority, are the traditions of Africa – the voodoo ceremony, or what the American novelist Zora Neale Hurston once described as 'the old, old mysticism of the world in African terms', in which women and children would serve at the heart of combat manoeuvres and which would be, at once, an organic expression of free life.[28] More so than political rhetoric and philosophy translated out of another revolution, these ceremonies began to articulate the common cause of the revolutionary class before it has come to know itself as a class.

This racialized collocation of class and war is pronounced in the mythic associations bestowed on the slaves' most effective military commander, Dessalines. A slave born in the colony, Dessalines was also 'performatively and ideologically African', in that, unlike Louverture, he rejected France and retained a political affinity with Africa and its voodoo traditions.[29] He was popularly known as Desalin Ogou, a name that alludes to either a warrior spirit or a god of war, and his leadership was modelled on such a title; it is said that he 'embodied a revolutionary lwa or lao, spoke Congo, and called his people the Incas of the Sun'.[30]

Such militancy would be a point of fear and fascination at the imperial core. Victor Hugo's anti-revolutionary novel of 1826, *Bug-Jargal*, tells the story of the insurrectionary phase of the revolution from the standpoint of a liberal slave-owner who is taken captive by a fierce military leader, Biassou – a character modelled on Dessalines. In one set piece, Biassou delivers a 'soldierly sermon of sorts' to his comrades, in which he calls for them to abandon any sort of patience with 'the enemies of humanity's regeneration, those whites, those colonists, those planters, those traffickers, *verdaderos demonios* vomited forth from the mouth of Alecto', and 'now be as implacable as the panthers and jaguars of the lands from which we were torn away'. The response to this speech is a spectacle of primitivism:

I won't make any attempt to describe for you the disquieting enthusiasm that took hold of the insurgent army after Biassou's exhortation. It was a discordant chorus of shouts, groans, and howls. Some beat their chests, others banged their cudgels and sabres. Several, on their knees or prostrate, were riveted to the ground in an ecstatic pose. Negresses lacerated their breasts and arms with the fishbones they use in lieu of combs to untangle their hair. The sound of guitars, tomtoms, drums, and balafos mingled with volleys of musket fire. It was as if all hell had broken loose.[31]

This is a liberal aesthetics of slave revolt, betraying the barely concealed racism that underpins such a worldview as well as the fear of genuine militancy. Written to terrorize but also titillate the white imperial reader, it is a reactionary inversion of the voodoo ceremony, an event that would serve the insurgent army as an expression of solidarity and liberation.

* * *

Before the revolt became revolution, seizing the state and enacting social transformation, the local economy was also reframed by external interstate conflict and – consistent with a dynamic we will encounter many times in subsequent chapters – class formations developed alongside, and in response to, imperial wars of extermination. In 1793, Napoleon declared war on Great Britain. In Saint-Domingue, the French plantation owners, wary of state-sanctioned revolutionary ideals, arranged for Britain to declare sovereignty over the colony, believing the British would preserve slavery. Britain complied, apprehending Saint-Domingue as a financial asset for the ensuing war against France and as insurance against further revolts in the Caribbean. Spain, which still controlled the eastern half of Hispaniola, entered the conflict to fight against France, invading Saint-Domingue in alliance with the rebel slaves, supplying them with food, ammunition, arms, medicine, naval support, and military advisors. Still serving the French, Louverture was at the head of this alliance and ran a line of posts between rebel and colonial territory.

On 29 August 1793, having adapted the language of the French Revolution to the context of war, he challenged the slave population to fight now for emancipation. 'Brothers and friends', he declared, 'I am Toussaint Louverture; perhaps my name has made itself known to you. You know, brothers, that I have undertaken vengeance, and that I want liberty and equality to reign in St-Domingue'. Note here the emphasis on political work combined with exhortations for unification. 'I have worked since the beginning to make that happen, and to bring happiness to all', he announced 'Unite yourselves to us, brothers, and fight with us for the same cause'.[32] On the very same day, two commissioners – the Jacobins Léger-Félicité Sonthonax and Étienne Polverel – declared a state of abolition. They did so in an attempt to secure the colony for republican France as opposed to either Britain, Spain, or the French royalists. The slaves were set free and fought as citizens of the republic, but only temporarily. Bonaparte would soon have Louverture arrested and deported, and would seek to restore slavery. 'Rid us of these gilded Africans, and we shall have nothing more to wish', Bonaparte wrote to Leclerc in 1802, dispatching the expeditionary force to Saint-Domingue.[33]

For some, including Danton, the slaves' temporary freedom was a momentary extension, or completion, of the French Revolution. Under the military leadership of Louverture, the forces made up mostly of former slaves succeeded in winning concessions from the British and expelling the Spanish forces. While Louverture and the insurgents liberated Saint-Domingue, unifying their territories in a lived commitment to emancipation, their ideology was exported from the colonial periphery back to the imperial core. Responding directly to the revolt, the French constitutions of 1793 and 1795 both included the abolition of slavery. The constitution of 1793 was never applied, but that of 1795 was implemented and lasted until it was replaced by the consular and imperial constitutions under Bonaparte. Louverture restored control of Saint-Domingue to France, and expanded that control over the entire island. In 1801, after taking control of Spanish Santo Domingo and freeing its slaves, he issued a constitution that called for universal abolition. In this interchange between Haiti and France is an articulation of what the postcolonial literary critic Priyamvada Gopal describes as the insurgent empire, wherein the 'enslaved and colonial subjects' are seen as not just the victims of 'imperial history and the subsequent beneficiaries of its crises of conscious', but as 'agents whose resistance not only contributed to their own liberation but also put pressure on and reshaped', in the global north and core states, 'ideas about freedom and who could be free'.[34]

That revolutionaries should expect nothing from the ruling classes, no matter how politically compatible they might otherwise claim to be, is one of the central lessons of Haiti, where slaves were not granted but instead won freedom. To echo E. P. Thompson's description of the English working class, in Haiti the revolutionary class was present at its own making – it freed itself from caste and mobilized as a class. On the first day of 1804, Dessalines, who had succeeded Louverture, baptized the independent republic 'Ayiti', an indigenous Taíno word meaning 'land of mountains'. He marked the founding with words that, despite his rejection of France, echoed Rousseau and would reverberate onward through revolutionary history. 'In the end', he announced on 1 January 1804, 'we must live independent or die'.[35]

* * *

If class war was first theorized in the global north when Marx and Engels responded critically to European and English history, here we find its practical inauguration in the global south, where it did not cohere with the movement of industrial proletarianization. Nor would it resolve into anything approaching the condition of parliamentary politics. To be clear, this is not to say that class war begins outside of capitalism. Rather than approaching Haiti as something other than capitalist, beginning here insists that decolonial combat, which resists capital in the form of enslavement, is itself a form of class war, in that its subjects are bound together in the first instance by their economic immiseration and then by that rebellion which destroys their economy and resurrects them as a new people. While Marx polemicized that instead of seeking universal emancipation for humanity the revolt only represented the liberation of people of African descent, here we will do better to follow Marxist thinkers of the Black Atlantic and the Black Pacific and to insist that, while Africa is key to the class character and military strategy of the rebels, their revolution repudiated capital in its specifically colonial manifestation, establishing in the place of racial capitalism a safe haven for all indigenous people and people of colour threatened by colonization, enslavement, and genocidal violence.

As Eric Williams, historian of the Caribbean and first prime minister of Trinidad and Tobago, famously set out in his doctoral thesis – later revised and published as *Capitalism and Slavery* – the plantation was in fact a modern institution relative to capitalist exploitation and the geopolitics of empire. 'The commercial capitalism of the eighteenth century developed the wealth of Europe by means of slavery and monopoly', he writes in the conclusion. 'But in so doing it helped to create the industrial capitalism of the nineteenth century, which turned round and destroyed the power of commercial capitalism, slavery, and all its works'.[36] Or let us affirm Christophe when he speaks of African inheritance in the triumphant language of post-revolutionary progress as a concrete universal fraternity of the kind the French Revolution promised in theory but refused in practice, or what might otherwise be described as the internationalization of class solidarity. 'We should understand', he announced, 'that we labor for the benefit of the human race generally, for the Black equally as for the White; for we are all brethren: let us recollect that African blood flows in our veins, and that we are under the necessity of exerting our utmost efforts to live in the great practice of society; our progress more or less influencing the opinions that the Europeans will form of us!'[37]

Going to war against the oppressors but also oppression itself is to close the gap between thought and practice at a moment in history when that gap and the ideological falsehoods it enabled were being used to celebrate the transformation of capitalism from its mercantile into its proto-industrial form, in which the slave-driven colonial economy and its resources guaranteed the material sustenance of ruling classes in the global north. And so, our story begins not with an industrial workforce picketing the factory gates or sabotaging the mineshaft, but instead with men and women denied access to the structural conditions for revolutionary immanence made available elsewhere and who nevertheless committed *en masse* to violent insurrection and insurgency. In mobilizing the slaves as a class, Haiti affirms actual combat as the forerunner to ideology, and its combat is both locally anti-colonial and systemically anti-capitalist. Class war emerges from the global south as a way of rendering absolute the ideals of liberty and equality, not as assumed universal rights but as contested resources denied those of a different race, to be seized and defended through combat.

Haiti's smoke was visible everywhere within capital's expanding empires. The methods, language, and emancipatory promise of the Haitian Revolution would provide tactics for waging war in and from the global peripheries as well as an idea of class that would find home in the first world. As an exceptional flashpoint in the decolonial campaign against slavery, the impact of the Haitian Revolution on the Caribbean and the rest of the Americas inspired collective revolt in Barbados in 1816, Guyana in 1823, and Jamaica in 1831–2. It would also resonate with mobilizing proletarians in the core states: in France, in North America, and in England. There, William Wordsworth would compose his 1803 sonnet for Louverture, that 'miserable Chieftain' who would soon die in 'some deep dungeon's earless den'. Wordsworth's poem apostrophizes that the rebel might 'take comfort' in a radical legacy embodied by his 'great allies', namely the 'exultations' and 'agonies' and 'love' and 'man's unconquerable mind'.[38] While this reads as pure idealism, and as an affirmation of the heroic individual at the expense of the revolutionary multitude, a more accurate poetic treatment of Louverture's legacy would be conceived of in an English prison sometime around 1849, drafted on flyleaves with a rook's feather for a quill and using blood and soot for ink. Written by the Chartist organizer and agitator Ernest Jones while imprisoned for insurrection, the epic 'New World, A Democratic Poem' would include these lines, conjuring new solidarities upon an image of scorched earth:

> Deep in the burning south a cloud appears,
> The smouldering wrath of full four thousand years,
> Whatever name caprice of history gave,
> Moor, Afrit, Ethiop, Negro, still meant slave!
> And, dire allies! to make their vengeance sure,
> Behind them tower Ogé, and Louverture.[39]

2

Army of Redressers

Fifteen years after Haiti first declared independence from France, between sixty and eighty thousand men, women, and children gathered on St Peter's Field in Manchester, a centre of Britain's industrializing north. On 16 August 1819, this crowd was demonstrating in the name of suffrage for English workers, who, consigned to poverty through mass unemployment during the depression caused by the long-running war with France, were also debarred from parliamentary redress. Modifying one of the best-known slogans from France and Haiti, one banner is said to have read 'Equal Representation or Death', with text accompanied by a bloodied dagger. Organized by the Manchester Patriotic Union, the demonstrators were to be addressed by the radical reformist Henry 'Orator' Hunt. Joseph Johnson, the union secretary, summoned Hunt from London with a description of the conditions in the north. 'Nothing but ruin and starvation stare one in the face', he wrote. 'The state of this district is truly dreadful, and I believe nothing but the greatest exertions can prevent an insurrection'.[1] Less a political ultimatum than a statement of fact, the meaning is clear: that without major reform there will be a deadly uprising. Hence, representation or death; no justice, no peace. Misconstruing this communiqué as the threat of insurrection instead of advocacy for its prevention by way of redress, the local magistrates prepared for armed conflict, summoning mounted paramilitaries with which to disperse the crowd. Soon after the meeting began, the Manchester and Salford Yeomanry – a local cavalry militia originally mustered to subdue labour agitation – moved to arrest Hunt and the other speakers. The cavalry galloped into the demonstrators, colliding with at least one woman, Ann Fildes, causing the death of her infant son. After Hunt's arrest, the magistrates summoned the 15th Hussars – a battle-hardened cavalry regiment of 600 men – to disperse the crowd. They charged with sabres, murdering eighteen protestors and injuring hundreds more.

The *Manchester Observer* christened this unilateral and unprovoked assault the 'Peterloo Massacre', a portmanteau that merged the local context of St Peter's Field with Waterloo, the site on which Britain defeated Napoleon four years earlier. 'Very many were necessarily ridden over in consequence', reads the article, 'as if they were eager to give a practical proof of the ardency of their courage, but which by the by was not previously to these exploits, in the estimation of many of the Waterloo kind'. The difference between a battle and a massacre is conveyed in the subsequent description:

> Had the military only attacked robust men, only wounded those who had offered them insult, only dealt out death and destruction with something like discrimination, much less infamy would have been their lot. But it is notorious, that some of our gentlemen who shall be nameless, only struck the quickest but the heaviest on those who were the most defenseless. The women seemed to be the special objects of the rage of these bastard soldiers.[2]

It is in this way, as the interclass localization of an international conflict, that antagonism entered the public imagination as an expression of war, with an idea of class solidifying through combat. Likewise, the militaristic preparations for this demonstration and its final defeat charged a conceptual circuit between class and war. 'The drilling, in the weeks preceding the meeting', notes E. P. Thompson, 'sometimes undertaken by old Waterloo men – and, on occasion, with staves at the shoulder like muskets, or hand-claps to simulate firing – gave colour to the prosecution

witnesses who spoke of a "military array"'.[3] Even if the prosecution's claims were exaggerated in order to exonerate the
murderers, and while the ultimate outcome was conservative
insofar as the government immediately passed legislation
suppressing meetings for the purpose of reform, the event helped
redefine class solidarity as revolutionary immanence. 'Beneath
this contingent response', writes Thompson, 'we must understand the profounder fear evoked by the evidence of the translation of the rabble into a disciplined class'.[4] That will be a consist-
ency about England during the first half of the nineteenth
century: class would be understood, by the industrial capitalists
and conservative politicians as well as the radical reformers and
committed revolutionaries, as a military threat against the
standing social order.

* * *

The affective shock of Peterloo furnished the revolutionary
imagination with a distinctly romantic inclination: a sense of
undaunted possibility that, in Georg Lukács's phrase, 'the soul is
broader and more vast than any destiny that life can offer it'.[5] If
militants in Haiti weaponized the republican slogan and the
cultures of voodoo, in England romance served as an expressive
mode for common cause and revolutionary antagonism; it was,
in both the poetry and prose of the day, a way of envisioning the
demolition of class hierarchies while at the same time figuring
the commons as a potential utopia.

Discussing this form of revolutionary romanticism, an
aesthetic mode that rejects 'both the illusion of a pure and
simple return to organic communities of the past and resigned
acceptance of the bourgeois present', the intellectual historians
Robert Sayre and Michael Löwy write that 'it aspires – more or
less radically and explicitly, depending on the case – to see the
abolition of capitalism and the creation of a utopian future
possessing some traits or values of pre-capitalist societies'.[6]
Indeed, the decades leading up to Peterloo were defined by the
vast enclosure of land across the British countryside, during
which, in village after village, the various commons were

privatized, with landless agricultural tenants restored as dispossessed workers, left with nothing to sell but their own labour. Simultaneously, in the domestic industries, small-scale manufacture was eclipsed by larger firms, so that the majority of self-employed artisans, including weavers, stockingers, and nail-makers, would become wage-earning outworkers with precarious employment. Romanticism, in this context, helps us see via 'the Blakean boundedness of the work of art' what the poetry critic Anahid Nersessian describes as 'a model for the positive attenuation of desire's impacts on a material world under evermore impossible duress', coinciding with both the private enclosure of common land and the onslaught of industrial modernity.[7]

With romance thus providing fertile soil for opposition to the dark satanic mills of capitalist industry, Percy Bysshe Shelley's ballad for the Peterloo martyrs, 'The Masque of Anarchy', remains the most legible romance of class war and offers a template for how it would be articulated in England. The poem addresses a 'vast assembly' of the emerging proletariat, 'ye calm and resolute' stood now before 'the tyrants', as a military force, describing their 'folded arms and looks' as 'weapons of unvanquished war'. As it thunders toward its climax, the blood spilled on St Peter's Field is given a speaking part. It delivers these slogans sanctioning the armed reassembly of an inchoate mass, their rebirth as a class, and with that the now familiar passage from struggle to antagonism:

> Rise, like lions after slumber
> In unvanquishable number!
> Shake your chains to earth like dew
> Which in sleep had fallen on you:
> Ye are many – they are few![8]

Here we encounter the sharpening of a national agon, a division of society into ye and they, but also a romantic projection of some future victory born from present defeat. As one of the empire's heraldic icons, the lion simile compares international conflict to class antagonism, addressing its dispensation, a still slumbering proletariat, as an army of 'unvanquishable number'. Hijacking the language of patriotic exhortation, the poem urges us to rise, cast aside our chains, and overwhelm the oppressors and exploiters. This reappropriation, which diverts the rhetoric of national chauvinism into an affirmation of proletarian insurgency, belongs to the class politics of the day.

* * *

During and after the Napoleonic Wars, revolutionary thought assimilated the geostrategic manoeuvres of the world's contending empires. Militants applied these ideas to a growing class divide, producing a view of the state as comprising two separate and irreconcilable, warring nations: us and them, north and south, labour and capital. And this division only widened throughout the First Industrial Revolution. To this extent, the large-scale, multiform, and disaggregate agitations, of which that bloody day on St Peter's Field was only one critical encounter, were themselves conditioned by the Napoleonic Wars with which they coincided. With commerce dominating social relations both at home and across the oceans, the cultural logic of international imperial warfare was returned to the site of modern capitalist enterprise, in the factory system as well as the mill and mining communities, and to the increasingly transparent exploitation. As the historian Peter Linebaugh describes it, 'the smoke of the factory and the smoke of cannon, the hapless soldier's cry and the orphan's cry, vast fortunes and the fortunes of war, war and the machine morphed politically into the military-industrial complex'.[9] That industrialization took place under the shadow of war lent social stratification a language of conflict. The factories and mills were reimagined as battlegrounds. Their beneficiaries and assailants were cast as enemy combatants.

The first shots of this battle were fired not at the capitalists, but at their capital. Earlier in the century, during the Luddite crisis that began in 1811, it was the capitalists' machinery that felt the first blows. In the initial wave of industrialization, technology was a source of acute misery. Its application served to undermine the livelihoods of weavers, croppers, and other textile workers. It also destroyed their communities. The stocking frame, the gig mill, and the shearing frame transformed skilled labour into unskilled piecework. Craftmanship and the putting-out system were rapidly displaced by heavy industry. Charlotte Brontë's *Shirley* describes this process from the standpoint of capital as a 'state of feeling' embodied in the figure of a Yorkshire industrialist, for whom 'it is not to be expected that he would deliberate much as to whether his advance was or was not prejudicial to others', who 'did not sufficiently care when the new inventions threw the old workpeople out of employ', and who 'never asked himself where those to whom he no longer paid weekly wages found daily bread'. Under such conditions of systemic immiseration – at a time when it 'would not do to stop the progress of invention, to damage science by discouraging its improvements', when 'the war could not be terminated' and 'efficient relief could not be raised' – the un- and underemployed were driven to revolt.[10]

'Misery generates hate', writes Brontë. 'These sufferers hated the machines which they believed took their bread from them; they hated the buildings which contained those machines; they hated the manufacturers who owned those buildings'.[11] In her novel, the uprising takes form as a regionally accented 'rioters' yell', which causes fear in the gentry and bourgeois alike precisely because it serves as an expression of class solidarity uniting the dispossessed and exploited:

> You never heard that sound, perhaps, reader? So much the better for your ears – perhaps for your heart; since, if it rends the air in hate to yourself, or to the men or principles you approve, the interests to which you wish well, Wrath wakens to the cry of Hate; the Lion shakes his mane, and rises to the howl of the Hyena; Caste stands up, ireful against Caste; and the indignant, wronged spirit of the Middle Rank bears down in zeal and scorn on the famished and furious mass of the Operative Class.[12]

Mobilizing with what cultural theorist Gavin Mueller describes as 'an astonishing level of organized militancy', attacks sanctioned in the name of the mythical leader 'Ned Ludd' destroyed hundreds of machines, and especially frames and frameworks.[13] These raids, which were accompanied by petitions, were partly successful. They earned the sympathy of local communities in such a way that protected the identity of militants from authorities and, after a three-month campaign from November 1811 to February 1812 in which attacks were launched almost every night, wages rose.

But the revolt was neither against the machines themselves nor against local mills and factories. Rather, it was directed against industry as a whole and capitalism as a system, where the mills and factories would, in Brontë's phrase, be reduced by violence to 'a mere blot of desolation on the fresh front of the summer dawn'.[14] While the Luddites could not turn the tides of history – by 1815 the spinning of cotton was mechanized, and by 1832 weaving was almost completely undertaken in the factory – they nevertheless inaugurated a militant class politics on English soil.

'In those pre-socialist times the working class was a crowd, not an army', the historian Eric Hobsbawm writes, describing this moment with an approving quotation from the trade unionist Rinaldo Rigola: 'Enlightened, orderly, bureaucratic strikes were impossible'.[15] But precisely because unionized or syndicated strikes were not yet a thing, the Luddites forced that transition, from crowd to army, by enacting what should have been impossible. In other words, the Luddites were a movement initially shaped by technical composition, militating at a time when workers had not yet been disciplined by the factory but instead laboured from their homes or in shops using their own tools and were often employed under individual contracts. Their initial composition may have been one of atomized and cellular action as opposed to organized collectivity, yet through those midnight raids and the individual acts of machine-breaking they built a new practice of solidarity. They therefore carried a strategic as well as a tactical value. Not only did they shut down specific worksites, but in doing so they created new forms of collectivity. Ultimately, these acts mobilized the propertyless as a class.

In addition to secret oaths, bonds of confidentiality, and literary writing around the mythical figure of King Ludd, the movement also made use of military ideology, self-describing as an army and engaging in recruitment drives. So reads a letter posted around Leeds in March 1812:

> To all Croppers, Weavers &c & Public at Large
> Generous Countrymen.
> You are requested to come forward with Arms and help the Redressers to redress their Wrongs and shake off the hateful Yoke of a Silly Old Man, and his Son more silly and their Rogueish Ministers, all Nobles and Tyrants must be brought down. Come let us follow the Noble Example of the brave Citizens of Paris who in the Sight of 30,000 Tyrant Redcoats brought A Tyrant to the Ground. By so doing you will be best aiming at your own Interest. Above 40,000 Heroes are ready to break out, to crush the old Government & establish a new one.
> Apply to General Ludd Commander of the Army of Redressers.[16]

If military ideology served to inspire and recruit, it was also utilized to threaten. In another letter, written to intimidate a shearing-frame holder in Yorkshire, the Luddites threatened to send a detachment of 300 combatants to destroy the frames if they are not disassembled by their owner. And, if given cause to mobilize, the Luddites would look to 'increase' the holder's 'misfortune by burning your Buildings down to Ashes and if you have Impudence to fire upon any of my Men, they have orders to murder you, & burn all your Housing'. Before signing off as 'the General of the Army of Redressers', the letter's author pledges to fight. 'We will never lay down our Arms', the letter reads, using the emphatic language of collective identification: 'But We. We petition no more that won't do fighting must'.[17] This is how the crucible of collective identity works: the 'we' belongs to 'fighting', just as class is made in war.

This emphasis on solidarity achieved through fighting found its way into a romantic poem by one of the most celebrated writers of the day, the inimitable Lord Byron, who, in his maiden speech for the House of Lords, spoke out against the Frame Breaking Act of 1812, which applied the death penalty to machine-breaking. 'The perseverance of these miserable men in their proceedings', declaimed the newly appointed Lord, 'tends to prove that nothing but absolute want could have driven a large and once honest and industrious body of the people into the commission of excesses so hazardous to themselves, their families, and the community'.[18] Amplifying these sentiments, Byron's 1816 'Song for Luddites' begins with this stanza:

> As the Liberty lads o'er the sea
> Bought their freedom, and cheaply, with blood,
> So we, boys, we
> Will die fighting, or live free,
> And down with all kings but King Ludd![19]

Combining international geopolitics with republican sloganizing, these lines are, like Shelley's ballad, haunted by the French Revolution as well as the Napoleonic Wars. And indeed, for Byron the crisis resulted from 'a double infliction' relative to both class and war, namely 'an idle military and a starving population', which, in the industrializing north, were headed toward bloody conflict. 'All the cities you have taken, all the armies which have retreated before your leaders, are but paltry subjects of self-congratulation', he had instructed the House of Lords, 'if your land divides against itself, and your dragoons and executioners must be let loose against your fellow-citizens'.[20] But perhaps what is most striking about this poem, so much more than its referential content, is the political work undertaken by its music. Note the emphatic rhymes, which conjoin the movement's figurehead to the actuality of warfare, but which also mark that imperative freedom as relative to collective being, doing so here as a literary echo of the pronominal repetition found in the militants' letters: 'we, boys, we' directs these redresses to freedom by way of the battlefield.

The Luddites thus announced themselves as something like the vanguard of an army who, in Friedrich Engels's description, 'are as yet the first levies en masse of the great revolutionary war, raised and equipped locally and independently, all converging to form one common army, but as yet without regular organization and common plan of campaign'.[21] For Engels, whom Marx had once encouraged to author a chapter on military history for the first volume of *Capital*, England provided the concrete grounds for class war, exemplifying the more general affinity between modern warfare and economic development under capitalism. His book on the working class in England, first published in 1845, describes class as a revolutionary problem whose solution was to be found in military discipline. The working class, he argued, was not yet a battle-ready proletariat; 'converging columns cross each other here and there', he writes, 'confusion, angry disputes, even threats of conflict arise'. The challenge, then, is to organize various independent bodies and movements into the one army. And this, for Engels, is the task of militants, to elevate those fighters to be the equals of their state and class opponents in terms of weaponry and discipline: 'The community of ultimate purpose in the end overcomes all minor troubles; ere long the straggling and squabbling battalions will be formed in a long line of battle array, presenting to the enemy a well-ordered front, ominously silent under their glittering arms, supported by bold skirmishers in front and by unshakeable reserves in the rear'.[22] What Engels sensed, having served in the Prussian Artillery before spending time in and around the factories of Manchester, was a coming conflict of unprecedented scale and ferocity. 'The war of the poor against the rich will be the bloodiest ever waged', he predicted.[23] While that war never arrived, the first half of the nineteenth century saw the opening up of numerous battlefronts, many of which hosted militants that understood their task as one of combat.

* * *

The demonstrators on St Peter's Field – like most other popular movements, from the Luddites through Chartism – were essentially reformist as opposed to insurrectionary, insurgent, or revolutionary. They threatened war and occasionally used military tactics but – unlike Engels – most seemed intent on redress, transforming the workplace or the parliament without abolishing either. As the historian of Chartism Dorothy Thompson avers, 'in Britain the road to reform was seen to lie through the enlargement of the political system to include the working class, not the overthrow of the system as such'.[24] However, their reformist goals remain inextricable from more radical ambition. Many of the military tactics deployed in this context are subordinate to the greater process of what Engels would describe as proletarianization – the organization and radicalization of the dispossessed and exploited, the forging of new group identities, and the creation of common spaces in which this future-oriented projection and its collective subject might thrive. This tendency is not just particular to outwardly reformist objectives of trade unionism and parliamentary representation; it finds home, too, in some of the most hopeful lines of the *Manifesto of the Communist Party*. 'The advance of industry', Marx and Engels were given to prophesy, 'whose involuntary promoter is the bourgeoisie, replaces the isolation of the laborers, due to competition, by the revolutionary combination, due to association'.[25]

If this, the revolutionary dialectic of modern industry, is a means by which capitalism was seen as engineering its own demolition at the hands of an organized working class, the organization of class as a battle-ready proletariat was also a matter of parliamentary representation, and so reform. While the Combination Act of 1799 and the Combinations of Workmen Act in 1825 rendered the organization of workers illegal, the fight for suffrage was not just an end in itself; it was a fight to establish the social conditions in which revolutionary warfare might take place. This is one reason why, for Marx, the proletarian demand for universal suffrage, in English conditions, was nothing short of 'a war slogan'.[26]

Chartism is the movement that most readily cohered with the logic of redress. It openly sought political enfranchisement. By the same token, however, the movement also comprised a militant faction for which warfare was seen to underwrite more peaceable demands. This faction was the result of both local agitations and the international context. The Reform Act of 1832, forced through by a coalition of working- and middle-class radicals, extended suffrage from the landed aristocracy to property owners and certain working men. Some members of the working class looked to this as the start of a meaningful coalition against the common enemy and as the beginning of more expansive democratization. Yet these hopes soon dissipated. The middle-class Whigs joined with the conservative elite to safeguard the Act of Union, ensuring the unity of Great Britain and Ireland under central rule from London, against Irish republican protestors. Having cut his teeth with the Irish republicans, the individual figure to have contributed most to Chartist militancy in the 1830s was Feargus O'Connor, who owned the weekly newspaper *Northern Star*, from which he agitated for the use of physical force. 'The arming of the whole community capable of bearing arms would be the finest means of preserving peace abroad', he wrote, 'and harmony and satisfaction at home'.[27] The movement was thoroughly divided on the question of physical force as a practical means to success or a political good.

Two widely circulated pamphlets exemplify this division. Colonel Francis Maceroni's *Defensive Instructions to the People*, based on uprisings in European cities, provided instruction for the assembly of barricades, lances, and burning acids as well as 'helpful hints' on how to use them. It argued that by using methods of asymmetrical guerrilla warfare, the state military might be subdued. 'The officers of the British army, as a class', he instructs,

> are the avowed supporters of the system which works so well for themselves; and are, consequently, the bitterest enemies to all reform. On this account, therefore, it becomes doubly necessary

to recommend them to the especial attention of our sharpshooters! And the higher their rank, the more attention should be paid to them! An infantry officer on horseback, for instance, should immediately receive the honours of at least a dozen rifles.[28]

Opposingly, Alexander Somerville's *Warnings to the People on Street Warfare* set out to neutralize this kind of militancy by arguing that an armed people, no matter how disciplined and organized, would be no match for the regular army and its artillery. Rather than simply embody one or the other perspective on the question of warfare, Chartism maintained armed militancy, embodied in the faction of physical force, alongside its more liberal reformist campaigns. In this way, armed militancy came to serve as a threat against which reformist demands could be prosecuted.

Charles Davlin's 1832 poem 'Questions from the Loom' makes this clear using a nautical metaphor. 'Whence arises, what constitutes power?' it asks the 'tyrants of earth!'[29] Apostrophizing the state, 'your bark is at sea, and your mariners sleep' while 'the dark gloom of thunder half shadows the deep', the poem nominates 'the raft of reform' as the only safe passage ashore, for to keep sailing will surely end with 'war's brazen trump' and 'the cannon's dead roar', a coming cataclysm rendered in language that will soon reverberate through the *Manifesto*. 'For the mob on the grounds you their franchise refuse' will, according to this poem, soon be armed and insurgent because with 'nought to protect' they 'can have nothing to lose'.

The relationship between democratic reform and physical force is especially clear in the Chartists' thinking about the work refusal or labour strike. This principal method of class antagonism will be theorized properly in subsequent chapters, but it is worth noting here that it emerged alongside other and more insurrectionary measures. In 1839, unable to set a date for a general strike's commencement, the *Northern Star* was emphatic that it should not take place until the working people were militarily prepared. 'ANY ATTEMPT TO BRING ABOUT THE SACRED MONTH BEFORE AN UNIVERSAL ARMING SHALL HAVE TAKEN

PLACE', intoned one article, 'WILL RUIN ALL'.[30] At the same time, O'Conner argued that all-out war would be preferable to a disorganized strike. 'I never will, with a certainty of my own dinner, recommend a project which may cause millions to starve. No; I would rather go to battle'.[31] But the strike and the battle would coexist with each other, and not just with the latter consigned to the supporting role of contingent threat.

While relatively peaceable three-day strikes took place in some northern cities, on 30 August 1839 a large Chartist meeting in Newcastle upon Tyne was dispersed with violent force by the police, and on the next day fighting broke out in Stockport, where a quantity of weapons said to belong to the Chartists had been seized. Small armed uprisings, organized in secret, began erupting in the industrial districts during the winter of 1939. The most significant of these, putting truth to both the militants' threats and the establishment's fears, took place during November in Newport, South Wales. The local miners were said to be arming in secret and plotting insurrection, so the gentry swore in special constables, imported soldiers, and prepared for battle. On the night of 4 November, miners stormed the city, armed with billhooks, scythes, saws, hammers, pickaxes, and pikes. Twenty-two were shot dead before the crowd dispersed, many more were wounded, and the three organizers were prosecuted for high treason. Exemplifying state suppression, this moment also inaugurated a period in which the Chartists would start invoking war as an organizational trope designed to consolidate interest and catalyze action.

The first ever recorded utterance of the phrase 'class warfare' is to be found in this period. The term appeared on 25 January 1840 in *Northern Star*. It came at the end of an article setting out the movement's positions and demands, which pronounces ritual bloodletting as the outcome of underrepresentation coupled with immiseration. 'Good must come to the nation out of this class warfare for pre-eminence', it reads, 'as from a compound of the most deadly poisons a wholesale medicine may be extracted'.[32] No longer a threat, something to be worried about in the future, but alive and deadly, here and now: the class struggle had already erupted into civil war. Revolution seemed more likely than ever.

* * *

Class war bedevilled the conservative imaginary. Published in 1845, the same year as Engels's report on class, Benjamin Disraeli's novel *Sybil: or The Two Nations* is set against the Chartist movement and presents modern class relations as both the result of warlike conditions and the promise of wars to come. In the first instance, the dispossession of working people is said to have resulted from an unspoken civil war, in the dissolution of the monasteries and enclosure of the commons. 'The monks', we learn from a travelling stranger, 'struggled against property and they were beat', leaving a landscape haunted by commonality. Looking at monastic ruins, the stranger describes them as 'the children of violence, not of time. It is war that created these ruins, civil war, of all our civil wars the most inhuman, for it was waged with the unresisting'. The ensuing conversations use this history to reframe faith as a kind of secular militancy. 'You lament the old faith', responds the novel's bourgeois hero, whom the stranger summarily corrects that any such faith is less about spirituality than it is about property, 'which under their administration so mainly contributed to the welfare of the community', and so embodies a form of collective ownership that 'expired' in England, with communal bonds replaced by 'aggregation under circumstances'. Aggregation, says the stranger, is more alienating than unifying, bringing workers together 'not in a state of co-operation, but of isolation, as to the making of fortunes', with each labouring for the enrichment of their own.[33]

The conversation finishes with a recognition of England's division into two irreconcilable states, the belligerent coexistence of which occludes any unifying sense of nation. 'Our Queen reigns over the greatest nation that ever existed', claims the hero, before he is again corrected that 'she reigns over two', the rich and the poor,

> between whom there is no intercourse and no sympathy; who are as ignorant of each other's habits, thoughts, and feelings, as

if they were dwellers in different zones, or inhabitants of different planets; who are formed by a different breeding, are fed by a
different food, are ordered by different manners, and are not
governed by the same laws.[34]

While this novel is remarkably sympathetic to Chartism –
although it explicitly favours an unblemished 'moral force'
Chartism against the sinister threat of the 'physical force'
Chartists – it nevertheless adheres to the author's particular
vision of a one-nation conservatism, which proposed paternalist
maintenance of social hierarchy as a way to obviate against
revolutionary ferment, and betrays the ruling class's reactionary
paranoia. The superannuated aristocracy fear the potential for
'revolution' brought about by large-scale industry. They were
particularly afraid of 'a very dangerous tendency to equality',
which was then taking form in the trade union and parliamentary reform movements. 'Equality', clarifies one lord, 'is not our
metier. If we nobles do not make a stand against the levelling
spirit of the age, I am at a loss to know who will fight the
battle'.[35]

The battle is fought, for these embodiments of the ruling
class, through a strategy of 'war to the cottage, peace to the
castle', which we should here observe is a near inversion of
Engels's prophecy of escalation. For Engels, 'the war of the poor
against the rich now carried on in detail and indirectly will
become direct and universal', in such a way that localized struggles will transcend their villages and their parishes or their
workshops and their factories. 'The classes are divided more
and more sharply', Engels opines, 'the spirit of resistance pene-
trates the workers, the bitterness intensifies, the guerrilla skirmishes become concentrated in more important battles, and
soon a slight impulse will suffice to set the avalanche in motion'.
Only then will the 'war-cry', patently a military slogan, will
resound across England: '"War to the mansion, peace to the
cottage!" – but then it will be too late for the rich to beware'.[36]

* * *

But actual warfare was never really what the Chartists had in mind. The distinction between revolution and reform, civil war and civil disobedience, is most clearly felt in the thinking of Ernest Jones, whom we encountered in the previous chapter. Jones had joined the Chartist movement in 1846 as a follower of O'Conner and as a journalist for *Northern Star*. In 1848, Jones's speeches were preoccupied with physical force which was framed, always, as retaliatory and defensive. 'We are not men of non-resistance and passive obedience', he would insist, 'we will not be the aggressors – but if we are struck, will return the blow and they must stand the consequence'. And this consequence, for Jones, required a unified class – without which 'a people is a mob; but with it, it becomes an army'.[37]

On 19 February of that year, *Northern Star* would publish an unsigned article by Jones and George Julian Harney under the title 'The War of Classes', here responding to fearful characterization of a 'formidable enemy' stalking the mining districts, 'an enemy already within our fates – the cruelty-oppressed working class of this country'. Under conditions of economic depression, in which 'furnaces are being blown out, and workmen deprived of employment', the threat of collective action looms: 'A strike is anticipated – one of those advancing waves which will certainly come, and which will as certainly sweep to annihilation the monstrous system, by which the Aristocracy and the Bourgeoisie have grown fat, at the expense of the outcast millions of the fellow-countrymen'.[38]

Unlike Marx and Engels, who would advocate for precisely that annihilation of the system, for Jones and Harney the object of war remains reformist enfranchisement:

Liberty was never yet gained without a struggle, and certainly such liberty as we seek – the political emancipation and social regeneration of the working classes – is least likely to form an exception to the experience of all time. Moral force is moral humbug, unless there is physical force behind it, and we have done next to nothing towards carrying the Charter, until we have secured the aid of those masses of physical force, which, even at present, though deplorably wanting in mental power, strike alarm into the minds of the supporters of the existing system.[39]

War, for the Chartists, was not the proletariat battling against an integrated class system. It was instead a means of carrying out reform within that system. 'The aim was not to overthrow the system', clarifies Dorothy Thompson, 'but to enlarge it'.[40] This is what Jones would mean by invocation of 'the working classes – the people – the great march of Democracy, that shall yet trample on the graves of all monopolies', not the gravediggers of capital, who would be announced by Marx and Engels in due course, but a constitution open to working people who would need, now as ever, to rally as a class.[41]

In June of that same year, Jones gave an inflammatory speech in East London advocating that the blow for liberty should be struck first in Ireland. Calling for Ireland's liberation from the British rule, he was immediately arrested and sentenced to two years in solitary confinement. It was in prison that he recast his political thinking as poetry, composing his poem about the Haitian Revolution as well as several lyrics about the life of the militant waging 'dreadful war' against 'deep-rooted prejudice and power' and hoping, romantically, to 'blast back centuries in a single hour'.[42]

* * *

While poetry might be the perfect medium for the militant who writes, not least because it supplies a literary object easily circulated and reproduced within revolutionary environments, it was the novel that would come to enshrine these struggles within the ideology of romance. In the literary critic Terry Eagleton's metaphor, the form of the novel had 'something like the importance of steam-power or electricity in the material realm, or of democracy in the political sphere'. Indeed, the novel was a mode of storytelling wherein 'art finally returned the world to the common people who had created it through their labor, and who could now contemplate their own faces for the first time'.[43] And it was to be one particular form of the novel, the 'condition of England' novel, that bore witness to the great division of society into two warring camps.

Published in 1854, just a few years after Disraeli's one-nation vision of England, Elizabeth Gaskell's sentimental *North and South* provides an exemplarily romantic articulation of this view of the country as two opposing forces. In Gaskell's novel, the industrialist mill-owner John Thornton explains the disciplinary measures within his factory to an elderly preacher, father of the novel's heroine, while trying to distance himself from the brutality of his precursors. 'Some of these early manufacturers did ride to the devil in a magnificent style – crushing human bone and flesh under their horses' hoofs without remorse', he says. 'But by-and-by came a re-action, there were more factories, more masters; more men were wanted. The power of masters and men became more evenly balanced; and now the battle is pretty fairly waged between us'. If this exchange is informed by the heightening of tension between mutually exclusive interests of two social groupings, the characters all seem to know as much. 'Is there necessity for calling it a battle between the two classes?' asks the preacher, as though to underscore the significance of this rhetoric. 'I know, from your using the term, it is one which gives a true idea of the real state of things to your mind'.[44]

Finally, after the decline of Chartism, a belated account of class war, its romantic coordination, and its relationship to both revolution and redress would live on in the work of the poet, designer, and socialist William Morris, for whom class society was understood, following Rousseau, as a state of perpetual warfare. 'War', he writes, 'or competition, whichever you please to call it, means at the best pursuing your own advantage at the cost of someone else's loss, and in the process of it you must not be sparing of destruction even of your own possessions, or you will certainly come by the worse in the struggle'.[45] Morris claimed that capitalism is defined by two intersecting modes of warfare: geopolitical and commercial, of nationalist and corporate competition, comprising imperial expansion and colonial domination, on the one hand, and a fight to monopolize production, on the other. Socialism, he argued, was the only viable alternative, a way of living together in 'peace and friendship instead of war' – and class antagonism, as a civil war already inherent to the way things are, might clear the path from capitalism to socialism:

> As things go, the workers are a part of the competing firms, an adjunct of capital. Nevertheless, they are only so by compulsion; and, even without their being conscious of it, they struggle against that compulsion and its immediate results, the lowering of their wages, of their standard of life: and this they do, and must do, both as a class and individually: just as the slave of the great Roman lord, though he distinctly felt himself to be a part of the household, yet collectively was a force in reserve for its destruction, and individually stole from his lord whenever he could safely do so. So, here, you see, is another form of war necessary to the way we live now, the war of class against class, which, when it rises to its height, and it seems to be rising at present, will destroy those other forms of war we have been speaking of; will make the position of the profit-makers, of perpetual commercial war, untenable; will destroy the present system of competitive privilege, or commercial war.[46]

To write these words at the century's end, in 1894, is to have internalized the history of class in England, especially from the militant decades of violent movements, between the Luddites and Chartism, when it was at its most warlike.

But it is also to read that history through subsequent political events, in particular from the standpoint of the Paris Commune of 1871 – a conflict that was, for Morris, 'a matter of war, simply and solely', and one that gave life to the promise or threat of revolution. 'Looking back on the events of that time', as he described the barricades, 'it would now seem as if the Commune had some chance of triumphing in that war. Paris was now well victualled, ammunition was plenty, and munitions of war generally, including guns; and there was no lack of men as brave as might be, as the result showed'. Knowing the Commune's bloody defeat, Morris reads the events of 1871 through the lens of English militancy, finding an explanation for Paris in the failures of England. 'The result might have been different', he speculates, 'if the Commune had wasted less time in parliamentary pros and cons, and addressed itself more to organising its splendid army'.[47]

To that end, Morris's utopian novel of 1890, *News from Nowhere*, is a thought experiment that imagines this alternative reality from the victorious standpoint of classless society. Overlaying these two contexts, England in the 1830s and 1840s with Paris in 1871, the novel projects the final climactic battle during which an army of workers overthrows class society to establish a communist London. 'The sloth, the hopelessness', we are told by a witness to the conflict, 'the cowardice of the last century, had given place to the eager, restless heroism of a declared revolutionary period'. Here, as in Paris, 'civil war' erupts from within a longstanding struggle and 'ordinary sense of war', defined as it has been by 'mere massacres on one side, and endurance plus strikes on the other', when working people act collectively and decisively upon reckoning with the mutual exclusivity of freedom and capital. While government, the state military, and the ruling and middle classes all collude in reactionary suppression, the proletarian insurgents succeed not only because of organizational capacity, sympathetic defection, and revolutionary instinct; they succeed, it is said, because of a solidarity that can only belong to them as the defining commonality of their class. 'The end', we learn, 'must be either absolute slavery for all but the privileged, or a system of life founded on equality and Communism'.[48]

3

Defend the City

Jules Vallès's novelization of the Paris Commune, *The Insurrectionist*, recalls a protest march in response to Pierre Bonaparte's murder of Victor Noir on 11 January 1870:

> There were two hundred thousand of them! When we put our heads out of the window, we saw a street rolling and overflowing like the bed of a vast river in flood. The pistols and knives were hidden, but the stirring weapon of the 'Marseillaise' was being openly brandished. The earth trembled under the feet of the multitude that seemed to be marching in step, and the refrain of the hymn was rising to strike the sky with its wing.[1]

Here, in the unification of this disparate multitude in martial lockstep, as well as in the display of a real and metaphoric arsenal whereby the republican anthem is as much the weapon as those concealed armaments, we clearly see the language of class war. 'These', we had been told, 'were fragments of an army seeking other fragments, shred of a Republic stuck together by the dead man's blood, the beast that Prudhomme calls the hydra of anarchy extending its thousands heads, all held to the body by a single idea, hot coals of anger glowing deep in two thousand ideas'.[2] But by the 1870s, 'La Marseillaise' had ceased to be the weapon it once was. What Vallès hears is no longer the battle hymn of revolutionary republicans or the chorus that once resounded through the jungles of Haiti. Between 1789 and 1870, the 'Marseillaise' had become the very opposite of radical: a commemorative and patriotic hymn to state. 'It does not inspire volunteers', reflects the militant, 'it leads flocks of sheep'. To sing the 'Marseillaise' in 1870 was to reckon with the inheritance of the previous century's revolution, and so with a political sequence that had ultimately led to the bloody suppression of proletarians in June 1848, coinciding with the arrival of France's Second Empire. The 'Marseillaise', adopted as the national anthem in 1795, would only give voice to raging conservatism. 'What was a fire gong in the night has become a tinkling bell around the necks of beasts', Vallès laments.[3] This is why the 'Marseillaise' was rewritten for the Commune of 1871, re-sharpened into a 'stirring weapon' with which to accompany a class of insurgents into war against their state.

The original chorus was a literal call to arms. 'To arms, citizens, form your battalions, let's march, let's march!' Losing nothing of this militancy, similarly begging the people to 'wake up' from a twenty-year sleep and send 'to battle your proud warriors', the revised version shifts the zone of conflict from one of international competition between states to a specifically urban revolt. Crucially, it replaced the imperial patriotism of citizens with the people's means of survival:

Sing freedom,
Defend the city,
March on, march on, without a sovereign,
The people will have bread.

The song might retain an emphasis on liberty, but here freedom is re-contextualized as social instead of a political or national problem. While the verbal action is militaristic in its calls to defend and to march, the referential nouns mark that militarism as relative to the means of subsistence for working men and women. Specifically, as the cause of any number of riots, and prized by socialists as a symbol for freedom from compulsion and unalienated life, bread secures this version of the 'Marseillaise' in its social dispensation amid the dispossessed workers. Bread is, for the anarchist Peter Kropotkin, the material form of collective riches that need to be requisitioned through combat. 'Under pain of death', he writes, 'human societies are forced to return to first principles: the means of production being the collective work of humanity, the product should be the collective property of the race'.[4] And this is what marked the social shortcomings of 1789. 'It was always middle-class ideas which prevailed', writes Kropotkin. 'They discussed various political questions at great length, but forgot to discuss the question of bread'.[5]

The focus on people's bread and the collective work of humanity is also, crucially, an emphatically multi-gendered conception, incorporating the unwaged labour of social reproduction, which takes place not only in the kitchen, bedroom, and nursery, but also at the marketplace, the site of barter as well as assessment of goods. At all levels, 'bread' rhymes conceptually with 'city'. Both are the result of collective labour undertaken by working people, both are necessary for social reproduction, and both are priced to absorb surplus value into profit. 'From their very inception', writes the geographer David Harvey, 'cities have arisen through geographical and social concentration of a surplus product. Urbanization has always been, therefore, a class phenomenon of some sort, since surpluses have been extracted from somewhere and from somebody, while control over the use of the surplus typically lies in the hands of a few'.[6] To 'defend the city' is therefore to enact what Harvey describes, after Henri Lefebvre, as 'the right to the city', a collective reclamation by workers both waged and unwaged of that which they produce and from which they have been alienated under the rule of private property. Less revanchist than revolutionary, to follow this version of the song is to take up arms as a class for the overthrow of class society. That is what it means to defend the city.

As with scorched earth in Haiti and machine-breaking in England, in Paris the technical composition of the combatants shaped military strategy, with a city's workers giving form to urban warfare and with the spaces of commerce – the streets themselves – transforming into battlegrounds. 'Let Paris bristle up with barricades', the Committee for Public Safety would announce, 'and from behind these improvised ramparts still hurl at her enemies her cry of war, of pride, of defiance, but also of victory; for Paris with her barricades cannot be wiped out'.[7] Barricades, the Commune's principal defensive utility, were constructed through a critical engagement with work by workers. According to Kristin Ross, leading interpreter of the Commune's political and cultural legacies, the shoe-maker Napoléon Gaillard, head of barricade construction, 'had himself photographed standing in front of the barricade he designed on the Place de la Concorde, in effect "signing" his creation, appropriating for himself the status of author or artist', a symbolic gesture consonant with a desire to raise the cultural status of work and workers as well as a vision of unalienated collective labour: 'I believe myself to be a worker, an "artist-shoemaker", and though making shoes, I have the right to as much respect from men as those who think themselves workers while wielding a pen'.[8]

But the barricades were not just about workers appearing in their capacity as workers. 'What the commune as political and social medium offered that the factory did not', Ross clarifies, 'was a broader social scope – one that included women, children, the peasantry, the aged, the unemployed. It comprises not merely the realm of production but both production and consumption'.[9] And so, the barricades were also a site of militancy against gendered divisions of labour. Headed by Elisabeth Dmitrieff – the Russian-born co-founder of the First International and a comrade of Marx in London – the Union des Femmes was established to organize the working women of Paris to fight on and around the barricades, to serve in ambulance stations and canteens, and to work for the emancipation of women. This union understood class as the preserve of no single gender and in opposition to all systems of exploitation and exclusion. 'Women of Paris', they proclaimed,

> will prove to France and to the world that they too, at the moment of supreme danger – at the barricades and at the

ramparts of Paris, if the reactionary powers should force her gates – they too know how, like their brothers, to give their blood and their life for the defense and triumph of the Commune, that is, the People.[10]

The city is not just a battleground then, and neither is its combat exclusive to the zones of productive labour; it is, as the interlock of myriad injustices, a social form to be requisitioned by a class, mobilizing as a class, for the re-composition of classless society.

* * *

During the nineteenth century, this kind of urban warfare was seen as endemic to Paris, where social and political conflicts that took shape locally would nevertheless transform world history. This is also a mode of conflict that enjoys pride of place in French literary history, where the defensive street barricade predominates as an artistic principle unto itself. On 5 June 1832, at the onset of an anti-monarchist rebellion, Victor Hugo famously stumbled his way into a barricaded street and was forced to hide from the crossfire between revolutionaries and the state. In his novel *Les Misérables*, published in 1862, he draws on this experience to immortalize the city's radical history as resembling a decidedly classical vision of the underworld:

In brief, the barricade had fought like a doorway of Thebes, and the tavern fought like a house in Saragossa. Those were obstinate defenses. No quarter was given, no discussion was possible. Men are ready to die provided they also kill. When Suchet cried, 'Surrender!' Palafox replied, 'After the battle with firearms comes the battle with knives'. Nothing was lacking in the capture by assault of the Hucheloup tavern, neither the paving-stones rained down upon the besiegers from the upper window and roof, causing hideous injuries, nor shots fired from the cellars and attics, neither fury in the attack nor rage in the defense – nor finally, when the door gave way, the frantic dementia of slaughter. The attackers, rushing into the tavern, their feet entangled in the panels of the broken door, found not a single defender. The circular staircase, cut in halves with an axe, lay in the middle of the lower room, where a few wounded men were in process of dying. All those remaining alive were on the upper floor, and from here, by way of the hole in the ceiling which had been the entrance to the staircase, there came a terrible burst of fire. Those were the last cartridges. When they had been fired, and when the heroic defenders were left with neither powder nor shot, each seized two of the bottles set aside by Enjolras, of which we have spoken, and held back the attack with these most fragile cudgels. They were bottles of brandy. We are depicting these somber aspects of the carnage as they happened. The besieged, alas, makes a weapon of everything. Greek fire did no dishonor to Archimedes, nor boiling pitch to Bayard. All forms of warfare are terror, and there is nothing to choose between them. The musketry of the attackers, although harassed and aiming upwards, was murderous. The edge of that hole in the ceiling was soon surrounded by dead heads from which hung long, streaming red threads. The din was indescribable; and a reeking cloud of smoke plunged the battle in darkness. Words are lacking to depict a horror that has reached this point. There were no longer men engaged in a struggle that was now infernal, no longer giants against Titans; it was nearer to Milton and Dante than to Homer. Demons attacked and specters resisted.[11]

Hugo's liberal pacifism strains here to depict insurrection as the social form of immortal diabolism, with fighters engaged in 'heroism become monstrous' and so universally condemnable or just plain evil. This is the kind of writing that would inform a critical assessment of literary narratives from the period made by Hugo's sometimes correspondent, the militant revolutionary Louise Michel, whom we will later meet on the barricades. 'Under the Empire', she would insist, 'literature was strange, as it always is when nations are slaughterhouses. Books were filled with foolishness, but there were forgotten corpses behind each page. All published writing smelled stale'.[12] For all its expressed nonviolence and political non-commitment, liberal formulations like Hugo's conceal within themselves the human cost of imperial decadence. Such ideology shaded into Hugo's response to 1871 and so to the movement and the militancy in which Michel would play a pivotal role. 'In brief', he demurred on 9 April, 'this Commune is as idiotic as the National Assembly is ferocious. From both sides, folly'.[13]

Though no more enthusiastic than Hugo, the novels of Émile Zola narrate urban warfare with its political and class coordinates. Zola's twenty-book cycle *Les Rougon-Macquart* sings an epic of the Second Empire from the moment of its inception to its demise in the Commune. Unlike Hugo, Zola is intent on displaying the foolishness and the forgotten corpses, on portraying the empire as a vast slaughterhouse of the working person. Indeed, the establishment of the empire via coup d'état in 1851 is accounted for in blood:

> But the strip of pink satin fastened to Pierre's button-hole was not the only red spot in that triumph of the Rougons. A shoe, with a blood-stained heel, still lay forgotten under the bedstead in the adjoining room. The taper burning at Monsieur Peirotte's bedside, over the way, gleamed too with the lurid redness of a gaping wound amidst the dark night. And yonder, far away, in the depths of the Aire Saint-Mittre, a pool of blood was congealing upon a tombstone.[14]

In his capacity as the originator of literary naturalism – a kind of storytelling that rejects any sort of romance to instead foreground an otherwise submerged, underclass perspective – Zola's narrative of the Commune is bound up with a profound sense of interclass antagonism.

For Zola, the Commune is an event through which the veiled civil war becomes open conflict, with struggle modulating at last into antagonism, as a dispossessed and exploited people enter history as a class. From peasants and colliers, to prostitutes and shopworkers, to soldiers and train conductors: Zola's novels are populated by a congeries of workers from every walk of life.

What makes them unique, according to Fredric Jameson, can be measured in comparison 'with the sentimental accounts of the poor' in writers like Hugo as well as in those English novelists, like Dickens, Gaskell, Brontë, and Disraeli. Here, writes Jameson, 'philanthropy and its pity and sympathy' are replaced by 'a sinister and radically different space', which at once encodes a fear of descent into poverty as well as the very real threat of a rising proletariat.[15] As many of the workers meet their grim destiny in various kinds of social murder, often after a brief foray into relative wealth, for the politicians, bankers, and property developers the menace of classed violence is ever present, like an atmosphere. And, as the cycle approaches its revolutionary terminus, those workers become an existential threat to the empire as a whole.

So ends *Germinal*, Zola's novel about the grisly failure of a mineworkers' revolt in northern France. 'Of course they had been beaten', we are given to reflect:

> They had lost money and lives; but Paris would not forget the shots fired at Le Voreux, and the blood of the Empire itself would drain out of this incurable wound; for even if this industrial slump was drawing to a close, and the factories were reopening one by one, a state of war had none the less been declared and peace was no longer possible.[16]

Or as we read in one of the urban novels, *Money*, in a portent of things to come: 'Behind the reddish smoke on the horizon, in the blurred and far-off parts of the city, could be heard a sort of muffled creaking, as of the imminent end of the world'.[17]

That apocalypse is delivered in full with *The Debacle*, Zola's novel of the empire's defeat during the Franco-Prussian War, which sends one young and embittered soldier, Maurice, back from the frontline to the heart of Paris, where he joins the comrades on the barricades. Driven by disillusionment with the state and its leaders, and by visions 'of a nation collapsing', Maurice enlists to fight against the Prussians. Later, after witnessing the capitulation to the enemy, and after experiencing the life of an infantryman in defeat, he is filled with militant opposition to the state for whom he had been so degraded on the battlefield. 'Maurice, having escaped the slaughter, trembling from the battle, felt only hatred for this so-called government of law and order, which, crushed in every encounter with the Prussians, had only been able to find courage when it came to conquering Paris'.[18] Having joined the people to seize the city, he then approves of 'the first violent measures, the building of the barricades blocking streets and squares, the taking of hostages, the archbishop, priests, former civil servants', and is transported away in the fury of the exploited and the immiserated. 'He saw the Commune as the avenging angel for all the shames endured', we read, 'as a liberating force bringing the severing iron, the purifying flame'.

Sentences such as these, which carry a vehemence their author would gainsay as madness beyond reason, characterize the Commune's place in this history of class war: they convey at once what it means to find common cause as a class against a designated enemy as well the solidification of that militancy through the experience of actual conflict. The Commune presents itself, from the ground zero of urban warfare, as the living force of social redemption. 'If Paris won the day', he fantasizes, 'he could see it, crowned in glory, rebuilding a France of justice and liberty, reorganizing a new society, having swept away the rotten debris of the old'.[19] While conceptually familiar, this dynamic is historically unique: in Paris, as with Haiti and England, class would cohere and mobilize under its own circumstances.

* * *

After the French Revolution and through the first half of the nineteenth century, the bourgeois republicans set upon themselves to disarm the workers, enacting measures that culminated in June 1848, when the proletarians were driven to insurrection and, after five days' struggle, were crushed under the heel of the empire. Founded on this military suppression of the economically dispossessed and politically disenfranchised, the Second Empire – which commenced with a coup d'état in 1851

– concentrated political power around the imperial court of Louis Bonaparte. Bonaparte's encouragement of speculation and industrialization enriched the national bourgeoisie as never before, all while denying Paris municipal rights. Geopolitically, the Second Empire appealed to a certain national chauvinism, demanding a restoration of the frontiers lost in 1814 – 'hence the necessity for brief wars and extension of frontiers', wrote Friedrich Engels. 'But no extension of frontiers was so dazzling to the imagination of the French chauvinists as the extension to the German left bank of the Rhine'.[20]

In July 1870, the French Empire declared war on Prussia. Less than two months later, on 4 September, they faced a humiliating military defeat, in which the emperor was taken prisoner following the Battle of Sedan. In Paris, an immense crowd of civilians descended on the seat of France's parliament, announcing the downfall of the Second Empire and the beginning of a new, third republic. That same month, the Prussian Army laid siege to Paris, while the French forces were either fighting in Metz on the Franco-German border or held captive in Germany. Because of this polygonal emergency, the Paris deputies formed a legislative government, and all Parisians capable of bearing arms were enlisted in the national guard, with the force now comprising a majority of workers who were openly antagonistic to the bourgeois government. And that government stood for capital. Prosper-Olivier Lissagaray, who fought on the barricades and whose account of the period was subsequently translated by Eleanor Marx, explains the forces of reaction as a military array: 'The red sun of civil discord melts veneer and all masks', he reflected. 'There they are side by side as in 1791, 1794, and 1848, Monarchists, Clericals, Liberals, Radicals, all of them, their hands raised against the people – one army in different uniforms. Their decentralization is rural and capitalist federalism; their self-government, the exploitation of the budget by themselves, just as the whole political science of their statesmen consists only in massacre and the state of siege'.[21]

Years later, in 1936, the anti-fascist Jean Cassou would describe that science as one with the city itself. 'The other class has organized itself scientifically', he claims, and 'has entrusted itself to implacable armies. Its leaders have long since acquired a clear vision of the situation. Not for nothing had Haussmann built broad, perfectly straight avenues to break up the swarming, tortuous neighborhoods, the breeding grounds for mystery and for the feuilleton, the secret gardens of popular conspiracy'.[22] All of this provided the material conditions for the 'organized apocalypse' of the Commune, a form of class power that would live and die under conditions of war. The national government, living out the death throes of an empire, would soon react with maximum hostility. 'They', Lissagaray wrote, 'seeing this Paris capable of engendering a new world, her heart swelled with the best blood of France, had but one thought – to bleed Paris'.[23]

On 28 January 1871, Paris officially capitulated to the Prussians, rendering all Parisians prisoners of war. Forts were surrendered, the city wall disarmed, weapons handed over. But the national guard maintained its weaponry, entering into an armistice with the victors, who, not permitted entry to the city, instead occupied a relatively small area of public parks. The Prussian conquerors, having encircled Paris for over four months, were now surrounded by armed workers who kept them to their allotted territory. 'Such was the respect which the Paris workers inspired in the army before which all the armies of the empire had laid down their arms', wrote Engels. 'And the Prussian *junkers*, who had come to take revenge at the home of the revolution, were compelled to stand by respectfully, and salute precisely this armed revolution!'[24]

By 18 March, the chief executive of the new French government, Adolphe Thiers – whom Marx described as a 'monstrous gnome' with 'class prejudices standing him in the place of ideas, and vanity in the place of a heart'[25] – deployed official troops to rob the national guard of its weapons and artillery, which had been paid for by public subscription and established during the siege. Like the city and the bread in the 'Marseillaise', the canon represented a collective good realized through the combined labour of the city: a material embodiment of class war. In Louise

Michel's recollection, the resistance was led by women in such a way to reveal the shifting ferocity of the state, directing away from the international antagonist and onto the enemy within, but it also revealed the potential for class solidarity through military defection. 'The women of Paris covered the cannon with their bodies', writes Michel. 'When their officers ordered the soldiers to fire, the men refused'. Thiers's attempt failed, defeated at once by class solidarity, yet this solidarity would be neither universal nor lasting. 'The same army', this was, 'that would be used to crush Paris two months later'.[26] Paris thus mobilized as one in defence of the guns. The antagonism between city and state had thus become what legendary communard Adrien Lejeune described as 'above all war, civil war'.[27]

Just over a week later, on 26 March, the Paris Commune was elected, and two days later it was proclaimed to the people as an autonomous social form enacted to improvise the organization of collective life according to principles of association and coop-eration. This was, for Marx and Engels, 'the political form at last discovered through which to work out the economic eman-cipation of labour', an insurrection of the producing against the appropriating classes. 'Yes', they write in astonishment,

> the Commune intended to abolish that class property which makes the labour of the many the wealth of the few. It aimed at the expropriation of the expropriators. It wanted to make indi-vidual property a truth by transforming the means of produc-tion, land, and capital, now chiefly the means of enslaving and exploiting labor, into mere instruments of free and associated labor. But this is communism, 'impossible' communism![28]

Or in Kristin Ross's formulation, the new sociality was one of 'communal luxury', an unprecedented way of living together that 'countered any notion of the sharing of misery with a distinctly different kind of world: one where everyone, instead, would have his or her share of the best'.[29] In order to achieve such a goal, the Commune swiftly abolished conscription and the standing army, in its place declaring the national guard, comprising all citizens capable of bearing arms, to be the sole military force. The reaction from Thiers was swift. On 1 April, he officially declared war. 'The Assembly', he announced, 'is sitting at Versailles, where the organization of one of the finest armies that France has ever possessed is being completed. Good citizens may then take heart and hope for the end of a struggle which will be sad but short'. This was, in Lissagaray's withering condemnation, the 'cynical boast of that same bourgeoisie which had refused to organize armies against the Prussians', here responding in greater force and with more enthusiasm than ever against the occupying army.[30] As with Peterloo, class antagonism appeared as a greater threat than imperial conflict, and the state acted accordingly.

* * *

With insurrection emerging under the yolk of empire – class war fought alongside wars of extermination – the Commune presented itself as anti-war without embracing liberal pacifism. As the General Council of the International Working-Men's Association wrote to its members in September 1870, the English workers were to offer an outstretched 'hand of fellowship to the French and German working people', because revolutionary solidarity is antipathetic to the fratricidal wars of nations: 'Whatever turn the impending horrid war may take, the alliance of the working-classes of all countries will ultimately kill war'.[31] This superficially paradoxical formulation of class solidarity as war against war – familiar now from Rosa Luxemburg's response to German militarization, but which also appears to guide Trotsky's extraction of Russia from World War One and Mao's tactical alliances during World War Two – was taken up by the Commune as a matter for both symbolic gesture and practical necessity.

Symbolically, the act that was to serve as the indictment of wars between peoples and as a promotion of international solidarity was the destruction of the grand Vendôme Column. Gustave Courbet, as president of the Federation of Artists and elected member of the Commune, proposed that the column, which had been cast from guns captured by Napoleon after the war of 1809, be disassembled. It was, in his words, 'a monument devoid of all artistic value, tending to perpetuate by its expression the ideas of war and conquest of the past imperial dynasty, which are reproved by a republican nation's sentiment'.[32] The practical act was the national guard's attempt to persuade the Versailles troops to join the Commune, just as they are said to have initially held fire on the cannons' guard. Accusing the government of inspiring civil war to escape responsibility for the defeat and dismemberment of France to the Prussians, the Commune reached out to the standing army. 'Citizen soldiers', they wrote, 'will you obey the impious order to spill the same blood that flows in your veins? Will you tear out your own entrails? No! You will not agree to become patricides and fratricides'. Finding common cause in the form of a shared enemy, the insurrectionists wanted 'the army to be returned to its homes in order to return hearts to their families and arms to their labor as quickly as possible', and so, they averred,

> soldiers, children of the people, let us unite to save the republic. Kings and emperors have done us enough harm. Don't sully your life. Orders don't stand in the way of conscience's responsibilities. Let us embrace in the face of those who want to set us at each other's throats in order to conquer a rank, obtain a position, or return a king.[33]

Missives such as this give clear expression to the emergence of class through and against war, to a movement thoroughly enmeshed in antagonism, with comrades hard-won at the expense of the state and defection now performing double duty as solidarity.

* * *

On all these points – on the necessity of transferring state military powers to the insurgent city, on the need to merge an army and a class as one – the Commune owed much of its ideological and practical thinking to the revolutionary activist Louis

Auguste Blanqui. Blanqui, having spent his adult life in and out of prison for insurrectionary activity, was not to see the Communards in action. Just a few months before the barricades went up around Paris, he was condemned to death by trial in absentia, and after eluding arrest for a week, he was finally imprisoned on 17 March 1871. Though in prison, Blanqui was elected president of the Commune, and his comrades offered to release all political captives if the Thiers government returned Blanqui, an offer that was refused.

For Blanqui, revolution takes place relative to war, and political violence is key to social transformation. 'War is war', he would insist, 'reciprocity is its fundamental law. Whoever lives by the sword dies by the sword. We owe nothing to persecutors and executioners except reprisals and the axe'.[34] Combining these arguments with revolutionary strategy, Blanqui's 1868 field manual, *Instructions for an Armed Uprising*, concluded with a letter template addressed to the army. 'Soldiers!' it begins: 'The people of Paris are taking up arms. Will you oppose them? In liberating France, it is you, above all, whom they are liberating. Are you not slaves like us, even more than us?' The political task here is to enable social coherence around a common interest, making conscious the class identity shared between soldiers and workers under the guise of international solidarity: to recognize and overcome barriers imposed by the state between the exploited persons of all nations. 'Everyone', he implores,

> workers and peasants of France, Germany or England, of Europe, Asia or America – everyone, all of us have the same toils, the same forms of suffering, the same interests. What do we have in common with this race of gilded idlers who are not content to live merely from our sweat but who also want to drink our blood?

The settling of common interests takes place alongside the nomination of a shared enemy, so as to direct collective ire against the commanders of state and beneficiaries of capital:

For them, for these arrogant men, a man of the people who falls, whether he be worker or soldier, is one less member of the rabble, nothing more. If they command you to fire, well, open fire on these very scoundrels themselves! The hour has come to punish their betrayals and to avenge your wrongs. You need no longer fear courts-martial. The people are here. Join their ranks; your cause is theirs.[35]

There is a calculus of class solidarity at work here, finding expression in the shifting pronominal register as it pivots between third and second person, between the hailed 'you' and two very different kinds of 'them', apostrophizing a transfer of allegiance from the state to the people, namely those workers with whom soldiers share a common interest in freedom from exploitation, no less than in mutual survival.

Beyond this kind of rhetoric and its urging of class solidarity, Blanqui's writings on the army proved instructive at a more practical level. 'The government has only one force behind it', he writes: 'the army. One can sense its presence in its contempt, its arrogance and its deceit. We should neither insult nor flatter this force. We should wrest it from the government's control'.[36] Accompanying directives to liquidate the standing army is the call for class discipline, the absence of which in June 1848 was a lesson hard-earned for the proletarians, who, according to Blanqui, failed because they lacked organization, throwing up barricades haphazardly and seeking arms not strategically but according to individual whim. 'While the insurgents smoke their pipes behind the heaps of paving stones', he cautions, 'the enemy successively concentrates all its forces on one point, then a second, a third, a fourth, and thereby systematically exterminates the whole insurrection'. By comparison, the official army possesses 'only two major advantages over the people: the Chassepot rifle and organisation. The latter in particular is tremendous, irresistible. Fortunately the army can be deprived of this advantage, and when it is, the insurrection gains the upper hand'. In order to gain that upper hand, the insurrection needs to learn from the army, to become organized with military discipline, to develop 'that sense of unity and solidarity which, in leading them to coordinate their efforts towards one and the same goal, thereby fosters all those very qualities that isolation renders powerless'.[37]

The makings of this organization, of the insurrectionary army, are already provided by the city itself, in such a way that Blanqui can insist with confidence that, even if the insurgents lack cadres with which to form and train columns, they can nevertheless 'improvise them on the terrain, during the action', precisely because they are already working people now conjoined in a moment of heightened military defection. 'The people of Paris', he says, 'will provide all the elements – former soldiers, ex-national guardsmen. Their scarcity will mean having to reduce the number of officers and non-commissioned officers. But this does not matter. The zeal, ardour and intelligence of the volunteers will compensate for this deficit'.[38]

* * *

The exemplary instance of this compensation is the legendary figure of Louise Michel, that critical correspondent of Victor Hugo and defender of the cannons. Born in 1830 as the illegitimate daughter of a serving maid, Michel would train as a teacher and, in 1865, open a school in Paris. There she involved herself in radical politics and committed herself to social revolution. 'We lived in the future', she would recall of this period, 'in the time when people would be more than beasts of burden whose work and blood other people made use of'.[39] Moreover, her commitment was specifically feminist, placing concerns about the subordinate role of women between commonality in class and the revolutionary horizon.

That same year, in 1865, Michel recomposed the national anthem into a militant poem, 'The Black Marseillaise', which combines its battle cry for a universal republic with an affirmation of gendered, maternal labour:

The universal republic
Rises into the burning skies

Covering the people with its wing
As a mother does her children
In the East the dawn whitens
Stand up, people, be strong and great
Stand up, why remain sleeping.[40]

If this is a poem that, as Michel said about sending it to Hugo, 'smelled of gunpowder', her experience in the subsequent years is that of war.[41] During the siege of Paris, Michel joined the national guard and, following the declaration of the Commune, was elected head of the Montmartre Women's Vigilance Committee, and so occupied a leading role in the revolutionary government. As a poet, her descriptions of the Commune vividly capture the sense of class solidarity amid bloody antagonism. She describes, for instance, the Commune taking power on 29 March as a triumph of the city whole, which gathers individuals into an oceanic force of seasonal renewal. 'A human sea', she writes, 'all baring arms, their bayonets pressed as tightly together as flowers in a field, with the sound of the brass splitting the air and the heavy beat of the drums'.[42] In April, she threw herself into armed struggle, planning to assassinate Thiers, carrying a rifle under her coat, and organizing ambulance stations. 'She fought and killed', writes her biographer, 'but she also dragged the wounded to safety and nursed them, Versailles and Federal both'.[43]

For Michel, warfare transcends individual preservation and speaks to some different faculty or order of being:

It wasn't bravery when, charmed by the sight, I looked at the dismantled fort of Issy, all white against the shadows, and watched my comrades filing out in night sallies, moving away over the little slopes of Clamart or toward the Hautes Bruyeres, with the red teeth of chattering machine guns showing on the horizon against the night sky.

In Michel's recollection, revolutionary warfare is unifying because it is also an aesthetic experience, affecting comrades as

83

might the most enrapturing artwork or composition during times of peace. 'It was beautiful', she adds, 'that's all. Barbarian that I am, I love cannon, the smell of powder, machine-gun bullets in the air'.[44] A survivor of the Commune, this experience of warfare so shaped her sense of militancy for years to come that she would consistently emphasize the mobilized class over anything like individual will. It shaped, in particular, a militant feminism. 'Women', she would insist, 'ought not to separate their cause from that of the rest of humanity; instead, they must take a militant part in the great revolutionary army. We are combatants, not candidates. We are brave and implacable combatants – that's all there is to it'.[45]

* * *

On 21 May, Versailles troops entered Paris under permission of the Prussians, who still held the northern and eastern forts. Arriving at night, recalls Lissagaray, 'the Versaillese were slaughtering within the walls of Paris and Paris knew it not. The night was clear, starlit, mild, fragrant; the theatres were crowded, the boulevards sparkling with life and gaiety, the bright cafés swarming with visitors, and the cannon were everywhere hushed – a silence unknown for three weeks'. This calm would not last, and neither would military discipline. Louis Charles Delescluze, the Commune's military commander, pronounced that it was 'now a war of barricades', with 'everyone to his quarter'. The organized combatants were thus formed into a decentralized and chaotic force – precisely what Blanqui had cautioned against. 'Enough of militarism!' read the proclamation, posted to walls across the city. 'No more staff-officers with their gold-embroidered uniforms! Make way for the people, for the combatants bare-armed! The hour of the revolutionary war has struck!'[46]

The city would burn as the state forces spent eight days massacring workers in the tens of thousands and arresting 38,000 more, many thousands of whom would be forcibly deported. The result is a grim counterpoint to communal luxury, a return to order under the iron rule of capital:

Order reigned in Paris. Everywhere ruins, death, sinister crepitations. The officers walked provokingly about clashing their sabres; the non-commissioned officers imitated their arrogance. The soldiers bivouacked in all the large roads. Some, stupefied by fatigue and carnage, slept on the pavement; others prepared their soup by the side of the corpses, singing the songs of their native homes.[47]

Before and during the Commune, militarism was seen as constitutive of class, a discipline necessary for uniting workers and soldiers in opposition to the state, but in its aftermath this dynamic would take on a newly sinister form – with class determining military-style capital punishment. Civilian bystanders and combatants alike were rounded up for interrogation and reprisal. 'If the resolute attitude of a prisoner betrayed a combatant', writes Lissagaray, 'if his face was unpleasant, without asking for his name, his profession, without entering any note upon any register, he was classed'. To be classed during this reactionary massacre meant certain death. 'The classed ones were at once delivered to the executioners, who led them into the nearest garden or court'.[48]

* * *

If Blanqui supplied the political ideology of the Commune and figures like Michel its proletarian lifeblood, Marx and Engels remain its sharpest and most influential interpreters. While class war in England and previous struggles in France were only ever preparatory, a suggestion of the coming insurrection, the Paris Commune prefigured a strategy for winning that war, and so for the abolition of all classes. The key lesson, for Marx and Engels, is that 'the working class cannot simply lay hold of the ready-made state machinery, and wield it for its own purposes', and must instead supplant a conservative view of competing nation-states with international solidarity among proletarians. 'No wonder that Louis Bonaparte', they write, 'who usurped power by exploiting the war of classes in France, and perpetuated it by periodical wars abroad, should, from the first, have treated the

International as a dangerous foe'.[49] Class thus reappears as a horizontal mode of social cohesion, one that leaps national and cultural boundaries, in opposition to the vertical hierarchies within any one state or nation. Collective recognition of class in this specific sense is, for Marx and Engels, the way forward to a world without capital.

'The very fact that while official France and Germany are rushing into a fratricidal feud', proclaimed the two communists, 'the workmen of France and Germany send each other messages of peace and goodwill; this great fact, unparalleled in the history of the past, opens the vista of a brighter future'.[50] Practically, however, the Franco-Prussian War and the siege of Paris also provided the conditions of possibility for the Commune, by eliminating the official army and replacing it with a national guard that mostly comprised working people. 'This fact', for Marx and Engels, 'was now to be transformed into an institution. The first decree of the Commune, therefore, was the suppression of the standing army, and the substitution for it of the armed people'.[51] Or as Walter Benjamin would famously argue, 'the Commune puts an end to the phantasmagoria that dominates the earliest aspirations of the proletariat', insofar as its success with the people and its suppression by the state 'dispels the illusion that the task of the proletarian revolution is to complete the work of '89 in close collaboration with the bourgeoisie'.[52]

The Commune inspired writers and revolutionaries the world over, from William Morris and Jack London, who both committed its lessons to speculative fiction, to the poet Walt Whitman, whose 'Songs of Insurrection' pressed for 'quenchless, indispensable fire', having cast his thoughts from the United States to Paris. 'Then courage!' we read in his 1871 cluster. 'European revolter! revoltress!'[53] While that influence extends to the militant tendencies within today's Occupy and ZAD or zone à defendre movements, its practical legacy is that it taught the proletariat how to fight as a class and for social revolution. The chief adherents to those lessons are to be found in Russia, where Lenin is said to have danced in the snow to mark the Russian

Revolution's seventy-fourth day, one more than the Paris Commune. 'The thunder of the cannon in Paris awakened the most backward sections of the proletariat from deep slumber, and everywhere gave impetus to the growth of revolutionary socialist propaganda. This is why the cause of the Commune is not dead', he would insist in 1911. 'It lives to the present day in every one of us'.[54] Here, too, the 'Marseillaise' would serve as marching song for the revolution of 1917, with its melody providing a sonic template for the Internationale, that great anthem of no state or nation but of class solidarity everywhere.

4

School of War

As C. L. R. James once noted, the plantations of Saint-Domingue incubated something 'much closer to the modern proletariat than any group of workers in existence at the time', a people of shared circumstance united as a class to bring a fiery end to a unilaterally exploitative social order. It is in this way, he says, that the Haitian rebels proved themselves 'subject to the same historical laws as the advanced workers of revolutionary Paris; and over a century later the Russian masses were to prove once more that this innate power will display itself in all populations when deeply stirred and given clear perspective by a strong and trusted leadership'.[1] In other words, the revolutionary affinities between Haiti and France as well as England and Russia suggest that not only is the fight for real freedom waged autonomously in discrete locations, but it is also articulated internationally, across sovereign borders, in order to blaze a narrative pathway between disparate zones of the world-system. That is why the story of class war takes place across so many different locations, all of which are linked by a shared opposition to social hierarchies and by a shared commitment to revolution.

From 1861 to 1865, the American Civil War comprised another such radical iteration of this idea when slaves in the South fought independently from what was happening in the North, and in so doing ensured the abolitionist victory. 'There came slowly to realization the fact that here was not only separate organization but a separation in leading ideas', writes W. E.

B. Du Bois, 'because, among Negroes, and particularly in the South, there was being put into force one of the most extraordinary experiments of Marxism that the world, before the Russian Revolution, had seen'. As with Haiti, England, and France – as well as Russia and China hereafter – class militancy in America took shape alongside and in contradistinction to state militarism. 'That is', Du Bois continues, 'backed by the military power of the United States', which was more interested in the establishment of a universal market than in freeing slaves, 'a dictatorship of labor was to be attempted and those who were leading the Negro race in this vast experiment were emphasizing the necessity of the political power and organization backed by protective military power'.[2] Similar to the formation of a national guard out of workers in Paris, slaves were recruited into service for the Union, first working as non-combatant labourers before going on to fill official regiments, entering the field of combat as soldiers in 1862. 'Without legal authority and in spite of it, suddenly the Negro became a soldier. Later his services as soldier were not only permitted but were demanded to replace the tired and rebellious white men of the North. But as a soldier, the Negro must be free'.[3]

While the North was winning battles against the Confederate Army, the slaves mobilized as a class, acting together and as one. 'This was the beginning of the swarming of the slaves', wrote Du Bois, 'of the quiet but unswerving determination of increasing numbers no longer to work on Confederate plantations, and to seek the freedom of the Northern armies'. But unlike the slaves in Saint-Domingue who threw themselves into armed insurrection, in America they 'showed no disposition to strike the one terrible blow which brought black men freedom in Haiti'. This is in part because they recognized themselves as the class on whose labour power another military victory would depend, thus presenting a potentially safer route to freedom. And so the slaves went on strike, transferring the labour power of half a million men and women from the Confederate planters to the Northern invaders, for whom they would work no longer as slaves but as wage labourers. In this way, writes Du Bois, 'the movement became a general strike against the slave system on the part of all who could find opportunity'.[4]

* * *

At the level of tactics, the slaves' rebellion was more akin to England than Haiti. Since the 1760s in England, the workers' strike had served as a dominant mode of social antagonism as well as a passage to class solidarity, and a means to political and workplace reform. Strictly speaking, the strike is a collective subtraction of labour power from the site of its employment so as to forcibly terminate enterprise and thereby demonstrate that workers are the irreplaceable agents of production. In this capacity, the strike has featured prominently in some of the literary works we have already encountered. Elizabeth Gaskell's *North and South* includes a somewhat didactic conversation between the novel's heroine and a local union leader, as if to explain strikes for a broad or middle-class readership. 'Why do you strike?' asks Margaret. 'Striking is leaving off work till you get your own rate of wages, is it not?' The explanation and its reception together reveal an unspoken conservatism in the liberal sympathizer:

> 'But', said Margaret, 'if the people struck, as you call it, where I come from, as they are mostly all field labourers, the seed would not be sown, the hay got in, the corn reaped'.
>
> 'Well?' said he. He had resumed his pipe, and put his 'well' in the form of an interrogation.
>
> 'Why', she went on, 'what would become of the farmers'.
>
> He puffed away. 'I reckon they'd have either to give up their farms, or to give fair rate of wage'.[5]

The strike's usual purpose is indeed renegotiation for a better or even sustainable rate of exploitation instead of more wholesale requisitions of property – wages as opposed to farms or plantations themselves. However, as a mode of antagonism, strikes are also conducive to discipline, solidarity, and a recognition of class power. To that end, Émile Zola in *Germinal* describes the coordinated onset of a strike in terms that will resonate here:

And suddenly that very Monday at four in the morning the strike had just broken out. When the Company had applied its new wage structure on the first of December, the miners had stayed calm. At the end of the fortnight, on pay-day, no one had made the slightest protest. All the staff from the manager down to the humblest supervisor thought the rates had been accepted; so there was considerable surprise in the morning at this declaration of war whose tactics and organization seemed to suggest the presence of a strong leader.[6]

For a strike to take place under the banners of war is consonant with revolutionary theory during the nineteenth century.

In communist thinking, the strike has traditionally been understood as a 'school of war', preparing the way for revolutionary combat. According to Engels, strikes are 'the strongest proof that the decisive battle between bourgeoisie and proletariat is approaching. They are the military school of the working-men in which they prepare themselves for the great struggle which cannot be avoided; they are the pronouncements of single branches of industry that these too have joined the labor movement'.[7] Marx was of a similar mind, insisting that strikes combine workers into a class. 'In order to rightly appreciate the value of strikes and combinations', he reflected, 'we must not allow ourselves to be blinded by the apparent insignificance of their economical results, but hold, above all things, in view their moral and political consequences'.[8] Strikes were, like the organizational forms that predominated in England and France after the Napoleonic Wars, preparatory and promissory, preserving a militant impulse against the threat of material foreclosure and ideological stupefaction; without this kind of collective obstinance, claims Marx with reference to the specific kind of racial subjugation we see in America, we are doomed to become 'apathetic, thoughtless, more or less well-fed instruments of production', an atomized people 'whose self-emancipation would prove as impossible as that of the slaves of Ancient Greece and Rome'.[9]

If, for Marx writing to Engels in January 1860, 'the biggest things that are happening in the world today are on the one hand the movement of the slaves in America started by the death of John Brown, and on the other the movement of the serfs in Russia', we can briefly skip ahead to the afterlife of those Russian serfs before returning forcefully to American soil.[10] Writing after the Russian general strike of 1905, Lenin clarifies the relations between strikes, class, and war. As it did for Marx and Engels, in Lenin's assessment the strike 'reminds the capitalists that it is the workers and not they who are the real masters', and 'reminds the workers that their position is not hopeless, that they are not alone', but it only issues such a reminder amid a context of 'terrible privations that can be compared only to the calamities of war – hungry families, loss of wages, often arrests, banishment from the towns where they have their homes and their employment'.[11] The ultimate value of strikes is that they 'teach the workers to unite; they show them that they can struggle against the capitalists only when they are united; strikes teach the workers to think of the struggle of the whole working class against the whole class of factory owners and against the arbitrary, police government'. And this, for Lenin, is precisely why socialists describe strikes as a 'school of war'. They are a proving ground on which 'the workers learn to make war on their enemies for the liberation of the whole people, of all who labour, from the yoke of government officials and from the yoke of capital'. Yet strikes are only one tactic among many: as a tactic they respond effectively only to certain zones and phases of capital. Specifically, the strike belongs to capitalism's productive phase or to economic zones dependent on human labour. To over-invest in the strike is, Lenin cautions, to forestall actual revolution; while the strike can win considerable improvements to the living and working conditions of some, they will not achieve emancipation, because the strike is ultimately reformist, as opposed to insurrectional or revolutionary. The school of war, Lenin reminds us, 'is, however, not war itself'.[12]

* * *

In America, that metaphor would take on altogether more literal qualities, as the school of war would regularly lead to actual warfare. This tendency has as much to do with the conditions of American capitalism as with the militancy of strikers. The global hegemony of the United States, as both an economic and a geopolitical superpower, was the result of industrialization – and its industrialization was, exemplarily, entwined with war. So writes world-systems theorist Giovanni Arrighi and a team of researchers in their global history of political transformation:

> At least potentially, this giant island was also a far more power-ful military-industrial complex than any of the analogous complexes that were coming into existence in Europe. By the 1850s the US had become a leader in the production of machines for the mass production of small arms. In the 1860s, a practical demonstration of this leadership was given in the Civil War, the first full-fledged example of an industrialized war.

The Civil War also revolutionized and concentrated the industrial and agricultural means of production, as waves of railway construction established privileged access to the planet's two largest oceans. 'A truly integrated US Continental System', Arrighi adds, 'was realized only after the Civil War of 1860–65 eliminated all political constraints on the national-economy-making dispositions of Northern indus-trial interests'.[13] This dynamic, in which actual war counter-signs accumulation while simultaneously giving it a mythic veneer, is the secret history of industrial capitalism in the United States.

In the canonical version of this argument, the historian Matthew Josephson describes the emergent capitalist class – whose ranks included Jay Gould, J. P. Morgan, Andrew Carnegie, and John Rockefeller – as a cartel of robber barons. Here we get a sense of the martial spirit of industrial capitalism, which found its energies liberated by war and enjoyed lucrative deals in food, produce, clothing, machines, fuel, and railways:

> Loving not the paths of glory they slunk away quickly, bent upon business of their own. They were warlike enough and pitiless yet

never risked their skin: they fought without military rules or codes of honor or any tactics or weapons familiar to men: they were the strange, new mercenary soldiers of economic life. The plunder and trophies of victory would go neither to the soldier nor the statesman, but to these other young men of '61, who soon figured as 'massive interests moving obscurely in the background' of wars.[14]

In short: capitalists in the United States consolidated their powers in and through war, exploiting political conflict to satisfy an enormous appetite for private profit, acquiring their social form through the battle's economy and culture. This explains why those same capitalists were so given to narrate their enterprise using the language of military bombast, adopting terms like 'captains of industry' and insisting that, for the continual triumph of large-scale industry, 'the war of finance is the next war we have to fight'.[15]

American literature has been alive to the historical apposition if not the mutual imbrication of social structure and military conquest. This tendency is at its most visible with *The Octopus*, a work of Zola-esque naturalism written by Frank Norris and published in 1901. Describing the conflict between independent wheat growers of the San Joaquin Valley in Southern California and the tentacular expansion of the Southern Pacific Railroad company, the narrative famously begins with a half-ironic invocation of the poetic muse on behalf of a young writer who will come to observe the clash between ranchers and the railroad. 'He was in search of a subject', we are told, 'something magnificent, he did not know exactly what; some vast, tremendous theme, heroic, terrible, to be unrolled in all the thundering progression of hexameters. That was what he dreamed, while things without names – thoughts for which no man had yet invented words, terrible formless shapes, vague figures, colossal, monstrous, distorted – whirled at a gallop through his imagination'. The unnamed subject, here, is capital, a dawning empire whose blood-drenched epic is still elusive. 'Oh', he later opines, 'to put it all into hexameters; strike the great iron note; sing the vast, terrible song; the song of the People; the forerunners of empire!'[16]

The social substance of such an epic is class conflict, and its combat often takes the form of strikes. As one railway driver insists, 'they've not got a steadier man on the road', even as his wages are slashed and his employment terminated, precisely because he has always been a scab. 'And when the strike came along, I stood by them – stood by the company', he says. 'You know that. And you know, and they know, that at Sacramento that time, I ran my train according to schedule, with a gun in each hand, never knowing when I was going over a mined culvert, and there was talk of giving me a gold watch at the time'.[17] Another character, who self-identifies as an anarchist, is said to owe his militancy to personal tragedy, for his wife was trampled to death by strike-breakers during the same conflict. 'Wait till you've seen your wife brought home to you with the face you used to kiss smashed in by a horse's hoof', he intones, 'killed by the Trust, as it happened to me'. Deeply opposed to any sort of moderation or compromise, which he describes as a bourgeois luxury – 'You could do it, too, if your belly was fed, if your property was safe, if your wife had not been murdered, if your children were not starving. Easy enough then to preach law-abiding methods, legal redress, and all such rot' – this 'blood-thirsty anarchist' advocates instead for violent action. 'That talk is just what the Trust wants to hear. It ain't frightened of that. There's one thing only it does listen to, one thing it is frightened of – the people with dynamite in their hands – six inches of plugged gaspipe'.[18]

* * *

There is, however, an anachronistic dimension to Norris's book, which is set during the 1890s. Before the final decade of the nineteenth century, the railway had already been converted into a site of struggle. More than that, opposition to the railway as a capitalist technology had morphed into antagonistic social practices that used the railway as their vehicle, producing a kind of mobile insurrection for which strikes would serve as catalyst. As strikes escalated beyond a relatively orderly form of rebellion, anchored in place and defined by employment, the railway provided such antagonism with high-speed transport, spreading solidarity at the pace of capital, opening onto armed conflict against the state as well as the employers and their trusts. Such escalation was new to the period after the Civil War. As the historian Paul A. Gilje writes, 'before 1865, most violent strikes were limited to cracked heads and were local affairs. After 1865, the rioting became national in scope'. Note the modulation from strike to riot, pivoting on the use of violence, before the two modes of antagonism are regrouped as warfare. 'In the great railroad strike of 1877', Gilje continues, 'workers fought the military from Baltimore to San Francisco. The dimensions of these labor wars continued to capture national headlines with battles at Homestead in 1892, Pullman in 1894, Ludlow in 1914, and Blair Mountain, West Virginia, in 1921'.[19] And while the escalation from strike to war often effaces the original form of struggle, with the strike vanishing from narrative description as the antagonism leaves the worksite and enters the battlefield, here we will discern how that movement shifts its organizational energy away from any one given workforce in order to mobilize as a class.

The multiple interlocking rail strikes of 1877 are exemplary and seminal events in such a movement, with workers in and around the railway industry organizing for, and committing to, an armed uprising. Taking place during the long depression that began in 1873 and lasted until 1879 – a downturn that wrecked the railroad companies, reduced track expansion, and decimated the railroad craft brotherhood – the strike started over wage cuts in Martinsburg, West Virginia. From there it spread up, down, and along the railways, with strikers taking up weapons, burning depots, and fighting off the forces of repression, only to be joined by workers from other industries, producing comprehensive general strikes that shut down entire cities. According to the writer and journalist Louis Adamic, this was a time of material hardship coupled with massively diminished union power:

Hundreds of thousands were suddenly thrown out of work. Wages were reduced. The reductions caused prolonged and desperate strikes. Every one of them failed. Some strikes were followed by lockouts, so that vast numbers of people could not get to work on any terms. Labor leaders were blacklisted. Between 1873 and 1880 real and nominal wages were cut to almost one-half of the former standards. Labor organizations went out of existence. There were no leaders to lead them and no workmen to pay the dues. In New York City alone the trade-union membership dropped from 45,000 to under 5,000.[20]

While the train brotherhoods were fragmented according to craft, didn't coordinate with other branches, negotiated their own labour agreements, and were universally opposed to strikes or disruptions, now the workers self-organized into their own secret union: a representative and coordinating body open to all craft workers. Their first meeting took place in Pittsburgh on 2 June 1877, where they pledged to unite across crafts: 'in short, unity of capital would be met at last by unity of labor'.[21] If this pledge gestured at an expanded though industry- or employment-bound sense of class, the conflicts themselves would take that principle further.

The strike's expansive scope was more than the result of the nearly absent labour unions. In fact, it occurred despite their presence, with warlike action fulfilling its pedagogical role in the place of older and ultimately conservative institutions. A manifesto issued by the workers in Westernport, Maryland, on 20 July warned the Baltimore and Ohio Railroad that, if wages were not restored, 'the officials will hazard their lives and endanger their property', and promised the kinds of sabotage pioneered by the Luddites in England: 'For we shall run their trains and locomotives into the river; we shall blow up their bridges; we shall tear up their railroads; we shall consume their shops with fire and ravage their hotels with desperation'.[22] True to their word, the strikers' tactics were violent and destructive, including the removal of coupling pins and brakes, the tearing up of tracks, making trains only run backwards, cutting telegraph wires, and shooting strike-breakers.

As a school of war, these strikes demonstrate a double movement of expansion and escalation, from local strike to wider conflict and from reformism to insurrection; and this, as the realized threat of war, proved decisive in the consolidation not just of railway workers but of oppressed peoples from many backgrounds into a unified class. So writes the labour movement scholar Robert Ovetz:

> Several thousand Irish packing-house workers armed with butcher knives were met by cheering Czech workers marching across the city to enforce the strike and force employers to raise wages. Gender differences were also dissolving in the strike. The Times estimated that 20 percent of the strikers and their supporters were women. The Chicago Inter-Ocean generated national attention with their report of 'Bohemian Amazons' whose 'Brawny, sunburnt arms brandished clubs. Knotty hands held rocks and sticks and wooden blocks'. A fence around one plant was 'carried off by the petticoated plunderers' and other similar portrayals of the powerful women who helped enforce the strike.[23]

Armed conflict serves as a shared language that leaps racial as well as gendered divisions to forge a provisional unity against interconnected systems of oppression. This tendency would be carried through to the climax of the movement in the general strikes in St Louis and East St Louis, where for a few days a multi-ethnic coalition of strikers shut down much of their industry and the cities were controlled by executive strike committees. Comparisons were made with the events that occurred six years previously in France. 'In St. Louis and East St. Louis', writes Ovetz, 'the strike went further as workers across the cities shut down all industry and became renown in the press of the time as America's "Paris Commune"'.[24] Adamic made the same comparison in his history of class violence in America. 'The underdog had given capitalism in America its first big scare', he writes. 'The memory of the Paris Commune of six years before was still fresh'.[25] Not just the memory, either; it was the very spirit of 1871, the commitment to solidarity through an expansive mobilization of class, that made the movement powerful.

* * *

The strike, however, was ultimately demobilized by a betrayal of this open-minded militancy and the solidarities it engendered. Not only did the strikers lack the means to coordinate between numerous dispersed localities and multiple sectors simultaneously, they were also beset by two interlinked and ultimately avoidable limitations from within their own ranks: unions and racism. On the one hand, the survival imperative made the existing craft unions cautious for fear of losing existing members, and their dues, and the brotherhoods were firmly entrenched within the mass of skilled railroad workers, thus making their longevity dependent on the overall success of the industry, which they were unwilling to harm. On the other hand, racism in the executive committee was instrumental in their repudiation of the strike, to the point of committee members giving racist speeches and cancelling rallies solely to prevent the attendance of non-white and immigrant strikers who had otherwise been at the forefront of the rebellion. As the historian Chris Carlsson phrased it in an assessment of how this 'uprising' made its way from the East to the West Coast, where similar prejudices were maintained at the expense of expansive solidarity, 'class war was in the air, but an air choking on racism'.[26]

It is in this way that the outcome of the 1877 strike bookends a period that opened with the Civil War. According to Du Bois, both black and white workers missed a strategic opportunity that could have delivered revolutionary social transformation. The slaves' rebellion 'presented the greatest opportunity for a real national labor movement which the nation ever saw', yet the subsequent labour movement 'never had the intelligence or knowledge' to realize or make good on its lessons. 'The labor leaders went into the labor war of 1877 having literally disarmed themselves of the power of universal suffrage', and the surcharge for disarming was that the remaining workers were forced back to the trains at reduced wages.[27]

In 1895, the socialist leader Eugene Debs reported to the United States Strike Commission that 'a strike is war; not necessarily a war of blood and bullets, but a war in the sense that it is a conflict between two contending interests or classes of interests'.[28] We should emphasize here that these two wars coexist, as they always have, on a continuum between struggle and antagonism, between veiled civil war and open conflict, and that the passage between them goes through not only violence but also class. Because armed insurrection so often has its origins in the labour strike, work becomes a common denominator for class belonging. We know this to be anecdotally true. In 1877, an emphasis on labour instead of class served as a regressive limitation, undermining the movement when unions were insisting on industrial isolation during a time of high unemployment. But it also captured the militant imagination in ways that could ultimately lead to a more expansive sense of class solidarity.

During an episode of real heroism, the fabled union organizer Mother Jones recalls an exchange with the National Guard during the Paint Creek-Cabin Creek strike of 1912, a conflict that served as prelude to the more infamous battles of Matewan and Blair Mountain. 'The strike was truly war', she insists, 'with murders and assassinations, with dynamite and prisons. The mine owners brought in gunmen. The President of the Union urged the miners to arm to defend themselves, their wives and daughters. It was Hell!'[29] She described placing her hand on the muzzle of a gun and claiming it as collective property.

> 'Sir', said I, 'my class goes into the mines. They bring out the metal that makes this gun. This is my gun! My class melt the minerals in furnaces and roll the steel. They dig the coal that feeds furnaces. My class is not fighting you, not you. They are fighting with bare fists and empty stomachs the men who rob them and deprive their children of childhood. It is the hard-earned pay of the working class that your pay comes from. They aren't fighting you'.

There are echoes of Paris in all of this, with the call for defection from the state military and the insistence on the collective ownership of armaments. War, however, is what happens if shots are fired, as defensive retaliation. 'Young man', she intones, 'I want to tell you that if you shoot one bullet out of this gun at those men, if you touch one of my white hairs, that creek will run with blood, and yours will be the first to crimson it'.[30]

* * *

Combining all of this into a single narrative, Jack London's 1908 novel *The Iron Heel* reads as an alternative history of 1877. Before this novel, London had lived an adventuresome life. Having laboured in canneries, mills, power plants, and on ships, and having been incarcerated for vagrancy, in 1897 he took part in the Klondike Gold Rush, which would become the setting of multiple stories, including the immensely popular *Call of the Wild*, published in 1903. He then worked as a muckraking journalist, writing on poverty and deprivation, as well as a war correspondent, covering the Russo-Japanese War of 1904. *The Iron Heel* aligns itself with the notion that, in a climactic war of world-historic proportions, an avenging class of the dispossessed and the exploited will finally have its victory against the impersonal machinery of accumulation. This reimagines London's accounts of strikes and class written in his capacity as a labour journalist, wartime correspondent, and committed socialist. In a pamphlet called *War of the Classes*, published in 1905, he described class war as 'the prime preachment of socialism', while insisting that a class of workers 'is bound to revolt from the sway of the capitalist class and to overthrow the capitalist class'.[31]

Using a narrative conceit popularized by Edward Bellamy and radicalized by William Morris, *The Iron Heel* is narrated from the standpoint of an imagined post-capitalist future, around the year 2600 AD – or what it calls year 419 in the Brotherhood of Man. It takes the form of the fictional 'Everhard Manuscript', an incomplete document written during the first and failed American uprising of a great class war. The attributed author is Avis Everhard, wife of Ernest Everhard, an organizer who in the early decades of the twentieth century led the insurgent 'labor caste' against the powers of oligarchy. The manuscript has been annotated by an historian, Anthony Meredith, who writes from the other side of a post-capitalist horizon, with all the hindsight that position enables. We know from these annotations that, beyond the present narrative, another world exists. What makes this so compelling – more so than the projected futures of Morris – is that, rather than isolate utopia from its embattled prehistory, it describes the means by which we might someday, somehow get there.

The story contained within the manuscript is exhilarating and absolute. It begins with a romance between Avis, who is the daughter of a renowned physicist, and Ernest, a socialist agitator that prophesies coming insurgency, when the workers will rise against an ascendant monopoly of trusts. 'Such an army of revolution', he predicts, 'twenty-five millions strong, is a thing to make rulers and ruling classes pause and consider. The cry of this army is: "No quarter! We want all that you possess. We will be content with nothing less than all that you possess. We want in our hands the reins of power and the destiny of mankind"'.[32]

Crucially, the tipping point that turns class struggle into class war is, as both Rosa Luxemburg and Bill Haywood were predicting around the time London was writing the book, a general strike. This strike, covertly organized between the United States and Germany, circumvents an imperial war of extermination in which the working classes of either state would be sent to their mutually assured destruction:

> The Oligarchy wanted the war with Germany. And it wanted the war for a dozen reasons. In the juggling of events such a war would cause, in the reshuffling of the international cards and the making of new treaties and alliances, the Oligarchy had much to gain. And, furthermore, the war would consume many national surpluses, reduce the armies of unemployed that menaced all countries, and give the Oligarchy a breathing space in which to perfect its plans and carry them out. Such a war would virtually

put the Oligarchy in possession of the world-market. Also, such a war would create a large standing army that need never be disbanded, while in the minds of the people would be substituted the issue, 'America versus Germany', in place of 'Socialism versus Oligarchy'.[33]

The strike is organized via coded cables between two belligerent states, but also spontaneously at the level of individual industries. The general strike is, in the most material sense, presented as the anti-systemic movement from which class unity and international solidarity are together born. 'And you saw what a general strike would do', reflects Ernest on this victory for labour. His assessment echoes Marx and Engels on the Paris Commune: 'We stopped the war with Germany. Never was there so fine a display of the solidarity and the power of labor. Labor can and will rule the world'.[34] With this sense of internationalism comes an enlargement of novelistic scale, so that the United States appears as just one front in a global conflict, wherein geopolitical machinations articulate local battles between capital and labour as separate but related parts of a sublime whole. 'The capture of the world-market by the United States had disrupted the rest of the world', we learn. 'Institutions and governments were everywhere crashing or transforming'.[35] It is this view of capitalism as an interstate system, one that is sedimented over an extended historical period, that corresponds to the rebel socialists' strategy for insurrection, combining local insurgency with semi-coordinated internationalism. 'The solidarity of labor is assured', muses Avis on the opening pages, 'and for the first time will there be an international revolution wide as the world is wide'.[36]

If the mood and tense articulate internationalism in the language of idealism, where this novel locates successful strategy is in messy on-the-ground tactics. In doing so, it offers a corrective for the missed opportunities in the slave rebellion of 1865 and again in the strikes of 1877. What we see is the revolutionary need for an expansive conception of class, one that transcends differences without ignoring them, and is built not with ideas but through action. And so, beyond the strikes, the narrative documents the fall of the American republic and the ensuing confrontations: the industrial battles, taking the form of more strikes as well as slowdowns and sabotage; the guerrilla tactics employed by an underground resistance, ranging from mutual aid to campaigns of terror; the coercive measures taken by the oligarchy, both ideological and repressive; and moments of open warfare, culminating in a battle that consumes all of Chicago, 'the industrial inferno of the nineteenth century', where the rebels face off against mercenaries and both sides are consumed by a massive, racialized, and well-nigh inhuman lumpenproletariat – or, to use London's terminology, 'the people of the abyss'.[37] Here the narrative reaches the same limit as the social movements that preceded it. Prejudice undercuts solidarity, so that the unemployed and immiserated are met not as part of one class – 'They're not our comrades', shouts one socialist – but as 'the refuse and the scum of life, a raging, screaming, screeching, demoniacal horde'.[38] With its disdain for the unemployed, and in the racist language it uses to portray them, the novel's socialism reveals itself to be as limited as the strike form is as a mode of antagonism, confined as they both are to an organization of typically white industrial workers. Such disdain ultimately guarantees the demise of the insurrection and the reproduction of an exploitative class system. 'As we waited on the platform', reflects Avis after the battle, 'three trains thundered past, bound west to Chicago. They were crowded with ragged, unskilled laborers, people of the abyss', whose purpose is swiftly clarified. 'Slave levies for the rebuilding of Chicago', says Ernest. 'You see, the Chicago slaves are all killed'.[39]

The novel's central lesson, learned in spite or even because of its prejudice, also belongs to both the slaves of 1865 and the railway workers of 1877. It is that a revolutionary class will be doomed to suppression and subsistence if it internalizes a hierarchical division within its own ranks by the promotion of certain industries or job titles at the expense of others, or by taking employment itself as a condition for class belonging. Despite enacting precisely this tendency, London is acutely conscious of what he criticizes as an 'aristocracy of labor', a phrase he uses to describe 'the traitors and their families' who betray the proletariat for the oligarchy. 'The members of the favored unions became the aristocracy of labor', he writes. 'They were set apart from the rest of labor. They were better housed, better clothed, better fed, better treated. They were grab-sharing with a vengeance'.[40] This formulation was not original to London. It had been used by Engels to describe English trade unions, and it was popularized by Mikhail Bakunin and Karl Kautsky in opposition to a perceived overemphasis on the industrial proletariat. It was also later theorized by Lenin, for whom it would designate a subsection of workers from the core states that opportunistically reap the material benefits of imperial exploitation taking place outside the nation. 'For they are', says Lenin of this grouping, 'the real *agents of the bourgeoisie in the working-class* movement, the labor lieutenants of the capitalist class, real vehicles of reformism and chauvinism'.[41] While the idea of the labour aristocracy describes accurately the prejudicial and chauvinistic forces that work to undermine revolution, we should add that this is a problem endemic to strikes, which outside of specific circumstances favour the individuated workforce over the unified class: the industrial workers and unionized 'brotherhoods' at the expense of all those whose struggle takes place beyond the wage relation.

If there really is continuity between the novel and subsequent movements, it is in a different but related aspect of its narrative. One of Trotsky's best-known theses, which is usually attributed to Lenin, is that capitalism decays into fascism, that the capitalist state meets its crises by aggressively suppressing proletarian as well as parliamentary democracy. 'Fascism', he wrote in his final article, 'is the continuation of capitalism, an attempt to perpetuate its existence by means of the most bestial and monstrous measures'.[42] While Trotsky was describing the emergence of Mussolini in Italy and Hitler in Germany, elsewhere he concedes that this idea finds its exemplary illustration in London's novel: 'The fact is incontestable: in 1907 Jack London already foresaw and described the fascist regime as the

inevitable result of the defeat of the proletarian revolution'.[43]
This is what Trotsky writes from Mexico, in 1932, having served
as commander general of the Red Army but now in exile at a
time when he was insisting the socialist state in Russia had lost
its revolutionary drive precisely because it had retreated from
internationalism to embrace patriotism, betraying the class solidarity in which that state was founded. 'Over the mass of the
deprived rise the castes of labor aristocracy, of praetorian army,
of an all-penetrating police, with the financial oligarchy at the
top. In reading it one does not believe his own eyes: it is precisely
the picture of fascism, of its economy, of its governmental technique, its political psychology!'[44]

Perhaps more than anywhere else, it will be Latin America
during the second half of the twentieth century that would come
to experience this grim tendency – indeed, after the 1973 coup
in Chile, London's novel would be reprinted with the ousted
president Salvador Allende's image on the dust jacket. But Latin
America only put into practice, often with sponsorship from the
United States, what Du Bois had long ago sensed during the
American Civil War, what we have seen repeat in 1877, and
what takes place in the pages of an otherwise radical novel. As
countless militants, from Amiri Baraka to Angela Davis, as well
as armed resistance groups like the Symbionese Liberation Army
and the Black Panthers, have together shown: while racism and
chauvinism are the enemies of class solidarity, the fight for real
freedom is one with a fight against a fascism that is intrinsic if
not indigenous to the United States.

5

Towards a Red Army

For Russia, 1917 was as much a year of war as it was a year of revolution. After the February Revolution, which had overthrown Tsarist autocracy, urban workers organized into soviets and criticized the provisional government for its continued fighting in World War One, which the soviets saw for the vast scene of imperialist bloodletting that it was, a catastrophe through which all working people were destined to suffer. The provisional government responded with military aggression, and hundreds of protesters were killed during the July Days protests, events that only contributed to the rising popularity of the revolutionary Bolsheviks. On 10 October, the Petrograd Soviet, led by Leon Trotsky, voted for an armed uprising against the state. On this, Trotsky sided with Vladimir Lenin, who had just returned from exile in Switzerland, and against Grigory Zinoviev and Lev Kamenev. After a day of skirmishes, a fleet of Bolshevik sailors entered the harbour, and tens of thousands of soldiers joined the uprising. Government buildings were occupied by force, and the Winter Palace, which had been the seat of the provisional government, was captured.

'The working class of the world has seized from its enemies the most impregnable fortress', Trotsky would announce, 'the former Czarist empire. With this stronghold as its base, it is uniting its forces for the final and decisive battle'.[1] Going into that battle, in January 1918, the Council of People's Commissars issued a decree that drew its strategic insight from the Paris Commune: 'The old army was a class instrument in the hands of the bourgeoisie for the oppression of the workers. The seizure of power by the workers and propertyless persons renders necessary the formation of a new army'.[2] These words announced the formation of the Red Army, a military force raised from peasants and workers to protect the newly founded revolutionary state against capitalism's military confederations, and to further the revolution's goal of international communism. Led by Trotsky, the army was categorically different from any preceding military formation. It took the form of an enormous state-sanctioned personification of class war. The questions shaping its organization were about class solidarity as much as fighting capacity. How, Lenin and Trotsky asked, should the armed wing of a socialist republic differ from that of a capitalist state? And to what extent should its program be determined by the social character of those it serves?

* * *

The primacy of class to war, and vice versa, was a prominent feature of both Lenin's and Trotsky's military writings. In 1924, Trotsky began his book on literature and revolution by invoking the army as the necessary condition for everything that might follow: 'If the victorious Russian proletariat had not created its own army, the Workers' State would have been dead long ago, and we would not be thinking now about economic problems, and much less about intellectual and cultural ones'. According to Trotsky, the literature of this period was likewise responsive to the revolutionary sequence, evolving in parallel with the military and the state, undergoing a forceful disintegration of the old institutions in favour of something new and unknown. 'The Revolution overthrew the bourgeoisie, and this decisive fact burst into literature. The literature which was formed around a bourgeois center, is no more. Everything more or less vital, which remained in the field of culture, and this is especially true of literature, tried, and still tries, to find a new orientation'. That search for a new orientation is, ultimately, a question of class. 'In view of the fact that the bourgeoisie no longer exists, its center can be only the people, without the bourgeoisie. But who are the people?'[3] In Trotsky's scale of revolutionary necessity, military power presupposes questions of economic growth, and together military power and economic growth condition the intellectual and cultural life of the people. Nevertheless, for the revolution's leaders and its military strategists, even bourgeois literature helped solve the problem of class and of how to mobilize potential combatants. While Trotsky would eventually compare his own prodigious literary output to the compendious recollections of Marcel Proust, here we can observe an exemplary instance of the determinate encounter between the revolutionary imagination and bourgeois literature in Lenin's reading of Leo Tolstoy.

In 1908, Lenin described Tolstoy as a mirror of Russia's heretofore unsuccessful revolutions. Opposed as he was to Tolstoy's politics – which favoured moral uplift over systemic upheaval – Lenin considered the novelist an embodiment of the contradictions in Russian society which needed to be worked through to develop a united class out of common interests. 'Tolstoy', asserted Lenin, 'reflected the pent-up hatred, the ripened striving for a better lot, the desire to get rid of the past, and also the immature dreaming, the political inexperience, the revolutionary flabbiness'.[4] We encounter that desire on the pages of Tolstoy's most celebrated work, *War and Peace*, a novelization of the Napoleonic invasion of Tsarist Russia that focuses on five aristocratic families who, between them, offer the reader a panoramic view of the Russian elite, their hopes and their fears, as well as their manipulation of state power through a period of war. In particular, we are shown the threat of an emergent revolutionary class. As civilians flee Moscow ahead of Napoleon's Grande Armée, Count Rostopchin – a real historical figure, the governor-general – speculates on a possible uprising from the workers and the peasants. 'What reason', asks Tolstoy's narrator, 'was there for assuming any probability of an uprising in the city? The inhabitants were leaving it and the retreating troops were filling it. Why should that cause the masses to riot?'[5] Questions like these remain unanswered in the novel, unlike matters of military and political gain. While Tolstoy expressed a burning desire for social transformation, in his pacifism he abjured anything like a strategy for making transformation happen, so that uprisings and riots only ever occupy the narrative space of quasi-mystical speculation. Essentially, the great Russian author was, like Victor Hugo in France and the realists in England, a liberal writer unwilling to match sympathy and sentiment with active commitment. In that stance, however, Lenin found an explanation of Russia's political quiescence despite the abject circumstances in which its subjugated people subsisted: 'Historical and economic conditions explain both the inevitable beginning of the revolutionary struggle of the masses and their unpreparedness for the struggle, their Tolstoyan non-resistance to evil, which was a most serious cause of the defeat of the first revolutionary campaign'.[6] Precisely because his writing lacked a commitment to revolutionary transformation, his politics were articulated in such a way as to explain deficiencies of Russia's immiserated masses during times of actual combat. What Lenin found when reading Tolstoy against himself was the image of a social world with an impulse towards insurrection but without the means for its success: the desire for war without a class to wage it. This contradiction provided Lenin with an essential lesson about Russian life and what would be needed to turn a moral imperative to aid the dispossessed into a military program for ending dispossession.

Tolstoy is justifiably revered as the unmatched scribe of the Napoleonic Wars – an author who depicts, as phrased by Russian literary critic Viktor Shklovsky, 'whole battles as if battles were something new'.[7] His reputation here rests upon the vivid descriptions of the Battle of Austerlitz and the burning of Moscow in *War and Peace*, which contains comprehensive accounts of the organization and command of both French and Russian armed forces, as well as his attempts to explain the machinations of military and revolutionary power as a kind of social inertia. 'Why war and revolution occur we do not know', he speculates. 'We only know that to produce the one or the other action, people combine in a certain formation in which they all take part, and we say that this is so because it is unthinkable otherwise, or in other words that it is a law'.[8]

It is here, via his critical reading of Tolstoy, that Lenin formulates the principles that would later underwrite the Red Army. Rejecting moral indignation and vague accounts of 'the people' and 'the masses' as 'a reflection of the flabbiness of the patriarchal countryside', Lenin instead advocates for class solidarity through social antagonism, which amounts to something like revolutionary discipline:

> It is said that beaten armies learn well. Of course, revolutionary classes can be compared with armies only in a very limited sense. The development of capitalism is hourly changing and intensifying the conditions which roused the millions of peasants – united by their hatred for the feudalist landlords and their government – for the revolutionary-democratic struggle. Among the peasantry themselves the growth of exchange, of the rule of the market and the power of money is steadily ousting old-fashioned patriarchalism and the patriarchal Tolstoyan ideology. But there is one gain from the first years of the revolution and the first reverses in mass revolutionary struggle about which there can be no doubt. It is the mortal blow struck at the former softness and flabbiness of the masses. The lines of demarcation have become more distinct. The cleavage of classes and parties has taken place. Under the hammer blows of the lessons taught by Stolypin, and with undeviating and consistent agitation by the revolutionary Social-Democrats not only the socialist proletariat but also the democratic masses of the peasantry will inevitably advance from their midst more and more steeled fighters who will be less capable of falling into our historical sin of Tolstoyism![9]

As with previous formulations of class war, the idea announces itself here as a literary figure: a metaphor that aspires to the conditions of objective description. The invocation of 'armies' emphasizes bellicosity between the propertied and the dispossessed, the feudalist landlords and the millions of peasants, while also gesturing to the way that modern capitalism – still

underdeveloped in Russia – might harden the agrarian peasantry into a revolutionary proletariat. But there is a significant
difference here as well. While we are dealing with a metaphor,
the fact remains that warfare is very much the concrete historical object of this description. Lenin is referring specifically to
defeat in an actual conflict and to the violence inflicted upon
insurgent peasants by Pyotr Stolypin, the Tsarist interior minister in whose honour the hangman's noose in Russia became
known as 'Stolypin's necktie'. Armies and classes are not just
analogous; under the conditions of generalized conflict they
have become nearly interchangeable. To be precise, the political
task is to make them more than just analogous, to make them
interchangeable, by converting a mass of unruly peasants into a
class of 'steeled fighters' via political education and military
discipline.

Tolstoy teaches rage and feeling but not organization and
strategy, and that Russia's working population embodied this
imbalance is why the 1905 revolution was defeated. An impulse
is not enough to defeat the state's armed wing. That history of
defeat, however, sharpened rage and feeling into a desire for
victory. And this required the means to reassemble the dispossessed masses into a real fighting force. Lenin would summarize
this position in class terms in 1910. 'The Russian people will
secure their emancipation only when they realize that it is not
from Tolstoy they must learn to win a better life', Lenin wrote,
'but from the class the significance of which Tolstoy did not
understand, and which alone is capable of destroying the old
world which Tolstoy hated. That class is the proletariat'.[10]

* * *

It is not hard to imagine that, less than a decade later and now
in a position of political and military leadership, these thoughts
would have returned to Lenin, brought back by the movements
and machinations of the Red Army. Mikhail Tukhachevsky, who
commanded the Red Army's western front during the civil war,
modelled himself on Napoleon to such an extent that the bourgeois press referred to him as 'Red Bonaparte' and Stalin would

later dismiss him as 'Napoleonchik', or Little Napoleon. This description echoes Tolstoy's depiction of Napoleon as pompous and vainglorious, as an absolute disappointment to the book's more sympathetic heroes: it is a negative judgement of Napoleon the man as well as his cultic glamorization, a mystifying and soporific hero worship, the inborn egotism of which ultimately countervailed against anything like class mobilization.

Tukhachevsky introduced Napoleon-style reforms to the Red Army, modernizing its armaments and imposing an army force structure – namely a division of labour between artillery, infantry, and cavalry – as well as developing the military concepts of 'operational art' and 'deep battle', ultimately working towards a more scientific approach to warfare. All this was underwritten by an ambition to transform the Red Army from a defensive militia into an offensive military force able to export revolution beyond the boundaries of the socialist state. His words bear lengthy quotation, not least because they apprehend as strategy the now familiar passage from class struggle to open and international revolution by way of civil war:

The outbreak of a socialist revolution in one State will inevitably produce an intensification of bourgeois dictatorship in neighbouring States, and the State where the proletariat has rebelled will immediately become the target for the thunderbolts of the entire bourgeois world. Such conditions give birth to civil war. This initially breaks out on a national scale, although the overthrown bourgeoisie does also receive support for its counter-revolutionary struggle from the world bourgeoisie. The civil war outgrows its national dimensions and develops into a major international class war, as the bourgeois world grows convinced that the defeated bourgeoisie of the country concerned is unable to recover State power; convinced too that the dictatorship of the proletariat, as it consolidates its position, is by its very existence becoming a threat to the tranquillity of world capital.

Thus, from the moment of insurrection, the proletariat joins battle not only with its own bourgeoisie, but also – unequally matched – with the bourgeoisie of the entire world. Thus, as it

develops, the struggle between the working class and the bourgeois class ceases to be purely a domestic one, and becomes an
international war in which the proletariat cannot restrict itself to
a passive role. An attack by a working-class revolutionary army
over the boundaries of a neighbouring bourgeois State can overthrow the power of the bourgeoisie there, and transfer dictatorship into the hands of the proletariat.[11]

While this Napoleonic military strategy promoted by Tukhachevsky
favoured lightning attacks conducted by mobile infantry and
enabled by advanced technological resources, ranging from artillery and munitions through cavalry and transport, for economic
and social reasons this was not entirely possible. Soviet Russia and
Napoleonic France were irreducibly different entities. While early
nineteenth-century France was the most economically and socially
advanced country in Europe, Russia, at the start of the twentieth
century, was one of the most backwards. Walter Rodney acknowledges this in his lectures on the Russian Revolution, originally
delivered to African students embarking on their own decolonial
revolution in socialist Tanzania. For him, the Russian Revolution
was unprecedented in its alliance between the peasant and the
worker. 'Yet this itself further exemplifies the laws of uneven and
combined development. In order to realize the Soviet state', he
says, 'it was necessary to draw together two factors – a peasant
war characteristic of the dawn of capitalist development, and a
proletarian revolution, which comes after capitalism has
matured'.[12] Russia's revolutionary masses were, for the most part,
agrarian peasants. They lacked the disciplinary order, technical
skills, and mechanical capability of a wholly industrialized workforce. For this material reason, and abjuring egocentric individualism, Lenin, Trotsky, and later Stalin all sought to circumscribe
military Bonapartism in favour of a distinctly class-based
militarization.

This redoubled emphasis on class as a problem relative to
uneven development is given full articulation in the futurist
poetry of Vladimir Mayakovsky. His 3,000-line tribute to Lenin
avoids the language of hagiography, replacing mournful elegy

with military epic to embrace 'the million-headed, million-handed class of workers', and affirm 'the purest, most potent communion, with that glorious feeling, whose names is Class'.[13] While the poem comprises a sometimes didactic recitation of Marx's original theory of class war – 'Marx', it says of Lenin's great antecedent, 'undertook to lead the proletariat to class war' – Lenin is shown as a master strategist of social revolution, viewing the world as a game of chess.[14] 'Turning face about from chess to living foes', we read, 'yesterday's dumb pawns he led to a war of classes until a human, working-class dictatorship arose to checkmate Capital and crush its prison-castle'.[15] In Russia, however, any such mobilization is an exceptional challenge for revolutionary leadership:

The peasant –

    'twas urged –

        would blaze his own tracks

and set up socialism

        without hitch or wrangle.

But no –

    Russia too

        goes bristling with stacks;

black beards of smoke

        round her cities tangle.

There's no god

    to bake us

        pies in the skies.

The proletariat

    must head

        the peasant masses.

Over capital's corpse

    Russia's highroad

        lies,

With Lenin

    To lead

        The toiling classes.[16]

Within this constellation of historical images, the peasant and the proletariat appear as two different 'toiling classes' standing together in solidarity 'over capital's corpse', having felled the common enemy. Rejecting the presumption of success without hard work – 'pies in the skies' without 'hitch or wrangle' – the poem emphasises the immense labour required to mobilize the agrarian peasantry and the industrial proletariat as a unified force. As with all the revolutionary situations we have encountered, here social antagonism and actual warfare provide the impetus to mobilization, with the transformation of the war among nations of 1914 – what the poem describes as a 'whole-sale, world-wide auction of mincemeat' – being converted into the civil war of 1917–22. 'What are we, peoples, arguing for?' Mayakovsky asks, ventriloquizing Lenin. 'Put an end to catastrophes, wounds and losses. Raise the banner of holy war against the world-wide bosses!'[17] From the international to the national and back again in two 'world-wide' conflicts: if the passage of revolution requires class solidarity within the nation, it also extends that solidarity beyond national borders.

* * *

This form of militancy, made of international solidarity, was one that the Red Army sought to concretize, making real what had heretofore been an ideal. The decisive battle was not simply a local antagonism or civil strife, and certainly not a conflict between nations. It was, instead, a world war against capitalism. Leon Trotsky, head of the Red Army from 1918 to January 1925, announced just such a struggle in March 1920 in a comment that would have profound implications for the revolutionary state's fighting forces. Recalling an old Tatar from the Samara province, a peasant man who had travelled to Moscow to thank the Soviet powers for liberating his village from Cossack despotism, Trotsky proceeded to explain that the combatants under his command were more than trained fighters; they are, he claims, the personification of class consciousness and political solidarity:

They know that people must be divided not by nation but by class. All honest working people form one family, whatever language they may speak and in whatever place of worship their fathers may have prayed. All oppressors, exploiters, parasites, aggressors, regardless of nationality, are enemies of the working people. The task of the soldiers of the Red Army, their sacred task, is to defend the poor against the rich. This is what distinguishes our army from all other armies in the world.[18]

To wage war on a system, to inhabit internationalism as a collective subject position, to live the communist ideal: this was the objective, the 'sacred task', that the Red Army seized in the early 1920s, a challenge that extends beyond internationalizing ambition and into the issues of public perception and social composition. It reads, in its shifting of ambition from the particular to the universal, as a radical and utopian pronouncement of why we fight. What makes the Red Army unique from other fighting forces, according to Trotsky, and what enables the movement of conflict across sovereign borders, is the class of its soldiers. Just as important here is the class of its adversaries: an entire social system comprising those who would benefit from its sustenance. What we encounter in this early vision of the Red Army is a militant recuperation of class, so that it is remade as an object of programmatic discipline and transnational cohesion, the primary purpose of which is to serve as a fighting force for the world proletariat against global capitalism. This is how class war becomes military doctrine.

We must also emphasize Trotsky's references to class as a fluid concept, the conceptual counterpart to an internationalist idea of war. Note how, after introducing class, he refers to 'working people' as well as 'the poor'. In both cases he does so in negative relation to the agents of capital. This is because, for the Red Army to serve as an anti-capitalist military, it needed to redefine class in a way that proved adaptive to the unevenness of capitalism and of capitalist dispossession. It also had to start with the fact that in Russia at the time of the civil war there was not yet a sufficiently large industrial proletariat. As with Lenin's reading of Tolstoy, what was needed was not just the mobilization of a proletarian army, but also the creation and expansion of a proletariat which could serve as the basis of a military force.

While Trotsky was calling for internationalism, he was doing so in a way that incorporated the social composition of the Red Army, for which Tukhachevsky's Napoleonic theory of proletarian combat presented real contradictions. Whereas Napoleon exported the values of 1789 via invasion and intervention, because 'the political transformations of society implied by the bourgeois revolution do not ipso facto demand mass participation from below', the Red Army under Trotsky's command was bound by its composition and its ideal.[19] It would therefore serve less imperial designs. In 1921, he spoke of how, 'in the great class war now taking place, military intervention from without can play but a concomitant, cooperative, secondary part. Military intervention may hasten the dénouement and make the victory easier, but only when the political consciousness and the social conditions are ripe for revolution'.[20] To make good on its leaders' ambitions, the Red Army would have to reconcile its social composition, which necessitated defensive instead of offensive warfare, with its commitment to internationalism, which invited expansion outwards and beyond the socialist state.

* * *

It was Victor Serge who was perhaps the writer most sensitive to the relationships between class and war as expressed in the Red Army during this time. Like Lenin and Trotsky, for whom 'imperialist war was the mother of the proletarian revolution', Serge claims to have known that imperial conflict would unleash the 'purifying tempest' of revolution. 'Revolutionaries', he would come to reflect, 'knew quite well that the autocratic Empire, with its hangmen, its pogroms, its finery, its famines, its Siberian jails and ancient iniquity, could never survive the war'.[21] Serge, born in Belgium in 1890, started political life as an anarchist. He participated in the Barcelona uprising of 1917 and was in a military prison in France during the closing months of World

War One, from which he was eventually returned to Bolshevik Petrograd and then to Soviet Moscow. His novels from the early 1930s provide a chronicle of the first revolutionary decade from the standpoint of a committed participant, often focusing on military matters. Later, he fell victim to Stalin's purges of the mid-1930s, events that forced him into exile in Mexico, where in 1947 he would die of a heart attack precipitated by his years in prison, which would come to occupy his writing in his final years.

'A revolution', Serge tells us, 'seems monolithic only from a distance; close up it can be compared to a torrent that violently sweeps along both the best and the worst at the same time, and necessarily carries along some real counterrevolutionary currents'. This description of the revolution as a contradictory force that was defined by and which would ultimately succumb to its own contradictions also draws on military language – in what is simultaneously figurative and actual, a metaphor of struggle and a description of an army's formation. 'It is constrained', he says of revolution, 'to pick up the worn weapons of the old regime, and these arms are double-edged. To be properly served, it has to be put on guard against its own abuses, its own excesses, its own crimes, its own moments of reaction'.[22] Narratively, and resonating with Lenin and Trotsky's vision for the Red Army, Serge's novels include the drive from local and national to international or world history, a drive that relates local battles to more global conflict.

In Serge's early novel *The Birth of Our Power*, written in 1931, we read a shift in the form of revolutionary energy from something like an undisciplined impulse or political ideal into the material actuality of the Red Army. We can measure this transformation via comparison of two passages. The first is from the opening chapter, set in Barcelona during a failed uprising. It describes the band of would-be revolutionaries, a group of anarchists:

There were at least forty or fifty of us, coming from every corner of the world – even a Japanese, the wealthiest of us all,

a student at the university – and a few thousand in the factories and shops of that city: comrades, that is to say, more than
brothers by blood or law, brothers by a common bond of
thought, habit, language, and mutual help. No profession was
foreign to us. We came from every conceivable background.
Among us, we knew practically every country in the world,
beginning with the capitals of hard work and hunger, and with
the prisons. There were among us those who no longer believed
anything but themselves. The majority were moved by ardent
faith; some were rotten – but intelligent enough not to break
the law of solidarity too openly ... No organization held us
together, but none has ever had as much real and authentic
solidarity as our fraternity of fighters, without leaders, without
rulers, and without ties.[23]

That this passage was written after the Stalinist betrayal, after
Serge's expulsion from the party, and with him facing targeted
harassment from the state, gives some biographical cause for its
romantic attachment to anarchism's consciously disorganized
multiplicity. It relishes the plurality of its social milieu, a disparate multitude held together by ideals alone: note the repeated
anaphoric injunction 'no'. There is no disciplinary limit placed
upon the revolutionaries. As the emphasis on that exceptional
Japanese combatant betrays, this is military formation without
common material interests. What Serge describes as 'real and
authentic solidarity' is precisely the kind of thing Lenin once
criticized as 'an infantile disorder', and which presented itself as
the very antithesis to Trotsky's disciplinary statutes for class
unity. It reads here as the kind of idealism professed by Tolstoy,
a warmly paternal mysticism that does not translate into a
successful fighting force. It is a beautiful aspiration, but its
beauty wants for the more concrete bonds that combine social
antagonism with class solidarity.

Now compare that description to this – taken from one of the
final chapters set aboard a vessel sailing from Paris to Petrograd,
in the wake of revolution:

We would have to be hard on ourselves, in order to be hard on others, since we were at last the power. It would be necessary to stop at nothing, or all would be lost. Would we be strong enough? Would we be worthy of you, Revolution? Would we be able to consent to the inevitable sacrifice of the best among us? Are we sufficiently tempered? The prisons, the poverty, the concentration camps from which we have come, the epidemics, the vanquished rebellions, the strikes, the trials, the death of our brothers, all of this has become a providential preparation ... Things never turn out the way one dreams about them. We must not be imprisoned by dreams or by theories. But then what guides remain? ... We need whole men, cast in a solid block, in work, in suffering, in rebellion; men born from this victory; men made for holding a rifle in the Red Guards as firmly as they hold their tools, able to carry out the tasks of organized revolt with the expert attention of sailors rabidly tightening a knot.[24]

This could hardly be more different, at the levels of form and style as well as in the stated content. The entire mood has changed. This writing is proleptic, forward-reaching: it gestures beyond itself. The 'we' is indicative of a people in process, a class in the making. Self-aware as it is, it knows that it is guided by dreams and theories. By the same token, it realizes that dreams and theories are insufficient for concrete programs. The grammar reflects this shift, from abstract ideation to real praxis – we have abandoned the indicative mode for the conditional, and so we have moved from the language of idealism to strategy and commitment. And there we find the keenest difference of all: the emergence of concrete solidarity from the interaction between military discipline and class consciousness. This is not the anarchist multitude of Barcelona, which thrived on difference no matter what; this is a proletarian army, whose skill and discipline is relative to their status and experience as workers, and so too this passage draws its aesthetic from the language of work, of tempering and casting, of holding tools and tightening knots.

Clarified by Serge's novel and its drift away from beautiful dreams to grim actuality is a further contradiction. This is one between the lived experience of a socialist army fighting a brutal civil war and the reckoning of a brilliant future built through international solidarity. These two things do not and cannot coexist: presumably the armed forces, like the state, are to wither away in the achievement of full communism. There would be no need and no excuse for this kind of military might if the Red Army were to achieve its goal. The actual warfare on which the idea of class war is dependent is simply a tactical compromise through which a revolution might be won. It is thus an army that serves as the precursor to its own abolition, a sublime work in progress that concedes its own status as such. Lenin described this kind of militarization as a necessary and difficult transitional phase central to the overall modernization of the revolutionary state. 'A new social class', he wrote,

> when rising to power, never could, and cannot now, attain power and consolidate it except by completely disintegrating the old army ... except by passing through a most difficult and painful period without any army ... and by gradually building up, in the midst of hard civil war, a new army, a new discipline, a new military organisation of the new class.[25]

That verbal formulation, 'gradually building' – or as it sometimes translated, 'gradually constructing' – is more referential than it might initially sound. What makes the Red Army unique within the history of class war is the result of this contradiction: the fact that it would always be – by necessity – under construction.

* * *

Any invocation of 'construction' within the Soviet 1920s cannot disarticulate from the way 'constructivism' became an operative term for the communist avant-gardes. Put simply, constructivism is an imperative in avant-garde art and radical literature to emphasize formal construction, the way an artwork has been made from actual labour and material resources, and to render art in the service of revolution. 'Whereas', writes Susan Buck-Morss, 'Le Corbusier proclaimed that a revolution in architecture could *substitute* for social revolution, the Bolshevik artists deployed themselves in an image-realm engendered *by* the Revolution'.[26] For Louis Lozowick, a Russian American artist and contemporary of the Soviet avant-gardes, constructivism 'borrows the methods and makes use of the materials common in the technical processes. Hence iron, glass, concrete, circle, triangle, cube, cylinder, synthetically combined with mathematical precision and structural logic. Construction scorns prettiness, seeks strength, clarity, simplicity, acts as stimulus to a vigorous life'.[27] It was in the world of architecture that constructivism primarily flourished. And not just in specific designs or particular buildings, but also in the transformation of urban space. The archetypal example of constructivism is Vladimir Tatlin's Monument to the Third International, which combined utopian aspiration with utilitarian ideals: a leaning cylindrical tower to be built from the geometric shapes and industrial materials of what Shklovsky would describe as 'iron, glass and revolution', twisting and turning in spirals that together represent the Leninist view of history as 'a development, so to speak, that proceeds in spirals, not in a straight line'.[28] Tatlin's tower was initially a response to the call for 'monumental propaganda' and intended as a central hub for the Communist International. But it should go without saying that the catalytic influence of the Red Army is discernible in constructivist artwork more generally.

A quick tour of constructivist artworks that wear this influence would begin with an improbable encounter between constructivism's neighbouring aesthetic, Malevichian suprematism, and the Red Army itself, or at least its predecessor in a moment of transformation: an old photograph that the art historian T. J. Clark dates to sometime around 1920. 'If one wants an image of the black square in action, in "revolution" – doing the work Malevich and his adepts seem truly to have thought it capable of – then the one I offer is a photograph that surfaced a few years ago', Clark speculates, 'apparently showing the Red Army on pause, maybe bivouacking, in a forest'.[29] The image depicts a battalion of soldiers in the middle of which, and surrounded by other flags, is the modernist artwork: a black square on white canvas hoisted aloft. While the origins of this photograph are unknown, it nevertheless presents a moment of convergence between two forms of construction: the military and the aesthetic. 'In any case', Clark concludes, 'what seems to me to matter most in the photo is again the sheer unlikelihood of the square's appearance – in a realm, for a purpose, whose co-ordinates we shall probably never know'.[30] That tour would continue through Alexander Rodchenko's photographs of military balloon training to the Stenberg Brothers' posters for *Battleship Potemkin*, before settling on El Lissitzky's lithographic print of 1919, *Beat the Whites with the Red Wedge*, which prophesied the Red Army's victory in the civil war, seen as a dynamic convergence of allegorical shapes.

* * *

If constructivism and militarization were twinned forces in the socialist imaginary, we can now see the personal circumstances that tempered the style of Serge's writing in combination with its historical content. 'For my books', he would later reflect, 'I adopted an appropriate form: I had to construct them in detached fragments which could each be separately completed and sent abroad posthaste; which could, if absolutely necessary, be published as they were, incomplete; and it would have been difficult for me to compose any other way'.[31] While lived experience lends his novels a constructivist quality, a sense that their rapid-fire historical descriptions are always provisional, tentative, or working towards some unknown and unknowable endpoint, we cannot separate that outward form from their preoccupation with a particular kind of class war, in which the army serves as a microcosm for the state. And so, upon arrival in Moscow, the administrative hub of the revolution, we are presented with a vision of class war as a mode of social construction that extends well beyond the battlefield. Here, in *The Birth of Our Power*, the Red Army has become not only a reflection of the economic base that sustains it but a mediation of the socialist economy as a whole:

In the language, in the slogans posted everywhere, in the only two newspapers published, among the men, we discovered one enormous uniformity of a single way of thinking, imperious, almost despotic, but supreme, terribly true, made flesh and blood at each moment through action. We found not the passionate mobs going forward under new flags to struggles begun anew each day in tragic and fruitful confusions, but a sort of vast administration, an army, a machine in which the most burning energies and the cleanest intelligences were coldly integrated and which performed its task inexorably. And that task was to strain ceaselessly, for commonplace, often invisible achievements, with forces which, each day, seemed to be the last; to live and to preserve day after day; it was also to make an exhausted country, on the point of falling back into inertia, rise above itself; it was, finally to resist and to conquer everywhere, at every moment, transcending all logic.[32]

After the imagination of legendary happenings, the kitsch and the myth of revolution, what reveals itself to our prodigal combatant is the actuality of a military-economic machine lurching towards the post-capitalist horizon. The Red Army's discipline courses through the socialist discourse network – 'the language, in the slogans posted everywhere, in the only two newspapers published' – in such a way as to elevate the revolutionary impulse to a real and working program. Here we encounter an endpoint to Lenin and Trotsky's revolutionary strategy. Class has been redefined and reclarified through the precepts of war. Militarization is now reshaping the economy and the class structure in its own image while simultaneously squaring off against a global regime preparing to fight and contain the revolution with everything it has. For Serge, the city is, like the army, an unstable formation, a moving immanence.

If Serge's literary legacy had an heir, then it was the war correspondent turned novelist who consciously modelled his accounts of the Red Army on Tolstoy's *War and Peace*. Vasily Grossman, in his 1960 epic *Life and Fate*, adapts Tolstoy's formal template in order to narrate the Red Army's heroic defence of Stalingrad against the Nazis. Like Tolstoy, he too would emphasize the moral dimension of his characters, both fictional and historical persons, in conjunction with the political and economic machinations in which they became ensnared. If, for Lenin, the significance of Tolstoy is that despite his social conservatism he nevertheless provided an impetus for the conceptualization of class war, to resurrect Tolstoy in the service of another conflict might therefore be significant because it reveals the premature abdication from class war in all but name. By this point in history, the transformative constructivist momentum had been replaced by something else entirely, dissipating into a nationalist impulse ultimately responsive to threats against the mother country. The Polish British writer Tamara Deutscher captured the political bathos of this repetition in an almost wistful review of the book's English translation. 'Grossman', she writes, 'recalls that once upon a time "the magic of the revolution" made people face prison, forced labour, homelessness, and even the scaffold for the sake of a better future. Maybe the sparks of this magic have not yet been extinguished'.[33] For the Red Army, class war had already become the great patriotic war.

While the official field regulations maintained an emphasis on class well into the 1930s and beyond – the first demand modern combat is said to make on the soldiers is 'class-based political education, which is the foundation of the healthy political morale of the unit and a guarantee of the revolutionary stanchness of the army and its fighters'[34] – the army would be understood no longer as constitutive of class but instead as a fighting force that went into combat to defend those that could not. This would be consonant with Stalin's resignation from internationalism in favour of socialism in one country, which became a state policy of isolationism and economic development in direct opposition to Trotsky's advocacy of permanent revolution. And, though it would not persist in its native lands, the Red Army's model of class war, in which an army not only absorbs but also militarizes the dispossessed on a massive scale, will be taken up elsewhere across the globe, inspiring commanders of newly socialist states having to fight off the forces of reaction – in China, in Vietnam, in Africa, and in Cuba – as well as self-governing militia groups in both the first world and the third, on the streets of Oakland to those of Oaxaca, from the jungles of Brazil to occupied Gaza.

6

Protracted Peoples' Wars

'The Chinese Revolution is a continuation of the great October Revolution'. Thus spoke Lin Biao, commander of the military forces responsible for two of the three major victories that enabled the communists to enter Beijing and seize power in 1949. For Lin, both of these events pursued 'the common road for all people's revolutions', with a Marxist-Leninist party leading a worker-peasant alliance into violent confrontation with the powers of reaction so as to build a new socialist system.[1] But continuation should not be equated with replication. Even if both the Chinese and Russian revolutions were based on worker-peasant solidarity, the two are radically dissimilar in their approaches to class and war. Whereas Russia's pre-revolutionary situation was of an absolutism defined by industrial concentration surrounded by rural agriculture, the Chinese revolution took place in a semi-colonial and semi-feudal country. As Lin makes clear, these differences articulate the geography of class within military strategy: 'The October Revolution began with armed uprisings in the cities and then spread to the countryside, while the Chinese revolution won nation-wide victory through the encirclement of the cities from the rural areas and the final capture of the cities'.[2] If the capture of Beijing in 1949 can be apprehended as proof of successful strategy, the communists' thought and practice of class war can be traced back to regional origins in the Jinggang Mountains during the late 1920s.

And it is there that this chapter begins, in October 1927 – ten years after the Bolsheviks seized Moscow and just under twenty years before the capture of Beijing. We join a small band of communist soldiers, numbering less than 1,000, who had fled for their lives into the mountainous border regions of the Jiangxi and Hunan provinces in southeast China. These soldiers barely survived the Autumn Harvest Uprising, one of three military operations undertaken to recover communist power in China. Earlier that year, Chiang Kai-shek, the leader of Kuomintang, the Chinese nationalist party, had terminated a four-year alliance with the Comintern, controlled from Moscow, and the Chinese Communist Party. The division between nationalists and communists was a response to events in the north earlier that year. In March, Shanghai's labour unions launched an armed insurrection against the northern warlords. Victorious, the workers successfully occupied and governed the city – except for international settlements, primarily controlled by British, French, and Japanese colonists, which remained autonomous. With both the right wing of the nationalist party and international investors fearing the communist demand for the return of international settlements, Chiang and the nationalist army were recruited to support capital, international as well as local, against the communists. On 9 April, Chiang declared martial law in Shanghai and three days later ordered the army to disarm the workers' militias. This resulted in more than 300 people being killed and wounded by sword and bullet. On 13 April, thousands of workers and students protested at the army headquarters. Soldiers opened fire, killing and wounding hundreds more. Chiang dissolved the provisional government of Shanghai, the labour unions, and all other organizations under communist control. And so, in an attempt to re-establish its influence, the Chinese Communist Party organized a series of insurgencies: the Nanchang Uprising in early August, the Autumn Harvest Uprising in September, and the Guangzhou Commune in December. All were suppressed by military force. Communism in China was driven from the cities.

The soldiers who made it to Jinggang were led by a young Mao Zedong, and within a year they would be joined by two other communist commanders, Zhu De and Peng Dehuai, who together formed the Chinese Red Army. In October 1928, Mao described their situation in a poem:

Low on the mountain our flags and banners
and on the peak an echo of bugles and drums.
Around us a thousand circles of enemy armies
yet we are rock.

No one cracks through our forest of walls,
through our fortress of wills joined as one.
From the front lines at Huangyang the big guns roar
Saying the enemy army fled in the night.[3]

These lines are exemplary of the thinking that guided the communists during their encirclement by the nationalist enemy. Such emphatic militarism – the guns and the army, but also the flags and banners, the bugles and drums – is representative of the collective from whose perspective the poem is written. It is also catalytic, shoring up the distinction between the embattled communists and 'the enemy army', thus uniting the soldiers as a class. That is what it means to self-describe as 'a fortress of wills joined as one', to be united in and through combat. Securing that sense of collective identity is the natural imagery that we find in both stanzas, in which the peasant soldier is one with their mountainous terrain so as to become the rock and the forest and in which heavy artillery is recast as a living creature that roars. While these metaphors recall classical Chinese literature with its elemental and animalistic transubstantiations, an aesthetic that will soon be appropriated to represent revolutionary social transformation, in 1928 this kind of writing suggests a bond between the revolutionary army and the materiality of their environment, between comrades and the land. In this way, the aesthetic prefigures what will become one of Mao's principal strategies: the expropriation and redistribution of the land away from private holdings and profit margins to the people that would use it for subsistence, those frequently rural communities alongside which and on whose behalf the communists would fight.

This emphasis on land is also emblematic of a semi-feudal situation in which the majority of working people depend on its resources as opposed to the wage for subsistence, and in which the landlord – more so than the industrialist – occupies the role of class enemy. Perhaps that is why the communists' 'forest of walls' is attributed to the plural possessive pronoun. Finally, the apparent preoccupation with displays of force can be read as an expression of political resolve, a reflection of the belief that only a strong army will seize and secure state power. 'Political power grows out of the barrel of a gun', or so Mao would later conclude, and in this formulation politics means class. 'Experience in the class struggle in the era of imperialism teaches us that it is only by the power of the gun that the working class and the laboring masses can defeat the armed bourgeoisie and landlords; in this sense we may say that only with guns can the whole world be transformed'.[4] This militancy, given early expression in the form of poetry, is the nascent form of what will eventually become revolutionary doctrine.

* * *

Class war was, for Mao, the principal engine of social transformation. 'War', he would insist, 'is the highest form of struggle for resolving contradictions, when they have developed to a certain stage, between classes, nations, states, or political groups, and it has existed ever since the emergence of private property and of classes'.[5] In China, from the 1920s until the moment of victory, class and war were understood as a mutually constitutive way to break with the system of semi-feudal, unevenly developed capitalism. 'A revolution', he says, 'is an insurrection, an act of violence by which one class overthrows another. A rural revolution is a revolution by which the peasantry overthrows the power of the feudal landlord class'. Crucially, this act is not only undertaken by the peasants; it is precisely what mobilizes them as a class. 'Without using the greatest force, the peasants cannot possibly overthrow the deep-rooted authority of the landlords which has lasted for thousands of years. The rural areas need a mighty revolutionary upsurge, for it alone can rouse the people in their millions to become a powerful force'.[6] Moreover, the language used to describe this ultimately violent process, the warlike passage from class struggle to open revolution, reflects the cultural specificity and class character of social transformation.

Of course, we can read as much in Mao's speeches and his poems. But we also read of such things in the historical fiction of and about the period, and especially those novels canonized as 'red classics', wherein revolution is dramatized using the kinds of language favoured by the revolutionaries. Published in the seventeen years between the establishment of the People's Republic of China in 1949 and the Cultural Revolution, which began in 1966, these included eight core novels: Wu Qiang's *Red Sun*, Yang Yiyan and Luo Guangbin's *Red Crag*, Liang Bin's *Genealogy of the Red Flag*, Liu Qing's *The Builders*, Yang Mo's *Song of Youth*, Zhou Libo's *Great Changes in a Mountain Village*, Du Pengcheng's *Protect Yan'an*, and Qu Bo's *Tracks in the Snowy Forest*. In different ways, all these novels foreground the peasantry as the agent of change and describe that change using the language of the classics. Plots are fluid and, oftentimes, narrative momentum is driven by descriptions of the natural landscape, itself an entity of violent transformation caused by thunderstorms and wildfire. These aesthetic tendencies resemble much older forms. According to Mao, who was a reader of 'the old romances', classical writing about premodern China offered visions of heroic warfare and moral good, as well as rhetorical forms worthy of adaptation. His reading of these texts was akin to Lenin's encounters with Tolstoy. Mao took them as informative and inspirational but primarily as a negative reflection of the material world and its unreconstructed social hierarchies. 'There was one thing peculiar about such stories', Mao would later reflect, 'and that was the absence of peasants who tilled the land. All the characters were warriors, officials, or scholars;

there was never a peasant hero'. Instead, the great myths of war 'all glorified men of arms, rulers of the people, who did not have to work the land, because they owned and controlled it and evidently made the peasants work it for them'.[7] By restoring the peasantry to such narratives, and by recasting the owners and controllers of the land as their enemies, Mao developed a narrative template for class war. That is, Mao established a way of apprehending modern social relations and inspiring comrades to fight. How all of this translated into collective military action begins with a new apprehension of class.

* * *

In 1926, Mao published a corrective to what he described as a political 'opportunism' that neglected accurate analysis of the extant social relations in China, which differ in some dramatic ways from those of Russia before 1917, and which also elude simple distinctions of bourgeoisie and proletariat. 'Who are our enemies? Who are our friends?' he asks. 'This is a question of the first importance for the revolution. The basic reason why all previous revolutionary struggles in China achieved so little was their failure to unite with real friends in order to attack real enemies'.[8] These questions are intended to reconstitute class militancy in opposition to a common enemy, namely 'all those in league with imperialism – the warlords, the bureaucrats, the comprador class, the big landlord class and the reactionary section of the intelligentsia attached to them'.[9] Unlike the 'vacillating middle bourgeoisie', the real class enemy in 'economically backward and semi-colonial China' exists in alliance with global capital. 'The landlord class and the comprador class are wholly appendages of the international bourgeoisie', writes Mao, 'depending upon imperialism for their survival and growth'.[10] Opposing this cartel of interests, the leading force of revolution is, for Mao, just as it was for Lenin and Marx, the industrial proletariat. Yet in an economically undeveloped country that social grouping remained small, employing in Mao's estimation around two million workers in railways, mining, maritime transport, textiles, and shipbuilding, all of which were industries dominated by foreign capital. But, answering that initial question of enmity and friendship with the numerically largest potential ally, Mao observed that the revolution's 'closest friends are the entire semi-proletariat and petty bourgeoisie', and so, in a primarily rural economy, political power belongs to an overwhelming majority of poor and semi-owner peasants.[11] An upsurge in the peasant movement is thus figured as the driving force of social transformation.

Mao's descriptions of revolution during the time when communism was establishing its fighting force are affirmations of class solidarity in language redolent of both the literary classics and the rural peasantry. 'In a very short time', Mao predicted in March 1927, while communists were being purged in Shanghai, 'in China's central, southern and northern provinces, several hundred million peasants will rise like a mighty storm, like a hurricane, a force so swift and violent that no power, however great, will be able to hold it back'.[12] This metaphor endows the peasant movement with a sense of natural inevitability, of world-historic destiny, but that will soon change to reflect the need for political work. In 1927, Mao was only reporting on the peasant movement: he wrote as an observer, with one eye on future mobilizations. In the subsequent decade, however, he would write as a combatant, sided with the peasants, and as such the elemental imagery would change, with agency replacing what had previously seemed inevitable: the 'mighty storm' of revolution would need to be summoned down to earth through collective organizational labour.

In 1930, and still in the Jinggang Mountains, Mao set out to remedy a perceived pessimism within the insurgency. And it was with another organic image – which, like the storm, would have carried both material familiarity and affective force for agrarian labourers – that Mao represented the coming war: fire. 'All China', he says,

> is littered with dry faggots which will soon be aflame. The saying, 'A single spark can start a prairie fire', is an apt description of how the current situation will develop. We need only look at the

strikes by the workers, the uprisings by the peasants, the muti-
nies of soldiers and the strikes of students which are developing
in many places to see that it cannot be long before a 'spark'
kindles 'a prairie fire'.[13]

While China is said to be riven at every level by contradiction
experienced by the dispossessed masses as immiseration, the
oppressors and the exploiters have together, by virtue of their
despotism, prepared the bonfire of their own annihilation. The
task for revolutionaries is to become the spark.

* * *

We see a return of the storm image in Zhou Libo's justly celebrated literary account of revolution in China, *The Hurricane*,
from 1948. Written by a communist organizer who had been
tasked with winning the trust of agrarian peasants during the
land reform movement during the 1940s, the novel not only
repurposes Mao's storm metaphor for its title but quotes it in its
epigraph. It is also self-conscious in utilizing narrative and
rhetorical forms particular to its social content. 'Language is the
medium with which a writer works', Zhou reflects, 'and if we
present peasant dialogue without using the language of the
peasants, the result will certainly be unrealistic. The speech of
peasants is characterized by richness of imagery, liveliness and
simplicity born of their rich knowledge of work on the land and
of struggle'.[14] As in Mao's writing, natural metaphors and
elemental imagery suggest both class solidarity and social transformation. The narrative dramatizes the challenges and the frus-
trations of the land reform team as they attempt to raise the
class consciousness of a rural village. Their moment of success
only arrives when Han – the vicious landlord – is brought to
heel by the villagers after whipping a young swineherd within
an inch of his life:

During the last fortnight, in their small group meetings the villagers had shed their former fears and acquired a new political
consciousness and courage to carry on the struggle. More and

more activists were appearing – they were like torches kindling fires everywhere. Han's cruelty to the little swineherd was merely another small instalment in a long series of crimes, but, now that the masses had been awakened, it was enough to ignite a great fire of hatred and revenge.

The flames were blazing higher and higher, up to the skies, burning down the feudalism which had obstructed China's progress for thousands of years, giving birth to a new society. The wrongs which the peasantry had suffered from generation to generation were the fuel for the fire.[15]

The social content of this extended metaphor coincides with our sustained thesis that a revolutionary class is enkindled through social antagonism. Here, commonality in struggle is expressed as something more than shared material interests: this tremendous, all-consuming blaze is one with the revolutionary passions of its subjects, those living 'torches kindling fires everywhere', who, in a moment of heightened conflict, finally recognize themselves as the force of renewal. In this sense, the passage quoted is both an illustration and an extension of Mao's thought: it clarifies that the revolutionary class is not made through moral and pedagogical re-education or through any other kind of instruction, compulsion, or direct leadership; the revolutionary class is instead a combustive entity fuelled by shared struggle, common interests, and – above all – social antagonism.

* * *

Class war in China combined a militarily tactical program for the annihilation of enemies with the painstaking establishment of power bases within and alongside the civilian population. In 1930, writing to Lin Biao, who during this time was his principal ally, Mao insisted that warfare alone, no matter how successful, would be insufficient to achieve social revolution. Reflecting on the guerrilla actions adopted in 1927, Mao argued that military tacticians do not fully appreciate what it means to establish, consolidate, and expand political power from within the areas under their control. Instead of building common cause 'by hard work', they overuse 'the easier method of roving guerrilla actions' directed toward some future absolute warfare: 'Once the masses throughout the country have been won over, or more or less won over, they want to launch a nation-wide armed insurrection which, with the participation of the Red Army, would become a great nationwide revolution'.[16]

In Mao's view, this strategy – according to which the communists must first win over the masses in all regions across the country, and only then establish political power – fails to understand that China is an unevenly developed, semi-colonial country, in which the 'subjective forces' of revolution have been disunited and greatly weakened. Like the revolutionaries active in Latin America during and after the 1960s, Mao argues for the development of material ties between potential combatants in established and defensible base areas. Revolutionary policy, then, is one of semi-autonomous and simultaneous organization, the deliberate cultivation of military strength through expansive class solidarity,

> of systematically setting up political power; of deepening the agrarian revolution; of expanding the people's armed forces by a comprehensive process of building up first the township Red Guards, then the district Red Guards, then the county Red Guards, then the local Red Army troops, all the way up to the regular Red Army troops; of spreading political power by advancing in a series of waves.

In this way, through the combination of roving guerrilla actions and the establishment of political bases among the people, it will be 'possible to create a Red Army which will become the chief weapon for the great revolution of the future. In short, only thus is it possible to hasten the revolutionary high tide'.[17] Practically, this policy determined military tactics in equal measure to political ideology, because it insists on understanding the interplay between the two, all of which is put in service of a single set of interrelated goals: namely, 'winning over the masses, . . . deepening the agrarian revolution and establishing

137

political power, and . . . expanding the Red Army and the local armed units'.[18]

* * *

Ding Ling's 1948 novel *Sun over the Sangkan River* – which, along with *The Hurricane*, was the recipient of the Stalin Prize for Literature in 1951 – is an equally impressive literary distillation of this theory in action. While this novel is less about individual heroes than the rural masses as a collective subject, at least one character stands out as an archetypal revolutionary. For Yumin, an illiterate peasant who describes himself as 'someone for rough work, to use a hoe, carry wood or drive a plough', the communist army proves inspirational, enacting a kind of revolutionary induction, which both heightens class consciousness and informs a sense of collective agency through military discipline. As a child, Yumin is said to have grown up 'like a little ox, able to thrive as long as he had grass to eat', and looking after his brother he would live according to the iron law of capital, that 'poor people must rely on their own strength to make a living', with no prospects for personal or collective redemption. 'If a day came when they couldn't take it any longer', he reflects, 'they would fall in their tracks and that would be the end of them'.[19]

Sent by the village landlord and war chief to deliver grain to the communists, he notices first that the 'soldiers were dressed just like the peasants, with the addition of a short gun in their belts and a corner of red silk showing', and that they 'were very friendly and kind'. Their meeting is transformative:

When he met the Eighth Route Army, they induced him to tell the story of his life. As he described to them the past that he seldom liked to think about, he realised for the first time how unhappy he had been, how lonely, oppressed and down-trodden! It was very comforting to have found friends for the first time in his life, and friends who were so concerned about him. Knowing that he was loved he felt happy and eager to live a better life. The fact that others had confidence in him made him want to live more purposefully. Especially when he realised that his difficulties and those of his uncle and many other poor people were all owing to the oppression of the rich.[20]

After this formative encounter, Yumin emulates the army in the development and promotion of self-discipline and sets out to inspire 'the poor youngsters who were his friends' so they too might share in a vision of revolution.

In Yumin, the town is said to have 'had its first communist that summer', and his is a commitment to practical militancy. 'That winter he had procured one blunderbuss and one local-made rifle, and secretly formed a militia', making the village a safe haven for the soldiers, over whom the militia would stand guard, and with whom he would recognize the growing potential for an entirely new social system. 'He was only concerned over the actual extent of their strength, the amount of strength they could muster, and whether they could completely overthrow the old forces in the village'. And this strength, required to 'overthrow the forces of feudalism once and for all', means that the army 'must keep close to the masses to have strength' and that – rather than impose military rule – 'the people must organise voluntarily to emancipate themselves'.[21] This dialectic is the very essence of Mao's vision of revolution, his model for class war.

But instead of working to inspire self-emancipation, in 1930 the Chinese Red Army – under the command of Shanghai-based, Moscow-directed Li Lisan, with Mao's support – was used to attack urban centres. The goal was to spark forms of urban proletarian revolt. This strategy, which accorded with Moscow's insistence that there will be 'victorious rebellion of the entire people only if they are linked with the new surge forward of the revolutionary wave in the proletarian centres', clarified the differences between those who emphasized building bases in the countryside and those who sought to use force to catalyze urban revolt.[22] The assault on cities was disastrous. The Red Army was swiftly repelled by nationalist forces, and many communists – including Yang Kaihui, Mao's wife – were executed. As such, 1930 marked a transitional period between the emphasis on pre-1927 urban uprisings and the later withdrawal to the countryside.

* * *

By mid-1934, the communists were forced by repeated Kuomintang encirclement and extermination campaigns to leave their mountainous terrain. As the historian Rebecca E. Karl notes, their 'decision to abandon the area was not taken lightly, and it was well understood that landlords and previous practices of social hierarchy would make a roaring return in the vacuum left by CCP withdrawal. Those left behind would be subject to the White Terror of reprisal'.[23] With military assistance from Nazi Germany, Kuomintang forces overwhelmed the Red Army, and in October evacuation began. Many of those left behind lost their lives, but it was to the locals that the heaviest reprisals fell. One 1935 report proudly describes the area as a site of holocaust, in language that effectively reverses the descriptions given to this place by the communists:

> There is not a dwelling that has not been burned, there is not a tree that has not been felled, there is not a fowl or dog that has not been killed, there is not an able-bodied man remaining, no smoke rises from the kitchen chimneys in the alleys and the lanes, the only noise in the fields is the wailing of ghosts.[24]

From there, some 86,000 communists set off on a 9,000-kilometre journey, leaving behind a rearguard that fought a bitter, three-year war against the Kuomintang. Chen Yi, who fought in the rearguard, composed poems on a bivouac and in the heat of battle. He describes a fight for survival as opposed to revolution, class struggle instead of class war. In autumn 1935, he learnt of a truce between the Chinese nationalists and Japanese imperialists that allowed the former to concentrate on hunting down the surviving communists. In response, he penned these lines:

The sky lours on Dayu Mountain,
storms over Europe and Asia cloud my eyes.
Traitors have sold the last handful of our soil.
The sky fills with red banners raised among war's beacons.[25]

The gravitational forces of political affect are here reversed, transforming destitution into enthusiasm, registered as the exchange of one sky for another. If these storms recall Mao's hurricane, they do so at some remove. The poem's speaker, camped in the wilds, is separate from and blinded by the tempest. Likewise, the land itself no longer provides for the communists and their people; instead, the enemies have sold it off along with national sovereignty. The poet wants us to understand that betrayal as the cause of real longing: what has been sold is more sensuous than any kind of property. The formulation 'the last handful of our soil' registers the land as a common material interest made even more crucial in its absence. The concluding image of the red banners and the war's beacons arrives as the sign of hope, a visually brilliant counterpoint to the grim actuality of defensive mountainous warfare. While the final line might at first glance seem unmotivated, or at least like fantastical wish fulfilment, its sensibility would in fact inform another poem.

The poem in question was written in 1935. It is a commemorative poem in which we can feel the affective distance between the rearguard and those marching north, with Chen having received notice of his comrades' successful undertaking of a treacherous river crossing:

Storm-lashed and homeless,
we sleep in the wild and every day change base,
with nothing but cold food to still our hunger.
Quietly we catch lice among the mountain flowers.
Pebbles can fill the sea with blood,
We rejoice that our distant army crossed the Jinsha.
As we peer out into the long lampless nights,
Our hair grays with the anguish of our love for China.[26]

The natural world is not just estranged but actively hostile. The wilderness offers annoyance, lice, and little in the way of nourishment. Despite the potential beauty of the mountain flowers, the mood is one of hardship, and despite the collective pronouns the overwhelming feeling is one of isolation. The fifth line, which alludes to a mythical bird determined to fill the sea with pebbles, enacts a volte-face of political emotion. By replacing the sea with blood, the poem relocates ancient myth within the modern setting of warfare and enacts a kind of revolutionary calculus: the bird's impossible task is reframed verbally as merely improbable, and the subsequent line – the second half of its sentence – shows how the possible has been realized, with the successful river crossing. This provides the material conditions for redemptive feeling: a single, isolated pebble will make little difference in the sea, but a whole army is the agent of transformation. However, this transformation will be gradual, at least from the standpoint of the rearguard, and this too is a source of challenge, with the comrades' greying hair now serving as a visual doubling of the inclement weather from the opening lines. Meanwhile, the evacuees apostrophized by Chen would undertake a circuitous journey through difficult terrain before arriving in Shaanxi in October 1935, almost a year later, where only 7,000 of the original 86,000 evacuees survived.

* * *

Just as international and imperial conflict has, since the eighteenth century, shaped the conditions of possibility for revolution, the period in Chinese history following the Long March transformed the social composition, military strategy, and political self-perception of the Chinese revolutionaries. Much of this is reflected in Mao's celebrated 1937 essay 'On Contradiction', which established the philosophical underpinnings of what we now call Maoism. The essay accounts for the fluctuations of class composition through different, related modes of war. 'In a semi-colonial country such as China', Mao writes, 'the relationship between the principal contradiction and the non-principal contradictions presents a complicated picture'. As in China's nineteenth century – a time beset by the Opium War of 1840, the Sino-Japanese War of 1894, and the Yi Ho Tuan War of 1900 – when Japan invaded in 1936, the contradiction between an aggressive imperialism and the semi-colonial country of China became the principal contradiction. Other contradictions – between the various social forces within that country as well as between competing modes of production, for instance – were relegated to secondary status. As Mao wrote, 'when imperialism launches a war of aggression against such a country, all its various classes, except for some traitors, can temporarily unite in a national war against imperialism'. This, however, is only a temporary state of affairs. Or more accurately, it is a volatile unity, concealing social antagonism within itself. Imperialist advance can just as easily result in the ruling classes of the semi-colonial country capitulating to empire, with the two forming an alliance in order to enact the joint oppression of the masses. 'At such a time', as what took place after 1927, 'the masses often resort to civil war against the alliance of imperialism and the feudal classes, while imperialism often employs indirect methods rather than direct action in helping the reactionaries in the semi-colonial countries to oppress the people, and thus the internal contradictions become particularly sharp'.[27] The pendulum swing between these two contradictions defined the period between 1937 and 1945. The Red Army, which had just over 40,000 fighters when the invasion began, grew to a force numbering one million, establishing revolutionary bases as insurance against Kuomintang betrayal – which, with all the inevitability of reaction, would arrive in 1946, in the form of a nationwide civil war against the communists.

In a series of reports, pamphlets, and lectures from the latter half of the 1930s, Mao expounded the fraught interrelation between decolonial warfare and class struggle. In December 1935, on the eve of war with Japan, he insisted that the main characteristic of the present conjuncture is that 'Japanese imperialism wants to turn China into a colony'.[28] Before formulating a tactics of resistance, he asks how the different social strata in China will meet this imposition. Maintaining the class distinctions he

143

theorized in 1927, he insisted that the workers and the peasants would demand resistance, and in this they would be joined by the petty bourgeoisie and the urban students. The necessary compromise would be 'to form a revolutionary national united front by combining the activities of the Red Army with all the activities of the workers, the peasants, the students, the petty bourgeoisie and the national bourgeoisie throughout the country'.[29] By contrast, the 'local tyrants and evil gentry, the big warlords and the big bureaucrats and compradors have long made up their minds. They maintain, as they have done all along, that revolution of whatever kind is worse than imperialism'. The material interest of the exploiters and the expropriators, which finds expression in the Kuomintang, is for Mao inseparably linked to global capital. 'They are', he writes, 'the running dogs of imperialism'.[30] The exception is the national bourgeoisie, made up of rich peasants and small landlords, a group which, when faced with annexation, will likely split, with some joining the resistance and others opposing it.

This is what it means to think and act in terms of a 'people's republic' as opposed to a 'workers' and peasants' republic', and to fight as a People's Liberation Army as opposed to the Chinese Red Army. The contradiction between the classes must be temporarily subsumed within the contradiction between empire and colony. 'By throwing off imperialist oppression to make China free and independent and by throwing off landlord oppression to free China from semi-feudalism', Mao claims, 'the people's republic will benefit not only the workers and peasants but other sections of the people too'.[31] If this, however, is more akin to a bourgeois-democratic revolution, a mobilization of the working and peasant classes on behalf of the modern state, comparable to the French Revolution and the English Civil War, what makes the strategy unique is the foreknowledge that it is one part of a greater, more radical movement. 'The change in the revolution will come later', says Mao. 'In the future the democratic revolution will inevitably be transformed into a socialist revolution. As to when the transition will take place, that will depend on the presence of the necessary conditions, and it may take quite a long time'.[32] Nevertheless, the point is not to wait for those conditions but to actively cultivate them, to become the spark that ignites the prairie fire – and the means to cultivation, for Mao, was to wage protracted war.

* * *

The concept of protracted war that Mao developed during the 1930s was a response to China's position in the face of the Japanese onslaught. As foundational to military strategy, protracted war acknowledged that Japan possessed greater military, economic, and organizational power but was reactionary and lacking in international allies. In contrast, China, with less military, economic, and organizational power, was in an era of political progress, waging a war that is liberatory, and supported by allied states. Recognizing in this asymmetry the potential for victory, to think through protracted war was to appreciate that a possible, if not probable, victory would only be achieved with patience. 'All the experience of the ten months of war proves the error both of the theory of China's inevitable subjugation and of the theory of China's quick victory', wrote Mao in 1938. 'The former gives rise to the tendency to compromise and the latter to the tendency to underestimate the enemy. Both approaches to the problem are subjective and one-sided, or, in a word, unscientific'.[33] Instead of either capitulation or haste, then, the strategy was to wage war over a long period, utilizing China's strengths – in numbers, class consciousness, and sheer geographic scale – to overwhelm Japan's superior military capacity. In short, to wage protracted war meant looking beyond the technologies of annihilation to emphasize the social dimensions of combat: 'We see not only weapons but also people. Weapons are an important factor in war, but not the decisive factor; it is people, not things, that are decisive'.[34]

The combined power of the people, who are not yet united in class solidarity, is presented in vivid metaphor:

> The richest source of power to wage war lies in the masses of the people. It is mainly because of the unorganized state of the Chinese masses that Japan dares to bully us. When this defect

is remedied, then the Japanese aggressor, like a mad bull crashing into a ring of flames, will be surrounded by hundreds of millions of our people standing upright, the mere sound of their voices will strike terror into him, and he will be burned to death.[35]

In literal terms, waging protracted war means engaging in acts of both attrition and annihilation, reducing enemy-occupied territory and wearing down their forces with guerrilla tactics. It also necessitated a practical commitment to uniting the people as a fighting force along lines of common material interest. Assuming correctly that people are the war's motive force and that they are united in their struggle, interests, and antagonism, the repudiation of empire becomes an instance of class war: a conflict through which classes are made and remade before that more distant horizon of social revolution. In this way, the decolonial conflict is at once a civil war and a world war. The logic of protracted people's war might be similar to democratic revolution, but a vast gulf separates it from the socially limited transformations seen of England, Europe, and America, all of which resulted in a dictatorship of the bourgeoisie. Instead, and more akin to Russia's dictatorship of the proletariat, the Sino-Japanese War built a unified front under the leadership of the communists, allying the proletariat and the peasantry, who commanded the greatest military force. It is with such a force, organized and built through both class and decolonial solidarity, that the communists would eventually defeat the Kuomintang armed forces, overthrow the government, and seize state power in October 1949.

Another of Mao's poems, written in April of that year, dramatizes the communists' feeling in the lead-up to victory after the capture of Nanjing, formerly the nationalists' capital. While peace talks during this time had proposed a division of China into communist and nationalist spheres (a compromise that was supported by both Russia and America), the poem reflects a lasting commitment to class war as the engine of revolution:

Storms sweep and lour on Mount Zhong,
as our mighty million-strong army crosses the great stream.
Tiger crouching, dragon coiling, the strategic point outshines its
    past,
while we heroically turn earth to sky and sky to earth.
Boldly we chase our worn-out foe,
rather than ape Xiang Yu the Conqueror, who preferred to fish
    for
compliments and fame.
If sentient, the skies in growing old
will find that in the human world seas become mulberry fields.[36]

Descending as though from within the storm, the People's Liberation Army enacts something approaching elemental transubstantiation, a kind of revolutionary alchemy, remaking the city into a strategic point for the communists, as though converting earth and sky into one another. Three allusions connect this scene to military strategy: the poet Yu Xin, for whom tiger crouching, dragon coiling describes concealed force, suggests comprehensive assault before any declaration of victory; the legendary military strategist Sun Tzu, from whose *Art of War* the fifth line is adapted, suggests pursuit of the enemy no matter how exhausted they might appear; and the ancient warlord Xiang Yu, who granted amnesty to a seemingly weakened rival, Liu Bang, before that rival would regain power and defeat him, provides an object lesson in mercilessness. These three allusions combine to produce an affirmation of military aggression until the very end. Or as C. L. R. James would have it, translating the lessons of the Haitian Revolution into a revolutionary slogan, 'the rich are only defeated when running for their lives'.[37] In the final two lines, in a moment that reverses the natural order of things and delivers on the revolutionaries' patience, 'the skies in growing old' hypothetically bear witness to human mutability, the miracle of revolution in which 'seas become mulberry fields', so that desolation is finally remade into abundance.

* * *

147

Less than half a year later, on 1 October 1949, at 3 p.m. in Tiananmen Square, Mao formally proclaimed the founding of the People's Republic of China and the formation of a Central People's Government. If, during the revolutionary years, the Chinese model of class war was located within the nation, it would subsequently be reinterpreted as a vehicle for international revolution. In 1965, Lin Biao would elaborate a grand vision of people's war on a global scale, with the international peasantry of the world's hinterlands surrounding and destroying the urban bourgeoisie of the core states. 'The contemporary world revolution', he insists, 'presents a picture of the encirclement of the cities by the rural areas', with the imperialists now headed by the United States rather than Japan, and on a global stage. 'In the final analysis', he says, 'the whole cause of world revolution hinges on the revolutionary struggles of the Asian, African and Latin American peoples who make up the overwhelming majority of the world's population'.[38] Indeed, protracted people's war would inspire anti-capitalist and national liberation movements the world over. From the communists of Cuba and Vietnam to the Naxalites in India and the Shining Path in Peru, as well as in decolonial movements across Africa and ideologically or culturally within the United States, each would see China's struggle as a model.

And, as Lin insisted, Mao's thought itself was turned into a weapon. 'What is the best weapon?' Lin asked. 'It's not the airplane, not artillery, not the tank, not the atom bomb. The best weapon is Mao Zedong Thought. What is the greatest military force? The greatest military force is people, armed with Mao Zedong Thought; it's courage and fearlessness of death'.[39] In 1967, the realization of this maxim was enacted in imperialist America when Huey P. Newton and Bobby Seale, cofounders of the Black Panther Party, purchased copies of the Little Red Book from a Chinese bookstore in order to resell them to students at UC Berkeley. While the profits were used to buy shotguns with which to intimidate the police, the content of Mao's book was no less enabling to their self-conceptualization. In Seale's recollection, Newton adapted straight from Mao's source text, only replacing peasant actors in uneven- and un-developed countries with a racialized vanguard of the working poor from the world's imperial core: 'Where the book said "Chinese people of the Communist Party", Huey would say "Change that to the Black Panther Party. Change the Chinese people to black people". When he saw a particular principle told in the Chinese terms, he would change it to apply to us'.[40]

7

For Complete
Disorder

'We are off', begins a notebook entry from the summer of 1960. 'Our mission: to open the southern front. To transport arms and munitions from Bamako. Stir up the Saharan population, infiltrate to the Algerian high plateaus. After carrying Algeria to the four corners of Africa, move up with all Africa toward African Algeria, toward the North, toward Algiers, the continental city'.[1] The author of these words is Frantz Fanon, a trained psychiatrist from Martinique, the French overseas territory in the Caribbean, who was then running arms and munitions through the Sahara Desert between Algeria and Mali. During the trip he envisaged a future unification in which the nations and cultures of Africa would stand together against a common enemy. If class war is a metaphor that wants to be literal, here a similar logic applies to metonymy. Algiers is one part of Africa, but it aspires to represent the continent as a whole. How it might do so is explained as the combination of revolutionary desire, military logistics, and geological materialism:

> What I would like: great lines, great navigation channels through the desert. Subdue the desert, deny it, assemble Africa, create the continent. That Malians, Senegalese, Guineans, Ghanaians should descend from Mali onto our territory. And those of the Ivory Coast, of Nigeria, of Togoland. That they should all climb the slopes of the desert and pour over the colonialist bastion. To

turn the absurd and the impossible inside out and hurl a continent against the last ramparts of colonial power.[2]

In the language of concatenation, we are privy to a vision of
insurgency in which a shared continent is both the goal and the
means of achieving that goal. Africa is a thing to be assembled
and created – the coalition of a people yet to come – and it is
being forged both practically and ideologically over a sprawling
landmass through decolonial warfare. Such an uprising is said
to assail the absurd and the impossible, because the local situation is one of profound inversion, with the riches and resources
of an entire nation siphoned off by an elect few. It is also because
victory would not be possible or even likely without absurd and
impossible measures of military strength. Arrayed against continental unity are the forces of colonial oppression and division,
with all the might of empire at their back: 'We must work fast.
Time presses. The enemy is still stubborn. In reality he does not
believe in military defeat. But I have never felt it so possible, so
within reach'. Opposition to that enemy serves as a calling forth
of Africa, a consolidation of its collective being through combat,
which in this revolutionary imagination takes the form of a
great awakening. 'We need only march, and charge', says Fanon.
'It is not even a question of strategy. We have mobilized furious
cohorts, loving our combat, eager to work. We have Africa with
us. A continent is getting into motion and Europe is languor-
ously asleep'.[3] What Fanon has described is the cultivation of
solidarities through wars of decolonization. It is, in short, the
dynamic form of class war.

If this revolutionary vision is a reimagining, under colonial
rule, of what we have seen elsewhere and at other times, then
Fanon knows the place of decolonial warfare within the history
of social revolution. He locates Africa's direct antecedent in
Mao's China. 'Fifteen years ago it was Asia that was stirring', he
says. 'Today 650 million Chinese, calm possessors of an immense
secret, are building a world by themselves alone'.[4] In China, like
Russia before it, class relations had not evolved into anything
like the clear opposition between proletariat and bourgeoisie

that we encountered with relative clarity in England, France, and the United States. Instead, Russia and China were shaped by semi-feudal social relations anachronistic to the core economies. This is why revolutionaries in those two states developed the political language and military logic of class war in new directions, with Trotsky's vision of the army as a force of modernization and Mao's strategy of protracted people's war, both of which understood combat capacity as a way of remaking class on unstable terrain. Not only did those revolutionaries emphasize solidarity between workers and peasants, they also recognized their enemy as the local front of imperial oppression and the material form of global capital. In 1956, Mao registered this as the cause for tricontinental solidarity. 'Our friends in Latin America, Asia, and Africa are in the same position as we and are doing the same kind of work', he announced, 'doing something for the people to lessen their oppression by imperialism. If we do a good job, we can root out imperialist oppression. In this we are comrades'.[5]

The Russian and Chinese revolutions, as well as those in Africa and Latin America, took place during a time when capitalism in the core states had moved into its imperial phase. Geopolitical expansion was deployed to defer class conflict at home and generate profits elsewhere. As Lenin famously defined it, imperialism is the monopoly stage of capitalism. This refers to the ascendance of finance as the merging of monopolist banks and large-scale industry, but also, in Lenin's accounting, 'the division of the world is the transition from a colonial policy which has extended without hindrance to territories unseized by any capitalist power, to a colonial policy of monopolist possession of the territory of the world, which has been completely divided up'.[6] This second characteristic of empire, the division of the world under colonial administration, was realized in blood during what has been called the 'Scramble for Africa'. After the Berlin Conference of 1884–5 sought to destroy competition between the industrially advanced core states by defining 'effective occupation' as the criterion for international recognition of a territory claim, there was redoubled enthusiasm for colonization as a way for the superpowers to exploit the new labour, new resources, and new markets of a subjugated continent. In 1870, on the eve of the Paris Commune, only 10 percent of Africa was under formal European control; by 1914, that colonization had increased to almost 90 percent of the continent, with only Ethiopia and Liberia still independent.

While in Russia during the 1920s and China during the 1930s social revolution was conditioned by uneven development and its incoherent class composition, African militants including Fanon confronted a different challenge: not uneven development, but enforced and systemic underdevelopment. Distinct from uneven development, underdevelopment is a relationship of interstate exploitation, a geopolitical analogy for the conflict between bourgeoise and proletariat. For the Guyanese historian Walter Rodney, writing in *How Europe Underdeveloped Africa*, colonialism exemplified 'the exploitation of one country by another', extracting resources and labour from one nation for the benefit of another nation, primarily through unequal exchange but also through foreign ownership of the means of production. 'When citizens of Europe own the land and the mines of Africa', argues Rodney, 'this is the most direct way of sucking the African continent. Under colonialism, the ownership was complete and backed by military domination'.[7]

Colonial Africa is subject to intersecting levels of exploitation and domination, which together complicate the class structure we have seen evolve in Europe and America. Rodney explains the difference in class relations between Africa and Europe:

Capitalism as a system within the metropoles or epicenters had two dominant classes: firstly, the capitalists or bourgeoisie who owned the factories and banks (the major means for producing and distributing wealth); and secondly, the workers or proletariat who worked in the factories of the said bourgeoisie. Colonialism did not create a capital-owning and factory-owning class among Africans or even inside Africa; nor did it create an urbanised proletariat of any significance (particularly outside of South Africa). In other words, capitalism in the form of

153

colonialism failed to perform in Africa the tasks which it had performed in Europe in changing social relations and liberating the forces of production.[8]

On one level, Africa is exploited absolutely by the imperial system, which causes economic retardation by draining the wealth and resources from the continent and sending it elsewhere. However, some Africans are still exploited by 'those who manipulate the system and those who are either agents or unwitting accomplices of the said system', and so, in working for the overthrow of imperial rule and the colonial system, militants also fight within and against a nascent class structure without the familiar divisions and commonalities. 'That European capitalism should have failed to create African capitalists', he speculates, 'is perhaps not as striking as its inability to create a working class and to diffuse industrial skills throughout Africa'.[9] In material terms, colonialism in Africa was prejudiced against the development of primary production outside of agriculture, investing instead in extractive industries like mining and timber-felling. In addition, when it came to work that required technical expertise, those professions would be overseen by colonist supervision. This ensured that for the greater part of Africa's modern history, modernizing class structures have been imposed incompletely or inconsistently, with a social hierarchy resulting from a multi-ethnic and tribal or communal society unevenly incorporated into a capitalist money economy, while the state as a whole is deprived of the basic means for subsistence.

* * *

If there is a narrative mode taken by war against the colonial system, then it is an allegorical one. As with Fanon's notebook and its projection of a unified Africa, each revolutionary action appears within its local context and simultaneously understands itself in correspondence with a more expansive idea of the nation and its geopolitical situation. The battle for Algiers is, in this sense, a battle for all of Africa. That's why Fanon describes it as the continental city. While the incommensurability between class and nation defined the organizational challenge faced by revolutionaries, here we can add that the allegorical relationship between class and colony, between emancipation and liberation, equips militants with revolutionary frames of reference as well as extra-economic targets that embody colonial occupation. In other words, class war in colonial settings is as much a fight against domination as it is a fight against exploitation, projecting a revolution that extends beyond the immediate conflict zones to embrace national and continental emancipation.[10]

In underdeveloped Africa, where class categories never formed as solidly as they did in the core states, the nation serves as an expansive myth that both precedes and stems from combat. Fanon understood this:

> Each man or woman brings the nation to life by his or her action and is pledged to ensure its triumph in their locality. We are dealing with a strategy of immediacy which is both radical and totalitarian: the aim and the program of each locally constituted group is local liberation. If the nation is everywhere, then she is here. One step further, and only here is she to be found. Tactics are mistaken for strategy. The art of politics is simply transformed into the art of war; the political militant is the rebel. To fight the war and to take part in politics: the two things become one and the same.[11]

What takes place in decolonial warfare is an attempt to construct the nation through social forms that are empowered by combat, with every local battle, every repudiation of the colonial occupiers, allegorically conjuring Africa into existence. Or as the political theorist Geo Maher writes, with 'the expansive myth of the nation, spontaneous revolts are knitted together into a complex revolutionary tapestry and the people rear up in unison'.[12]

We find a successful mobilization of this kind of allegory in the words and actions of Thomas Sankara, leader of an anti-colonial revolution that transformed the French Republic of Upper Volta into Burkina Faso in 1983. In a speech that simultaneously accounts for the extant social structure and galvanizes a fighting force against it, he insisted that, in colonial Africa, 'the enemies of the people are both inside and outside the country'.[13] Beginning with local hierarchies, Sankara proclaimed the enemies as those who take advantage of social and bureaucratic positions, who serve corporate shareholders, who seek approval from the commercial world, who exploit in order to enrich themselves – either through trade or industry – and those that enable such figures, from politicians to religious leaders. And surrounding the local economy are other enemies, those outside the borders:

> They base themselves on unpatriotic people here in our midst at every level of society – civilians as well as in the army; men as well as women; young as well as old; in the town as well as the country. The enemies of the people are there. The enemies outside the country are there: these enemies are neo-colonialism; they are imperialism.[14]

The local hierarchies and the global empire are thus combined into one adversary. After naming each enemy, Sankara repeats a phrase with only slight variation as a kind of decolonial incantation. 'These are enemies of the people', he begins. 'They must be combated. We will combat them together with you'.[15] This call to arms deploys allegory in a calculated attempt to forge an alliance, to build class solidarity on nationalist grounds between the civilian population and the state military. There is a grammar of induction at work here in the movement between the collective 'we' and the apostrophic 'you' in opposition to the enemy 'they', who is both local and global. Indeed, we sense an inverted echo of the Paris Commune and its calls for military defection away from the state and to the people. 'For the first time', Sankara explains,

> we see an army that wants power, that wants democracy, and that genuinely wants to link up with the people. For the first time, too, we see the people coming forward in massive numbers to stretch out their hands to the army. That's why we believe that

this army, which is taking control of the destiny of Upper Volta, is the people's army.[16]

Mediating between local people and imperial geopolitics, between class and colony, is the army: the collective embodiment of warfare.

* * *

As is so often the case, in this colonial setting class war arrives in the aftermath of imperial war. Sankara had undergone officer training before leading a popular coup against the previous military ruler, and Fanon likewise had experience in the armed forces of the state: he had lived and fought through two wars, and between them gained a lesson in decolonial solidarity. During World War Two, at age seventeen, he joined the French Free Forces to fight against the Nazis for the liberation of France. Following this, he studied medicine and psychiatry at the University of Lyons, completing his training in 1951. Two years later he was appointed to run the psychiatry department of the Blida-Joinville Hospital in Algeria, where he lasted only a few years, resigning his post in 1956 after insisting that psychiatric healthcare under the 'systemic dehumanization' of colonial rule is impossible: 'Madness is one of the ways that humans have of losing their freedom', he wrote in his letter of resignation. 'And I can say that, placed at this junction, I have measured with terror the extent of the alienation of this country's inhabitants'.[17] That same year he joined the Algerian National Liberation Front, or FLN, fighting against the French occupation of Northern Africa. He would go on to write about World War Two and the Algerian War of Independence in relation to each other – specifically, about how European armies militated against racial solidarity by separating West Indians from Africans. 'Before 1939', he recalled, 'the West Indian who volunteered in the Colonial Army, whether he was illiterate or knew how to read and write, served in a European unit, whereas the African, with the exception of the natives of the five territories, served in a native unit', which led to a racialized hierarchy wherein the West Indian was taken as superior to the African but subordinate to the European.[18] A similar dynamic pertained to the enlistment of Algerians in the French army. Both Muslim and European Algerians fought in World War Two but were required to serve in segregated units. The divide-and-conquer strategy for containment would be repeated in the colonies. Though it might be a given that ruling class power is a structure of foreign occupation, that structure also subsumes and modifies extant hierarchies. 'The first tactic of the colonial countries consists of basing themselves on official collaborators and feudal elements', says Fanon, and African militants would know this to be true.[19]

While the introduction of imperial rule in Africa created a series of single-crop economies dependent on foreign capital – alongside both indigenous and occupying classes of bureaucrats, reactionary intellectuals, and traders – outdated social forms were nevertheless preserved and cultivated. Kwame Nkrumah, who led the Gold Coast to independence from Britain in 1957, accounted for such tribal atavism in traditional Marxist terms, describing colonization as the suppression of communal ownership in favour of private property. 'At the opening of the colonial period', he asserts, 'the peoples of Africa were passing through the higher stage of communalism characterized by the disintegration of tribal democracy and the emergence of feudal relationships, hereditary tribal chieftaincies and monarchical systems'.[20] Indirect and foreign rule utilized local chiefs as tools for administration, and they exploited tribal conflict to strengthen colonial power. This helps us better understand the markedly different social dynamics presupposed by decolonial warfare. In contrast to colonialism, which deploys separatist and regionalist forms to preserve its own power by encouraging chieftaincies and confraternities, decolonial warfare is totalizing in its liberatory violence and nationalist in its opposition to customary groups.

It was Amílcar Cabral who perhaps made this argument most forcefully. Cabral was the leader of the nationalist guerrilla movement against Portuguese colonial rule in Guinea-Bissau and Cape Verde, a movement that won independence in 1973 only months after Cabral's assassination. According to him, armed struggle was a kind of development in and of itself. 'The armed liberation struggle implies', he says, 'a veritable forced march along the road to cultural progress'.[21] His argument in favour of warfare illustrates how social antagonism materially underwrites class solidarity in the colonial context:

> The armed liberation struggle requires the mobilization and organization of a significant majority of the population, the political and moral unity of the various social classes, the efficient use of modern arms and of other means of war, the progressive liquidation of the remnants of tribal mentality, and the rejection of social and religious rules and taboos which inhibit development of the struggle (gerontocracies, nepotism, social inferiority of women, rites and practices which are incompatible with the rational and national character of the struggle, etc.).[22]

Utilizing a form of protracted people's war, or what Che Guevara describes as deep warfare, Cabral, like Mao, insisted that combatants live off the land alongside the civilian population. Trained as an agronomist, he instructed soldiers to teach peasants better farming techniques so they could increase productivity and be better able to feed their families as well as the armed forces who, when not engaged in combat, tilled and ploughed the land alongside the locals. For this reason, he says, 'the armed liberation struggle is not only a product of culture but also a determinant of culture', a constitutive force for class solidarity against colonial occupation.[23]

* * *

France had occupied Algeria since the invasion of 1830, after using scorched-earth tactics to annihilate the native rulers in a genocidal conflict rooted in the contests over political legitimacy sparked by the Atlantic revolutions of the eighteenth century, especially that of Haiti. 'Although the crisis of colonial legitimacy that resulted from the Haitian Revolution differed in important ways from the crisis of political legitimacy engendered by the French Revolution', writes the historian Jennifer E. Sessions, 'together they pushed forward the processes of military conquest and settlement colonization that made Algeria not just a French colony, but ultimately part of France itself'.[24] Algeria was immensely profitable for France. In terms of trade, it accounted for between one-third and one-half of French imperial commerce and, by the 1930s, had become France's primary external trading partner. The struggle of Algerian people assumed form in a movement for national liberation. Founded on 10 October 1954, the National Liberation Front (FLN) absorbed extant nationalist organizations and parties and created an armed wing, the National Liberation Army, which by 1957 had enlisted around 40,000 combatants, many of whom had previously been in the French Army during the French-Indochina War of 1946-54, where the imperial state lost its Vietnamese colonies.

The Algerian War started on what has become known as Toussaint Rouge, or Red All-Saints' Day, when, early on 1 November 1954, FLN guerrillas launched coordinated attacks on military and civilian targets using tactics borrowed from both the French wartime resistance and the Viet Minh. After the attack, the FLN broadcast its demands from Cairo, announcing itself as 'a group of responsible young people and dedicated militants, gathering about it the majority of wholesome and resolute elements', and claiming that now was the time to escalate the national movement 'into the true revolutionary struggle at the side of the Moroccan and Tunisian brothers'. The announcement insisted on a strategy that would employ 'every means until the realization of our goal', hoping to galvanize 'action abroad to make the Algerian problem a reality for the entire world', though also wanting to limit bloodshed by taking up 'an honorable platform for discussion with the French authorities'.[25] This platform was never granted. Instead, French paratroopers – many of them also veterans of both World War Two and the French-Indochina War – commenced a colonial war infamous for its savagery. 'This was', reflects the writer Elaine Mokhtefi, 'the start of a nasty, deadly, eight-year war, which pitted a technologically advanced, well-armed European nation (the fourth most powerful military establishment in the world) against a ragtag army of peasants and barely literate villagers'.[26]

In 1956, the FLN called a nationwide general strike and planted bombs in public spaces, continuing hit-and-run shootings and bombings through the spring of 1957. Specializing in ambushes and night raids, and avoiding direct contact with superior French firepower, the internal forces targeted army patrols, military encampments, police posts, and colonial farms, mines, and factories, as well as transportation and communications facilities. Jean Lartéguy, a former soldier and popular journalist, wrote this moment into his 1960 novel *The Centurions*, about a French airborne battalion who are held captive by the Viet Minh and then deployed in Algeria. 'I knew them well', writes Lartéguy in the novel's preface, 'the centurions of the wars of Indo-China and Algeria. At one time I was one of their number; then, as a journalist, I became their observer and, on occasion, their confidant'.[27] Upon arrival in Africa the soldiers find themselves surrounded by terror. 'Horror reigned in Algiers', we read, 'to the sound of wailing ambulance sirens and in the midst of shattered shop windows and pools of blood hastily sprinkled with sawdust'.[28]

While Lartéguy is no friend to revolution – and is often included on reading lists for counterinsurgency training – his novel captures the mood of the occupation:

Algiers became a paratroop city. It got used to living to the silent, stealthy tread of patrols in camouflage uniform who, with a blank expression on their faces and a finger on the trigger of their guns, paced up and down the narrow lanes and stairways. The paratroops did not mingle with the local population; they lived on their own, outside the town and its customs, like occupants from another planet. They answered no questions, refused the wine and sandwiches that people offered them. They broke the strike, they destroyed the bomb network, but even the best-informed journalists could not tell 'what was going on'.[29]

This is an affirmation of colonial domination in prose form as well as in narrative content, with writing degree zero here serving as a reflection of the paratroopers' violent anonymity: their existence above and in opposition to the people, answerable to nobody while nevertheless highly visible, like a negative image of the guerrilla cell. This is deliberate. The paratroopers claim to have learned a new kind of warfare from the communists who held them captive, people for whom war is both social and military, 'a mixture of everything, a regular witches' brew ... of politics and sentiment, the human soul and a man's ass, religion and the best way of cultivating rice, yes, everything, including even the breeding of black pigs'. For the paratroopers in Algiers, this social arrangement was inverted into something closer to fascism, with the military engaged in black ops, which was then affirmed as an ideal. 'Have you noticed that in military history no regular army has ever been able to deal with a properly organized guerrilla force?' asks one of the French paratroopers. 'If we use the regular army in Algeria, it can only end in failure'. Instead, a call is made for France to have two armies. One for display: 'an army that would be shown for a modest fee on every fairground in the country'. Another would be the real fighting force, 'composed entirely of young enthusiasts in camouflage battledress, who would not be put on display but from whom impossible efforts would be demanded and to whom all sorts of tricks would be taught'.[30]

* * *

If Lartéguy's novel is one of colonial domination, the obverse narrative, written from the perspective of decolonial insurgency, is found in the memoirs of Zohra Drif, a young woman who was transformed by militancy as she joined the armed wing of the liberation movement. 'In Algiers', she reflects, 'particularly since March 1956 and the institution of the special powers, our helpless and unarmed people lived every night in anguish and fear, powerless against the fury and terror of the combined police and army forces, not to mention the *ultras*'.[31] The situation she describes is local and contemporary, but it is also continental and historical. In other words, it is the lived experience of colonial underdevelopment:

> Our nineteenth century was one of mass slaughter that made rivers of our ancestors' blood flow, thousands of hectares of their land burned and seized, and countless cities, towns, and villages ransacked and set alight. Our twentieth century was no better; the massacres of May 8, 1945, and August 20, 1955, ended up serving as fuel for the fire that our brave combatants lit on November 1, 1954, and that would not be extinguished until our country's liberation, and rightly so. We had always believed that our misfortune, our bondage, our negation as a people and nation went hand in hand with the system of settler colonialism. As a result, we always believed that our liberation and our affirmation would come with the end of colonization. We had always considered it better to die with honor in the armed struggle for dignity and liberation than to survive in the disgrace of tolerating colonization – and by settlement, at that.[32]

Drif and her friend Samia commit to serve the movement as what they describe as 'volunteers for death', agents of anonymous terror using bombs to shock the colonial world into consciousness.

After training and preparation, which involves the psychological management of fear through reading works of militant literature ranging from the French Revolution to Victor Serge, they sneak timed explosive devices into venues populated by French settlers. They choose their own targets: 'The Milk Bar symbolized colonial modernity in the service of the Europeans, their offensive carefree attitudes, their shameful indifference to our woes, and the arrogance of the colonial regime – especially since the café-bar abutted Place Bugeaud, named for the sinister exterminator of our people'.[33] The attack is narrated as a moment of suspense. 'Suddenly', Drif recalls, 'the Milk Bar was before me, all white, transparent, and shining: the hubbub of happy conversations, laughter, questions, youthful voices, summer colours, the smell of pastries, and even the distant twittering of birds in Bresson Square'.[34] After a 'huge explosion' followed 'by the sound of shattering glass' and the 'sight of people screaming and running everywhere', Drif and Samia go into hiding. 'Now', says Samia, 'we are real *moudjahidate*. We really are part of the guerrilla army'.[35]

When the attack is reported in the colonial press, Drif reads this as a minor victory, telling us the articles 'showed that the Europeans and their administration had suffered a blow to their certainties and their arrogance, that they had indeed been rattled and surprised'.[36] Interpreted as confirmation of the action's success, this comes to be read as evidence of an effective strategy:

> All this reaffirmed our conviction that our leaders' objective had been largely achieved: jar the Europeans out of the indecent tranquility and peace in which they had swooned, while only the 'natives' had been subject to a total war since the outbreak of the national liberation struggle. 'They want Algeria? Well! Algeria is at war, so let them taste the bitter reality!' That was our message to force them to open their eyes and realize that every day, thousands of 'natives' were bombed, besieged, arrested, tortured, executed, or disappeared so that 'peace, tranquility, innocence', the interests of the European population and the *status quo*, could be preserved and maintained. The FLN had achieved a major objective: to show our people that it was able to protect them, and especially to keep its word by striking blow for blow and hitting the heart of the European city.[37]

While the bombing is intended to serve the ideological or political as opposed to a more strictly military side of struggle, this strategy, namely terrorism, has occupied revolutionary thought for several centuries.

Lenin and Trotsky famously dismissed terrorism as adventurism, an atomizing violence that works against class solidarity. 'If it is enough to arm oneself with a pistol in order to achieve one's goal', asks Trotsky, 'why the efforts of the class struggle? If a thimbleful of gunpowder and a little chunk of lead is enough to shoot the enemy through the neck, what need is there for a class organisation?'[38] If, in the latter half of the twentieth century, terrorism would be taken up by militant groups like the Weather Underground and the Red Army Faction, whose failure to inspire wider movements might be viewed as confirmation of Lenin and Trotsky's critique, it was also utilized in other colonial settings as well as in ongoing wars against occupation and apartheid in Palestine, Sri Lanka, and elsewhere. In these settings, where exploitation and domination are conjoined, we might distinguish between decolonial terror and the violence of colonial domination, and in doing so clarify terrorism's place within specifically decolonial revolutions. 'Terror and counterterror are in fact two faces of one and the same reality', writes the political theorist Achille Mbembe. 'On the one hand, the terrorist project aims to effect the collapse of a society of rights, whose deepest foundations it objectively threatens; on the other, antiterrorist mobilization relies on the idea that extraordinary measures alone will enable enemies to be overcome and that state violence ought to be able to bear down on these enemies unreservedly'.[39]

Recalling the arc of class war, terrorism in colonial settings might therefore serve the function civil war does in Marx and Engels's narrative of escalation. That is, it creates a passage between class struggle and open revolution, which raises anew the question of solidarity. If the violence of counterterror leads to what Mbembe describes as 'domination without responsibility', as in the kind of social detachment found in Lartéguy's account of the paratroopers, decolonial terror aspires to the exact opposite: to inspire and activate solidarity.[40] This, in turn, will serve as the guiding hypothesis of Fanon's masterpiece from 1961, *The Wretched of the Earth*, a handbook of revolutionary theory inseparable in both form and content from the violence of Algiers.

* * *

Fanon's contention can be summarized in a single sentence: 'Decolonization, which sets out to change the order of the world, is, obviously, a program of complete disorder'.[41] Unlike many other works of revolutionary theory, this one does not affirm the proletariat as the subject of history but, instead, places the lumpenproletariat front and centre. Fanon's theory of revolution begins not with the workers of the world but with the starving peasantry of colonial countries, those men and women cast 'outside the class system', abandoned absolutely, who will – in Fanon's formulation – be 'the first among the exploited to discover that only violence pays'. It is a theory that begins with an account of colonialism as the terrain of war. 'Colonialism', he says, 'is not a thinking machine, nor a body endowed with reasoning faculties. It is violence in its natural state, and it will only yield when confronted with greater violence'.[42] Colonialism establishes its own battlefield through social division, arraying force against force and arming either side. 'The colonial world is a world cut in two. The dividing line, the frontiers are shown by barracks and police stations. In the colonies it is the policeman and the soldier who are the official, instituted go-betweens, the spokesmen of the settler and his rule of oppression'.[43] Liberation from the colony will always be violent because it requires – indeed demands – the forceful extirpation of the entire colonial system and the seizing of power by those who have been dispossessed, enslaved, and exploited under that system. 'The naked truth of decolonization evokes for us the searing bullets and bloodstained knives which emanate from it. For if the last shall be first, this will only come to pass after a murderous and decisive struggle between the two protagonists'.[44] There cannot and will not be an accord between the two zones, between the colonized and the colonizer; instead, 'destruction of the colonial world is no more and no less than the abolition of one zone, its burial in the depths of the earth or its expulsion from the country'.[45]

If we can hear the echo of Marx and Engels in this, for whom the bourgeoisie produces its own gravediggers, elsewhere Fanon echoes Mao, for whom the revolution is no dinner party:

It cannot come as a result of magical practices, nor of a natural shock, nor of a friendly understanding. Decolonization, as we know, is a historical process: that is to say that it cannot be understood, it cannot become intelligible nor clear to itself except in the exact measure that we can discern the movements which give it historical form and content.[46]

Decolonization is, in other words, a process whereby the subjugated forcibly and existentially terminate the mechanisms of subjugation no less than the subjugators. Here the practice of violence, qualitatively and quantitively heightened to the point of warfare, is what defines that process and its people. In other words, what took place in Algeria might be the formation of a new class through decolonial violence, the mobilization of the colonially dispossessed as a revolutionary army:

The practice of violence binds them together as a whole, since each individual forms a violent link in the great chain, a part of the great organism of violence which has surged upward in reaction to the settler's violence in the beginning. The groups recognize each other and the future nation is already indivisible. The armed struggle mobilizes the people; that is to say, it throws them in one way and in one direction.[47]

This linking, which takes its language from both the history of colonial enslavement and the communist critique of capital, is not just a matter of individual consciousness, of thinking and feeling; it is also the result of social interdependence, a sociality wherein each militant is responsible for every militant. In other words, what Fanon discovered in decolonial warfare is practical solidarity, the construction of a revolutionary class, which is the very opposite of what he had encountered in the imperial armies during World War Two.

* * *

The solidarity described by Fanon was aspirational, a drive towards unity in opposition, but also the result of military contingency, wherein guerrilla fighters would adopt a cellular sociality so that each operation group would comprise a handful of combatants known to each other but anonymous within the movement. This organization structure will be familiar from the French resistance to Nazi occupation, but it has more immediate precedent elsewhere in decolonial Africa: not least from the Mau Mau uprising of Kenya during the 1950s, when hundreds of thousands of rebels swore an oath to each other and their cause but retained a structure of anonymity. 'Nearly everybody was a member of the Movement', writes the Kenyan novelist Ngũgĩ wa Thiong'o,

> but nobody could say with any accuracy when it was born: to most people, especially those in the younger generation, it had always been there, a rallying center for action. It changed names, leaders came and went, but the Movement remained, opening new visions, gathering greater and greater strength, till on the eve of Uhuru, its influence stretched from one horizon touching the sea to the other resting on the great Lake.[48]

This is no mere political gesture or fraternal ideal. Rather, it is an expression of the necessary anonymity of guerrilla combat under colonial domination, similar to what the Algerian insurgents hoped for by organizing into small, semi-autonomous cells. 'Threatened by the colonial government with yet another eviction', writes the historian Caroline Elkins, 'sometime around 1943 the Olenguruone residents radicalized the traditional Kikuyu practice of oathing. Typically, Kikuyu men had taken an oath to forge solidarity during times of war or internal crises; the oath would morally bind men together in the face of great challenges'.[49]

Ngũgĩ's 1967 novel *A Grain of Wheat* is set during a Kenyan village's preparations for their independence-day celebration, Uhuru, during which two former resistance fighters plan to publicly execute the traitor who broke oath and betrayed Kihika, a revolutionary war hero who was captured and hanged by the British. In a flashback, the novel's protagonist, Mugo, recalls when Kihika tried to recruit him for an underground resistance movement, and how Kihika explained the oath as a unifying force, consolidating commitment. 'But what is an oath?' asks Kihika.

> For some people you need the oath to bind them to the movement. There are those who'll never keep a secret unless bound by an oath. I know them. I know men by their faces. In any case how many took the oath and are now licking the toes of the whiteman? No, you take an oath to confirm a choice already made. The decision to lay or not to lay your life for the people lies in the heart.[50]

Elsewhere, Kihika insists that to swear the oath is a commitment to solidarity amid conflict. 'In Kenya', he says, 'we want deaths which will change things, that is to say, we want true sacrifice. But first we have to be ready to carry the cross. I die for you, you die for me, we become a sacrifice for one another'.[51]

* * *

What we encounter across these regional contexts – in Guinea-Bissau, the Gold Coast, Burkina Faso, Kenya, and especially in Algeria – is the creation of solidarity through warfare. When Fanon says that decolonization is 'the veritable creation of new men', and that 'the "thing" which has been colonized becomes man during the same process by which it frees itself', we should emphasize that this creation, or becoming, is a collective phenomenon of solidarity, one that pertains utmost to those who are forced to live outside the formal hierarchies of exploitation and domination, thus shaping a class formation without the organizational benefit of any recognizable class structure.[52] In doing so it elevates the colonized from a political status as 'hordes of vital statistics, those hysterical masses, those faces bereft of all humanity, those distended bodies which are like nothing on earth, that mob without beginning or end, those children who seem to belong to nobody, that laziness stretched out in the sun, that vegetative rhythm of life', to an active fighting force that can reclaim its humanity through armed and open combat.[53]

At the level of individual consciousness – and here we can recall Fanon's work as a psychiatrist – revolutionary warfare is a force of redemption that 'frees the native from his inferiority complex and from his despair and inaction', and 'makes him fearless and restores his self-respect', insofar as armed conflict shows that 'liberation has been the business of each and all and that the leader has no special merit'. Exceeding the elevation of the individual subject, decolonial warfare brings together disparate persons and unites them in the service of social transformation. 'The mobilization of the masses, when it arises out of the war of liberation, introduces into each man's consciousness the ideas of a common cause, of a national destiny, and of a collective history'.[54] And within this logic we find a decolonial redefinition of terrorism, for when 'violence represents the absolute line of action', it performs double duty as a concrete measure of commitment to emancipation.[55]

While this infusing of the revolutionary imagination and decolonial warfare took shape on the continent of Africa, the commitment to violence as expansively and allegorically political would find its form in the practice of guerrilla warfare. In the guerrilla war, notes Fanon, every militant 'carries his warring country between his bare toes'.[56] On that score, Africa corresponds with other struggles for national liberation within the global south, especially those in Latin America. There, the military action of guerrillas would serve as a principal form of class struggle and armed propaganda a means of recruitment.

Closing a circuit between the two continents, on 25 April 1965, Che Guevara travelled to the Congo, meeting with an elite group of volunteer guerrillas from Cuba, the vast majority of them black, with whom he was to train indigenous combatants and fight against the puppet regime of former Belgian colonists and international mining companies. For Guevara, this was more than a gesture of altruistic solidarity. It was a way of preserving revolutions in Latin America – against which imperialism is said to hold Africa as a reserve. 'When the people's war develops in all its magnitude in the regions of Latin America', he says,

> it will become difficult for it to keep exploiting on the same scale the great natural wealth and markets that are the basis of the power of imperialism. But if Africa meanwhile calmly develops its system of neocolonialism, with no great commotion, investments could be transferred there – this has already begun – as a way of ensuring the survival of imperialism.

With these words, allegory once again makes itself felt within the space of decolonial warfare. The task of revolutionaries was, here as ever, to understand each local battle within the framework of global struggle, and so to recognize 'its duty within the great struggle of the peoples of the world' and 'to give consistent support to the movements that offer hope of a real and serious mobilization for victory'.[57]

8

The Armed Nucleus

From 1952 until 1959, the island of Cuba was under the dictatorship of Fulgencio Batista, a military general backed by the United States and aligned with the owners of the island's largest sugar plantations. Under his rule, forms of collective action such as the right to strike were outlawed, and he saw to the transfer of both the lucrative sugar industry and around 70 percent of arable land into foreign ownership. With support from the United States, his regime enacted violent domestic repression, utilizing the secret police to carry out mass violence, including torture and public execution. Fidel Castro, then a qualified and working lawyer, attempted to bring criminal sentences against the Batista regime. Having reached a legal and political deadlock, Castro went on to found an insurgent movement, developing a clandestine cell system, publishing an underground newspaper, stockpiling weapons, and recruiting and training militants, often hailing from the poor districts of Havana. In this, he emulated the nineteenth-century independence fighter José Martí, who rejected Spanish rule with its racialized class hierarchies, and instead advocated for a war of national liberation. 'For myself', Martí wrote on the day of his death, 18 May 1895, 'I understand that a nation cannot be made to go against the spirit that moves it, or to do without that spirit, and I know how to set hearts on fire and how to use the ardent and gratified state of those hearts for incessant agitation and attack'.[1]

It was to a similar line that Castro would soon commit, and on 26 July 1953 he led a raid of 165 rebels in an attempt to seize a military barracks in Santiago de Cuba. The raid was disastrous, and Castro was imprisoned. Upon his release two years later, he left Cuba for Mexico with his brother Raúl because, in his own words, 'all doors of peaceful struggle have been closed to me'. In Mexico, Fidel and Raúl befriended the Argentine doctor Ernesto 'Che' Guevara as well as the Spaniard Alberto Bayo, a veteran of the Spanish Civil War who would instruct the rebels in the practicalities of combat. On 25 November 1956, in Tuxpan, Veracruz, Castro boarded a leaky yacht, the *Granma*, with eighty-one militants armed with ninety rifles, three machine guns, around forty pistols, and two handheld anti-tank guns. The *Granma* made land in the mangrove swamps at Playa Las Coloradas, at the southeastern tip of Cuba. After initial attacks from Batista, only nineteen rebels made it to their rallying destination.

Two years later, on 2 January 1959, Castro's chief commandants – Guevara and Camilo Cienfuegos – led columns into the capital city, Havana. Castro joined them a week later, and symbolically delivered Cuba to those who aided the insurgents. In his victory speech, he appraised a people remade by conflict, a revolutionary class mobilized through social antagonism:

> When I hear talk of columns, of battle fronts, of troops, I always reflect. Because here our strongest column, our best unit, the only troops capable of winning the war alone are the people. No general can do more than the people. No army can do more than the people. I was asked what troops I would prefer to command, and I answered I would prefer to command the people. Because the people are unconquerable and it was the people who won this war, because we had no army, we had no fleet, we had no tanks, we had no planes, we had no heavy guns, we had no military academies or recruiting and training teams. We had neither divisions nor regiments nor companies nor platoons, but we have the confidence of the people, and with this alone we were able to win the battle for liberty.[2]

These words are more than an expression of socialist ideology, in which the state is returned to the people. Specifically, the methods by which Castro and his comrades waged war against Batista combined military tactics with a material dependence on the support of an oppressed population living under dictatorship, who provided not only soldiers but food, shelter, medicine, and information. Correspondingly, the combatants' relations with the people were key, and they set out to inspire revolt not only through their armed propaganda but also by working in solidarity with rural communities.

This form of fighting, guerrilla warfare, was born out of necessity, taken up here and elsewhere by the outgunned and outnumbered. But it also contains within itself the form of a new sociality. The guerrillas mobilized with the oppressed against the system of their oppression. 'This attitude', wrote the journalist and historian Richard Gott, 'owed much to Frantz Fanon, who emphasized the desirability of creating a new type of society through violent, revolutionary struggle. To paraphrase Marshall McLuhan, the method had become the program'.[3] As a mode of conflict to which the remaking of class is as much a part of the process as it is the stated objective, guerrilla combat epitomizes class war.

* * *

Revolutionaries have long been drawn to guerrilla warfare by the need to fight asymmetrically as partisans against forces of greater number and technical capacity. This has been true since the Peninsular War of 1808–14 between France and Spain, from which the term 'guerrilla' derives its English origins as a translation of the Spanish *guerra*, or war. According to Marx, the Spanish resistance to French invasion had achieved something believed impossible. 'As Don Quixote had protested with his lance against gunpowder', wrote Marx, 'so the guerrillas protested against Napoleon, only with different success'. In Marx's estimation, the potency of the guerrilla movement is an index to revolutionary potential; and its dissipation, by contrast, a reflection of counter-revolutionary inertia. 'Beginning with the rise of whole populations, the partisan war was next carried on by guerrilla bands, of which whole districts formed the reserve and terminated in *corps francs* continually on the point of dwindling into banditti, or sinking down to the level of standing regiments'.[4]

While Lenin, Trotsky, Mao, and Fanon also wrote about and practiced forms of guerrilla warfare, it would be Latin America, especially after the Cuban Revolution, that was to become synonymous with the guerrilla. Covered with jungles and thick with swamps and mountains, it became home to numerous guerrilla movements that have carried out assassinations, hijacks, kidnappings, robberies, and attacks on military, political, and economic targets. Aside from offering hospitable terrain, the fact that the continent functions in the capitalist world-system as a site of resource extraction, much like Africa in the previous chapter, made it a key locus of guerrilla action insofar as overseas imperial interests would rely on and so frequently install dictatorships. These antagonisms heightened during the Cold War, when Latin America was also taken to be contested terrain in the fight against global communism by the geographically proximate superpower, the United States, which sponsored right-wing dictators and roving death squads across the region, and ensured a steady supply of arms, funds, and military training to counter-revolutionary forces under the guise of anti-narcotics initiatives.

In the words of Salvador Allende, Chile's democratically elected socialist leader who was later deposed in a US-backed coup, Cuba and Latin America share one fate. For Allende, Castro provided a revolutionary object lesson in how to defeat the forces of reaction. 'They are all underdeveloped producers of raw materials and importers of industrial products', wrote Allende in reference to Cuba and the rest of Latin America. 'In all these countries imperialism has deformed the economy, made big profits and established its political influence'.[5] Significantly, Allende's argument resembles the metonymy used by Frantz Fanon, in which, we recall, Algeria became a cipher for all of Africa: 'The Cuban revolution is a national revolution, but it is also a revolution of the whole of Latin America. It has shown the way for the liberation of all our peoples'.[6] After the Cuban

Revolution, militants applied its practical lessons up and down the continent, fighting against local dictatorships and foreign oppression, colonial domination and economic exploitation. Pre- and post-dating Cuba's revolutionary inspiration, this kind of insurgency became something like a cultural tradition. The Sandinista National Liberation Front in Nicaragua, the Revolutionary Bolivarian Army in Venezuela, and the Zapatista Army of National Liberation in Mexico all adopted the names and personae of legendary fighters, just as Castro took inspiration from José Martí. Such figures, for Castro, spoke in

> the genuine voice of the people: a voice that breaks forth from the depths of coal and tin mines, from factories and sugar mills, from feudal lands where rotos, cholos, gauchos, jibaros, the heirs of Zapata and Sandino, take up the arms of liberty; a voice heard in poets and novelists, in students, in women and children, in the old and helpless.[7]

* * *

This kind of inspiration, of revolutionary traditions reenacted in the voice of the people, can be seen too in what is perhaps the most celebrated Latin American novel, Gabriel García Márquez's *One Hundred Years of Solitude*. Márquez's book was shaped, both thematically and aesthetically, by the guerrilla movements of the continent. 'Many years later', reads its opening sentence, 'as he faced the firing squad, Colonel Aureliano Buendía was to remember that distant afternoon when his father took him to discover ice'.[8] Alongside its pitch towards a sense of wonderment, this sentence foreshadows an execution that will never arrive but forever seems likely. As we eventually learn, Aureliano's military title is owed to his service as an exemplary guerrilla, a combatant who led 'thirty-two armed uprisings'. Notwithstanding this opening, his is a death forestalled until old age and which takes place by natural causes, far from any battlefield, after he already 'survived fourteen attempts on his life, seventy-three ambushes, and a firing squad'.[9] Gifted with prophetic foresight, Aureliano starts political life as something very different from the guerrilla he would eventually become. In fact, he first identifies with the Liberals in opposition to Conservative rule but only does so at a remove from anything like political commitment let alone militancy. 'Because of his humanitarian feelings', the narrator tells us, 'Aureliano sympathized with the Liberal attitude with respect to the rights of natural children, but in any case, he could not understand how people arrived at the extreme of waging war over things that could not be touched with the hand'.[10] Soon enough, however, after witnessing an atrocity at the hands of Conservative troops, he takes up arms and strikes out on a 'mad operation' against military occupation with 'twenty-one men under the age of thirty ... armed with table knives and sharpened tools', taking a garrison by surprise, confiscating their weapons, and executing their leaders. He is eventually proclaimed by his troops as the 'chief of the revolutionary forces of the Caribbean coast with the rank of general'.[11] Aureliano's progression from identifying with the Liberals against the Conservatives to his eventual adoption and mastery of guerrilla warfare is a process of learned militancy, and one that resembles the life of Márquez's close friend, Fidel Castro, in taking up arms only after the failure of political reform.

When Aureliano does turn away from the state's political apparatus, however, it is a turn towards the people, engaging in covert operations that ultimately serve to build force through solidarity:

At the end of three months they had succeeded in arming more than a thousand men, but they were wiped out. The survivors reached the eastern frontier. The next thing that was heard of them was that they had landed on Cabo de la Vela, coming from the smaller islands of the Antilles, and a message from the government was sent all over by telegraph and included in jubilant proclamations throughout the country announcing the death of Colonel Aureliano Buendía. But two days later a multiple telegram which almost overtook the previous one announced another uprising on the southern plains. That was how the legend of the ubiquitous Colonel Aureliano Buendía began.

Simultaneous and contradictory information declared him victorious in Villanueva, defeated in Guacamayal, devoured by
Motilón Indians, dead in a village in the swamp, and up in arms
again in Urumita. The Liberal leaders, who at that moment were
negotiating for participation in the congress, branded him an
adventurer who did not represent the party. The national government placed him in the category of a bandit and put a price of
five thousand pesos on his head. After sixteen defeats, Colonel
Aureliano Buendía left Guajira with two thousand well-armed
Indians and the garrison, which was taken by surprise as it slept,
abandoned Riohacha. He established his headquarters there and
proclaimed total war against the regime.[12]

Despite moments like this, which read like the gathering of intelligence from multiple battlefronts, Márquez's novel is less about
the guerrilla movement itself, which tends to appear only in the
narrative margins, than it is a harmonization of narrative form
with how the guerrilla movement would describe its own
actions. For example, one of the eccentricities of this novel is
that so many characters share the name Aureliano, including the
guerrilla's seventeen children, making them virtually indistin-
guishable and practically uncountable. While this renders the
family unknowable and anonymous, like members of any clandestine cell system, for Fredric Jameson it is also analogous to
'the ancient cosmologies of atomism', a philosophy in which

> the very concept of the atom produces a multiplicity of other
> atoms, identical to itself; the notion of the One generates many
> Ones; the force of attraction that pulls everything external into
> the internal, that absorbs all difference into identity, now subverts
> and negates itself, and the repulsion into which attraction
> suddenly turns acquires a new name: war.[13]

If this is how a family drama modulates into an epic of war, it is
likewise how the band of twenty-one men wielding cutlery
somehow become several thousand armed guerrillas. And if that
impossible multiplication resembles the revolutionary process

that took place in Cuba between 1956 and 1959, in which nineteen rebels became a revolutionary people's army, it also resembles the rhetoric of the guerrillas, who often described themselves as the nucleus of revolution. The nuclear metaphor – which reappears all throughout revolutionary discourse in Latin America – serves as a local counterforce to the superpower rivalry that defined the Cold War era and the Cuban Missile Crisis, a zero-sum contest beneath which rival armies fought in the continental wilderness, where the guerrilla and its people enact something approaching a nuclear fission of revolutionary solidarity. More than any one novel, however, if there is a narrative form belonging to guerrilla warfare, that form is what might be described as the field manual.

The field manual is an instructional handbook that combines anecdotal evidence and personalized illustration with lessons from history, technical information about military operations and weapon manipulation, and the explicitly ideological content of political philosophy and revolutionary propaganda. It was these works that another celebrated Latin American author, Argentine novelist Julio Cortázar, took inspiration from when crafting an experimental novel about a guerrilla cell working in Paris to undermine Argentina's military dictatorship and their attempts to construct for themselves a paraphysical 'bridge', the kind of thing apprehended by William Morris and Jack London, between lived reality and a post-capitalist future. Invested in the idea of literature as the preserve of revolutionary memory – as a prismatic home to military tactics and ideological commitments – the book chronicles the lives of the cell but also takes the form of a manual: a scrapbook of revolutionary history made for Manuel, the infant son of one of the guerrillas, from whom the novel derives its title, which translates as *A Manual for Manuel*.

Like the instructional pamphlets we have encountered by Francis Maceroni, Louis Auguste Blanqui, and Mao Zedong, the field manual is best thought of as a portable pedagogical device, a material object to be read by the guerrilla. A fictional 'autobiography' of Castro describes the form accurately when noting its own brevity in contradiction to the apparent author's infamous verbosity, insisting that 'in my case, logically, the reader in mind is none other than the revolutionary combatant', and so literary form must follow social function. 'Revolutionary works can't be merely objects of display on a high shelf, or designed to be read on a lectern'. Instead, 'the ideal would be a book that is easy to get rid of in case of a police raid and that fits easily in the pocket of one's field uniform or doesn't weigh much at the bottom of your backpack', where it fits comfortably 'along with smokes, munitions, and dry rations'.[14]

While fictions such as these predominate within Latin American literary culture, our primary interest for this chapter will be in three field manuals that were carried in the packs of guerrilla fighters. They were also written by three men who each – unlike the magically unstoppable Aureliano Buendía – met state suppression: Che Guevara, Régis Debray, and Carlos Marighella. In October 1967, Guevara was captured and executed in Bolivia. In April of the same year, Debray was arrested in the small Bolivian town of Muyupampa and sentenced to thirty years in prison. And in November 1969, Marighella was ambushed by police in São Paulo, where he was shot to death.

* * *

Up in the Sierra Maestra mountains, Guevara was the only non-Cuban to fight along Castro in his guerrilla army, and it was there that he tested his political beliefs and military strategies, eventually commanding the rebel army. His experiences in Cuba confirmed to him that guerrilla combat was an essential and exportable mode of revolution – the guerrilla movement, he would later reflect, 'has diverse characteristics, different facets, even though the essential will for liberation remains the same'.[15] Or, as Michael Löwy has summarized, Guevara's perspective on revolution – his 'signal insight' – is 'that class struggle is more than an economic struggle; it is a struggle to become more fully human through the creation of ever widening sociabilities, of a boundless horizon for human enrichment'.[16]

It is in his field manual of 1960 that Guevara's surest

conceptualization of the guerrilla can be found. Written the year after he and the rebels marched victoriously into Havana, the document was planned, according to Guevara, as a counter-point to 'the defeatist attitude of revolutionaries or pseudo-revolutionaries who remain inactive and take refuge in the pretext that against a professional army nothing can be done, who sit down to wait until in some mechanical way all neces-sary objective and subjective conditions are given without work-ing to accelerate them'.[17] The operative idea here is work. The actions taken by the guerrilla combatants are, when left alone, insufficient to bring about revolution. Instead, the revolutionary work is both the product of given conditions and the basis for new conditions. The guerrilla's task is to conduct propaganda by deed through military operations which debilitate the enemy army, but also to apply affirmative measures that are revolution-ary in social character: distribution of land to the peasants, the organization of cooperatives, the establishment of a court and an administration, the promulgation of revolutionary laws, so that the guerrilla force appears to the people as a desirable alter-native to the incumbent state, its economy, and the extant social order. The guerrilla is, in this view, a catalytic force of transfor-mation, embodying that which they hope to bring about. Guevara's central wager for the guerrilla thus echoes Mao's theory of protracted people's war, insofar as the guerrilla *foco* – namely a group that would serve as the point of focus for popular discontent – is the armed vanguard of the people, and as such is an organic expression of their material common interests.

Guevara outlines the two belligerent forces: the army of the state and capital and, standing in opposition, an armed people. 'On one side we have a group composed of the oppressor and his agents, the professional army, well-armed and disciplined, in many cases receiving foreign help as well as the help of the bureaucracy in the employ of the oppressor'. Opposing this confederation are those who have taken up arms, flanked by a much wider social milieu: 'the people of the nation or region involved', as he describes them. 'It is important to emphasize that guerrilla warfare is a war of the masses, a war of the people. The guerrilla band is an armed nucleus, the fighting vanguard of the people. It draws its great force from the mass of the people themselves'. As in the revolutionary propagation of Márquez's novel, this kind of atomic proliferation is the guarantee of success both on and off the battlefield. 'The guerrilla band is not to be considered inferior to the army against which it fights simply because it is inferior in fire power. Guerrilla warfare is used by the side which is supported by a majority but which possesses a much smaller number of arms for use in defence against oppression'. The proof that support from the people is indispensable is found when comparing the guerrilla column to bandit gangs. 'They have all the characteristics of a guerrilla army, homogeneity, respect for the leader, valor, knowledge of the ground, and, often, even good understanding of the tactics to be employed. The only thing missing is support of the people; and, inevitably, these gangs are captured and exterminated by the public force'.[18] Unlike the bandit, the guerrilla is wholly dependent on help from the civilian inhabitants of the combat zone, without which they are doomed to failure.

Class solidarity is the mediating substance between the guerrilla and the people, as well as between political ideals and military strategy. 'The Rebel Army', Guevara reflects, 'was already ideologically proletarian and thought as a dispossessed class; the urban leadership remained petty bourgeois with future traitors among its leaders'.[19] While the asymmetry of guerrilla warfare determines the practicalities of conflict, emphasizing the necessity of hit-and-run attacks, the most favourable ground for the guerrilla comprises those zones otherwise inaccessible to a large standing army: dense forests, steep mountains, impassable deserts, marshland, all of which Latin America has in abundance. While the guerrilla must possess good knowledge of this terrain in order to exploit the paths of entry and escape, the possibilities of speedy manoeuvres, as well as good hiding places, this terrain also corresponds with the class formation of the guerrilla force. And here we return to our nuclear metaphor. 'We might also ask', writes Guevara, 'if the members of the guerrilla band should be drawn from a certain social class. It has already been said that this social composition ought to be adjusted to that of the zone chosen for the center of operations, which is to say that the combatant nucleus of the guerrilla army ought to be made up of peasants'.[20] This, too, shapes political ambition in a concretely practical way:

> All this indicates that the guerrilla fighter will carry out his action in wild places of small population. Since in these places the struggle of the people for reforms is aimed primarily and almost exclusively at changing the social form of land ownership, the guerrilla fighter is above all an agrarian revolutionary. He interprets the desires of the great peasant mass to be owners of land, owners of their means of production, of their animals, of all that which they have long yearned to call their own, of that which constitutes their life and will also serve as their cemetery.[21]

Land rights are the historical truth of guerrilla warfare, and a truth that is not exclusive to Latin America. With every struggle against constituted power in locations where the dispossessed must otherwise live from the land, in China and Africa as well as in Vietnam and Cuba, whatever the ideological aims that may inspire the fight, the economic aim is determined by the aspiration towards land ownership – because without it there can be no survival. Land is an essential factor in the life of the peasant, and so a defining feature of the guerrilla's program.

The close association between the guerrilla fighters and the peasant masses is not an assumed fact; rather, it is something that must be built progressively. Likewise, the relationship between the army and the people, the guerrilla and the peasant, cannot be that of top-down, dictatorial leadership. If 'the initiators of guerrilla warfare, or rather the directors of guerrilla warfare, are not men who have bent their backs day after day over the furrow', they will instead be revolutionaries 'who understand the necessity for changes in the social treatment accorded peasants, without having suffered in the usual case this bitter treatment in their own persons'.[22]

While it is recommended that the guerrilla seize in 'the heat of the war those moments in which human fraternity reaches its highest intensity' to stimulate 'all kinds of cooperative work', for Guevara this cooperation between civilian and combatant occurs spontaneously, delivering simultaneously a proof of revolutionary ideals and the sociality required for military victory:

> It happens then (I am drawing on the Cuban experience and enlarging it) that a genuine interaction is produced between these leaders, who with their acts teach the people the fundamental importance of the armed fight, and the people themselves who rise in rebellion and teach the leaders these practical necessities of which we speak. Thus, as a product of this interaction between the guerrilla fighter and his people, a progressive radicalization appears which further accentuates the revolutionary characteristics of the movement and gives it a national scope.[23]

It is in this way – via the simultaneous militarization of class and the labouring of the military – that an army evolves exponentially and explosively, as though by process of nuclear fission. As Löwy explains: 'A people's army and the people become revolutionary, the two progressively merging into a more or less homogeneous bloc. From that moment onward, the guerrilla movement becomes practically invincible and is able progressively to defeat, demoralize, and overcome the army of the bourgeois state'.[24] Looking towards Cuba's future and the future of revolution in Latin America, Guevara suggests that this unfolding of class and war is the true meaning of revolution. 'An army that is linked in such ways with the people', he would reflect, 'that feels this intimacy with the peasants and the workers from which it emerged, that knows besides all the special techniques of its warfare and is psychologically prepared for the worst contingencies, is invincible'. The army is, then, 'the people in uniform', and, conversely, the people are the army: an omnipresent rearguard made capable through association with the guerrilla and by participating in the revolution.[25]

* * *

The second of those field manuals for guerrilla war is from Régis Debray, a student of Louis Althusser who relocated to Latin America in the late 1960s. Befriending revolutionaries, including Castro and Guevara, the Paris-born Debray lived and worked with guerrillas, combining an education in academic Marxism with the experience of revolutionary combat. 'At their invitation', writes the historian Robin Blackburn, 'Debray became the only man to have personally witnessed the travail of the revolutionary movement in every major Latin American republic in a series of visits from 1961 to 1967'.[26] To better understand the Cuban Revolution and its meaning for Latin America, Debray interviewed guerrillas, sometimes at the site of their victories, and was granted access to numerous unpublished documents, including military communiqués. This allowed him to develop political and military conclusions against the continental backdrop, all of which he combined into a comprehensive revolutionary injunction. The resulting text, *Revolution in the Revolution? Armed Struggle and Political Struggle in Latin America*, was printed for wide distribution in January 1967 in Havana. It criticized the strategy of emergent movements, acted as a supplement to Guevara's theorization, and ultimately clarified a vision of class war for Latin America. It is a book that, in Jean-Paul Sartre's frequently quoted assessment, 'removes all the brakes from guerrilla activities'.[27]

The premise of Debray's book is that Cuba inaugurated a new way of conducting revolution, and that this novelty cannot be repeated elsewhere in Latin America by directly exporting the legend or myth of 'twelve men who disembark and whose numbers multiply in the twinkling of an eye, no one knows quite how'. What the contemporary attention given to 'surface glitter' mystifies, or even suppresses, is the reality of an 'insurrectional process' from which 'truths of a technical, tactical, and even of a strategic order' will need to be elaborated and internalized by future revolutionaries.[28] Similarly, Debary is adamant in his refusal to superimpose the lessons of Lenin or Mao or any other movement onto Latin America. 'One may well consider it a stroke of good luck that Fidel had not read the military writings of Mao Tse-tung before disembarking on the coast of Oriente', we are reminded. 'He could thus invent, on the spot out of his own experience, principles of a military doctrine in conformity with the terrain. It was only at the end of the war, when their tactics were already defined, that the rebels discovered the writings of Mao'.[29] What this belated discovery of the nearest precedent meant is that, in addition to devising a mode of combat matched to the locale, the guerrillas were denied the luxury of an intellectual or aesthetic relationship to war. Instead, they had to live it, and in doing so learn quickly from confrontations with a well-armed enemy.

Rather than myth and legend, what should be taken from Cuba, echoing the lessons of Bolivar and Martí more so than those of Lenin and Mao, is the privileged role assigned to tenacity, or relentless military aggression, in the revolutionary sequence. According to Debray, revolution without insurrection is no revolution at all, and guerrilla warfare is the embodiment of this theory, bringing about positive change in lockstep with a total demolition of the state:

> In Latin America today a political line which, in terms of its consequences, is not susceptible to expression as a precise and consistent military line, cannot be considered revolutionary. Any line that claims to be revolutionary must give a concrete answer to the question: How to overthrow the power of the capitalist state? In other words, to break its backbone, the army, continuously reinforced by North American military missions? The Cuban Revolution offers an answer to fraternal Latin American countries which has still to be studied in its historical details: by means of more or less slow building up, through guerrilla warfare, carried out in suitably chosen rural zones, of a mobile strategic force, nucleus of a people's army and a future socialist state.[30]

The interdependence of military and political lines is intended to safeguard against the importation of military misconception under the guise of political belief. Beginning from the conviction that revolution – and nothing short of revolution – is going to serve the people of Latin America, the guerrilla is said to oppose a politics of reform and, with that, every political measure that might hamper military capacity.

As an instructional manual, Debray's book presents its injunctions in the form of targeted critique aimed at specific misconceptions, disputing the concept of self-defence, the separation of armed propaganda from real combat, and over-reliance on bases and the party – all of which, it is said, detract from the real practice of war. The defeat of worker and peasant self-defence movements in Colombia and Bolivia are said to mark the final demise of reformism. They end 'the epoch of relative class equilibrium' and mark the 'beginning of another, that of total class warfare, excluding compromise solutions and shared power'.[31] Where Debray departs from other revolutionaries – including Guevara – is in his steadfast insistence that warfare be total and that combatants remain wholly independent from the civilian population. 'Self-defence is partial', he says. 'Revolutionary guerrilla warfare aims at total war by combining under its hegemony all forms of struggle at all points within the territory'.[32] What this means is that the guerrilla should actively avoid protective integration into a sympathetic social milieu, because doing so hampers their effectiveness as guerrillas, rendering them immobile and their violence tactical and passive, as opposed to actively making a strategic revolutionary contribution.

There is, for Debray, grim irony in defensive warfare. 'By choosing to operate at this level, it may be able to provide protection for a limited time. But in the long run the opposite is true: self-defence undermines the security of the civilian population'.[33] Moreover, if the guerrilla were to take on a role as community organizer this would be catastrophic, for the purpose of organizing meetings and public gatherings is 'simply to denounce the inhabitants to the forces of repression and the political cadres of the police: it is to send them to prison or to their grave'.[34] By way of contrast, the guerrilla force's isolated militarism is itself the best protection against repression, which ultimately relies not on tactical defence but on the strategic and progressive destruction of the enemy's military power, so as to completely neutralize all threat of reprisal. In this turn, Debray's argument becomes the mirror opposite of Guevara's. 'In order to destroy one army, another army is necessary, and this implies training, discipline, and arms. Fraternity and bravery do not make an army. Witness Spain', he adds, 'and the Paris Commune'.[35]

Commonality nevertheless prevails at the level of class. Debray insists categorically that class solidarity, as opposed to political or ideological concessión, is what sustains revolutionary force. 'No political front which is basically a deliberative body can assume leadership of a people's war', he writes, 'only a technically capable executive group, centralized and united on the basis of identical class interests, can do so; in brief, only a revolutionary general staff'.[36] This is the negative lesson of the French Revolution and the English Civil War, that ideological concessions are, in the duration of revolutionary time, not in the service of national liberation or social transformation. Any foundation less solid than class solidarity will be as provisional as the compromises made in its name. This will be true unless leadership 'descends from the blue sky of agreements that transcend classes and sets his feet on earth in the very midst of its vulgar society of classes and takes his place at the head of one of them'.[37] The guerrilla army must therefore choose sides in what can only be understood as class war. 'Precisely because it is a mass struggle ... the guerrilla movement, if it is to triumph *militarily*, must *politically* assemble around it the majority of the exploited classes', because only they can ensure – via the general strike or generalized urban insurrection – the transfer of revolutionary energy from the small band of guerrillas to the mass movement. For this to work, however, the guerrilla must first be recognized by the masses as the force of their redemption, operating via 'the class alliance which it alone can achieve, the alliance that will take and administer power, the alliance whose interests are those of socialism – the alliance between workers and peasants'.[38]

It is on this point that Debray echoes Guevara. He concurs that the social factions within the revolution each have something to learn from one another, and that something is learned in war, where 'the shared existence, the combats, the hardships endured together, weld an alliance having the simple force of friendship'.[39] War, then, provides a foundation for class solidarity, providing the revolutionary conditions wherein individualist bourgeois psychology – and here Debray uses a simile that could have come from Márquez – 'melts like snow under the summer sun'. As was the case in Cuba, but also in China and Africa, this accounts for the fact that the worker-peasant alliance will often find its connective link in a group of revolutionaries from bourgeois extraction who must – as Debray quotes from Amílcar Cabral, whose thinking would also be adapted by Huey P. Newtown – 'commit suicide as a class in order to be restored to life as revolutionary workers, totally identified with the deepest aspirations of their people'.[40] The life of the guerrilla, as one amid a band of other fighters, generates the conditions for this kind of transfiguration. If strikes are the school of war, guerrilla warfare might be the university of revolutionary leadership, a forcing ground that materially reconditions social being around class solidarity.

* * *

Guevara and Debray both argued against guerrilla deployment into urban and suburban zones, emphasizing instead the wilderness of the jungle and the mountain range. Both shared Castro's view that 'the city is the cemetery of the revolutionaries and resources', a military and political graveyard for the guerrilla movement. While both appreciated the strategic value of an urban underground, especially when building towards general strikes and generalized insurrection, its activities are confined to the levels of intelligence, propaganda, and sabotage, or of generating conditions of mass unrest through disruption of commercial and industrial activity. This is because every encounter between the guerrilla and the city is a threat to military cohesion. 'As we know', quips Debray, 'the mountain proletarianizes the bourgeois and peasant elements, and the city can bourgeois-ify the proletarians'.[41] On the one hand, the city offers bour-geois comfort, a reprieve from sleeping unwashed and hungry in hammocks or on the ground; on the other, the city is enemy territory, where the guerrilla is susceptible to assassination, kidnapping, or torture. In these ways, as a threat to both morale and security, the city is hostile terrain for the movement as a whole.

And yet, by the 1960s, the Latin American poor were becoming increasingly urbanized, with informal barrios, shan-ties, slums, and favelas growing around the city outskirts. For Mike Davis, writing in *Planet of Slums*, it was during this decade that Venezuela 'went from being 30 percent urban to 30 percent rural'.[42] As in other countries on the continent, injections of North American capital led to the establishment of an automotive industry in Brazil, the most populous nation in Latin America, while, in the wake of several droughts, hundreds of thousands of peasants drifted from the interior northeast to the south-central region, and especially São Paulo, now Brazil's economic heart. It was in reaction to this kind of urbanization and its potential entanglement with guerrilla insurrection that Brazil entered a military dictator-ship in 1964, commencing a period in which squatter settle-ments were forcefully displaced from the city outskirts with the aid of public security forces. Or as Davis summarizes, 'evoking the threat of a tiny urban *foco* of Marxist guerrillas, the military razed 80 favelas and evicted almost 140,000 poor people from the hills overlooking Rio'.[43] Even if the city cannot be the optimal zone for guerrilla warfare, it has a significant role to play in Latin American revolution.

Carlos Marighella's *Mini-manual of the Urban Guerrilla* was published in 1969 in São Paulo. Marighella had served office for the Brazilian Communist Party before he was expelled and went on to found Ação Libertadora Nacional in 1967, a dedicated guerrilla organization which, during its active years, robbed banks to finance insurrectionary warfare and kidnapped public figures to exchange for jailed revolutionaries. In a 1969 declaration addressed to 'the Brazilian people', issued for wide release when the group kidnapped the American ambassador Charles Elbrick, they announced the intention of their activities. 'This is not an isolated action', they declared.

> It is another of the innumerable revolutionary missions we have carried out, which include bank raids to finance the revolution and recover money extorted from the people by the bankers; attacks against barracks and police stations to obtain the arms and ammunition needed to overthrow the dictators; attacks on jails holding revolutionaries; sabotage of buildings connected with government repression; and execution of government executioners and torturers.

For these militants, all of that would be subordinate to a greater struggle, the vanguard of which might be elsewhere than the urban centres. 'In fact our kidnapping of the American ambassador is only one more operation in the revolutionary war which is progressing daily, and which this year entered its rural guerrilla stage'.[44]

Carrying on this positive identification with 'our people', the manual compiled by Marighella emphasizes, in its written dedication, the importance of class solidarity forged through guerrilla combat, and gestures towards the necessity of armed conflict in opposition to dictatorship. The dedication reads as an incendiary call to arms for city dwellers:

> To the brave comrades – men and women – imprisoned in the medieval dungeons of the Brazilian Government and subjected to tortures that even surpass the horrendous crimes carried out by the Nazis. Like those comrades whose memories we revere, as well as those taken prisoner in combat, what we must do is fight. Each comrade who opposes the military dictatorship and wants to oppose it can do something, however small the task may seem. I urge all who read this mini-manual and decide that they cannot remain inactive, to follow its instructions and join the struggle now. I ask this because, under any theory and under

any circumstances, the duty of every revolutionary is to make the revolution.[45]

With this, and in keeping with the arguments of Guevara and Debray, the urban guerrilla is understood as subordinate to its rural counterpart. The urban guerrilla joins but does not initiate the struggle. They are, rather, one part of 'the upsurge of revolutionary war in the country', which manifests itself 'in the form of urban guerrilla warfare, psychological warfare, or rural guerrilla warfare', with that former group requiring a strategy of its own, distinct from what is happening in the jungles and the mountains. 'The urban guerrilla is not afraid to dismantle and destroy the present Brazilian economic, political and social system, for his aim is to aid the rural guerrillas and to help in the creation of a totally new and revolutionary social and political structure, with the armed people in power'.[46] The urban guerrilla is insurrectionary, then, insofar as they exploit proximity to state machinery to inflict as much damage as possible.

Though it might be assumed that the urban guerrilla would emerge from the vast surplus populations gathered around the city, the point is rather that this guerrilla is, as was the case for both Guevara and Debray, not so much an expression of this or that social milieu but an agent of class solidarity: the atomic core of a new sociality. 'As of now', says Marighella,

> the men and women chosen for guerrilla warfare are workers; peasants whom the city has attracted as a market for manpower and who return to the countryside indoctrinated and politically and technically prepared; students, intellectuals, priests. This is the material with which we are building – starting with urban guerrilla warfare – the armed alliance of workers and peasants, with students, intellectuals and priests.[47]

Within this broad coalition, semi-autonomous groups are assigned tasks based on their sphere of influence and expertise. The worker, for instance, is well placed to exploit industrial activity, 'constructing arms, sabotaging and preparing saboteurs and dynamiters, and personally participating in actions involving hand arms, or organizing strikes and partial paralysis with the characteristics of mass violence in factories, workshops and other work centers'.[48] Whereas the primary goal of the rural guerrilla is to destroy enemy force, the urban guerrilla has two discreet tasks: the demoralization of military regimes and associated repressive forces and material expropriation from the ruling class.

The social character of the guerrilla's armed alliance reveals itself in opposition to the enemy, this ruling class, which is presented as an interconnected and embodied mesh of international forces who will be forced to fund their own demise. 'By expropriating the wealth of the principal enemies of the people, the Brazilian revolution was able to hit them at their vital center, with preferential and systematic attacks on the banking network – that is to say, the most telling blows were levelled at the businessman's nerve system'.[49]

Bank robberies are dialectical in the way decolonial warfare is allegorical: they are both local and global, simultaneously attacking the agents of domination and the system of exploitation, undermining local business and state governments as well as foreign investment, especially in the companies that insure and reinsure banking capital. To expropriate from these interests is to enact insurrection while also supporting the guerrilla movement financially, providing the means to purchase supplies and munitions. 'The tremendous costs of the revolutionary war must fall upon the big businesses, on the imperialists, on the large landowners, and on the government too – both federal and state – since they are all exploiters and oppressors of the people'. Here, as with the landlords in China, revolutionary action finds impulse through reprisal. 'Men of the government, agents of the dictatorship and of foreign imperialism, especially, must pay with their lives for the crimes they have committed against the Brazilian people'.[50]

* * *

As the guerrilla movement bloomed in the jungles, swamps, and mountains of Latin America, it inspired militants across the world, including those from core states of the imperial north. Many followed the example set by Latin America, not least the Weather Underground, the Symbionese Liberation Army, and the Black Liberation Army in the United States, all of whom waged class war using guerrilla tactics, setting out to fulfil the role of 'armed nucleus' for wider movements and in solidarity with the global south, often opposing wars of imperial conquest, especially the United States' invasion of Vietnam. Elsewhere, in Europe, the Red Army Faction were especially active in Germany during the 1970s.

Like the autonomia movement we will encounter in the next chapter, who fought as a class in the wake of fascism, the Red Army Faction responded to the perceived failure of denazification and to the collusion between state and capital. As they announced in a dispatch after their execution of the former SS officer turned president of the German Employers' Association Hanns Martin Schleyer: 'After 43 days, we have put an end to [his] pitiful and corrupt existence ... As compensation for our pain and suffering ... his death is meaningless ... THE STRUGGLE HAS ONLY BEGUN. FREEDOM THROUGH ARMED ANTI-IMPERIALIST STRUGGLE'.[51] They also explicitly drew a line between themselves and other guerrillas. 'The concept of the urban guerrilla comes from Latin America', they confirmed, 'there, like here, it is the method of revolutionary intervention by generally weak revolutionary forces'. As with so many of the revolutionaries we have encountered, the taking up of arms was a refusal of the need to wait for what Guevara described as the 'necessary objective and subjective conditions' to instead accelerate social antagonism through acts of terror. 'The urban guerrilla struggle', they wrote, was 'based on an understanding that there will be no Prussian-style marching orders, which so many so-called revolutionaries are waiting for to lead the people into revolutionary struggle'.[52]

Instead of waiting, they set out to create the conditions for struggle through direct action, to mobilize a people into open revolution by way of civil war. 'The Red Army Faction and the urban guerrilla represent the only faction and practice which draws a clear line between ourselves and the enemy, and is therefore subject to the sharpest attack. This requires that one have a political identity, and it presumes that a learning process has already occurred'.[53] As Ulrike Meinhof, one of the RAF's leaders and its primary theorist, would describe this brand of militancy, theirs was a desire for escalation in which the vanguard action hoped to become the nucleus of a social movement. 'If one sets a car on fire', she would insist, 'that is a criminal offence. If one sets hundreds of cars on fire, that is political action'.[54]

9

Fighting after Fascism

Antonio Gramsci was not in Italy when Benito Mussolini took power in October 1922. While Mussolini and his Blackshirt paramilitaries were marching on Rome to seize control of the government, Gramsci was in Russia as a representative of the newly formed Italian Communist Party (PCI). Intending to return to the country early the next year, the political situation at home and the warrants issued for the arrest of much of the PCI's leadership forced him into two years of exile. When he did finally return in 1924 after his election to parliament granted him immunity, and in order to lead a united front of leftist parties against Mussolini's government, the political atmosphere in Italy was very different from the one he left behind. With the arrival of fascism, Gramsci sensed a catastrophic if popular abdication from revolutionary commitment. He wrote about this moment in an article published in October 1924 for *L'Unità*, the organ newspaper of the PCI:

> The worker, the peasant, who for years has hated the fascism that oppresses him believes it necessary, in order to bring it down, to ally himself with the liberal bourgeoisie, to support those who in the past, when they were in power, supported and armed fascism against the workers and peasants, and who just a few months ago formed a sole bloc with fascism and shared in the responsibility for its crimes.

Emphasizing the need for civil war and class solidarity, a liquidation of not only fascism but of the bourgeoisie that created it, he insists that the 'essential task' for all communists, the 'fundamental idea' to which all revolutionaries must subscribe, is class war, or at least its soviet variant. 'Only the class struggle of the mass of workers and peasants will defeat fascism', he asserts. 'Only a government of workers and peasants can disarm the fascist militia'.[1]

A few years later, in November 1926, the fascist government cracked down on all dissent, enacting a series of repressive emergency laws in response to an attempt to assassinate Mussolini. In the round-up that followed, Gramsci was one of the many arrested, and he was sentenced to confinement on the small island of Ustica off the coast of Sicily. This was followed by two decades of imprisonment in Turin under brutal conditions intended, in the words of the fascist prosecutor, to 'stop his brain from functioning'.[2] Gramsci's health, already poor, deteriorated horrifically. 'His teeth fell out, his digestive system collapsed so that he could not eat solid food, he had convulsions when he vomited blood and suffered headaches so violent that he beat his head against the walls of his cell'.[3] Despite all of this, he remained active as a revolutionary theorist. His theoretical writing from this time, which the historian Perry Anderson once described as mere 'hieroglyphs' of 'the true, obliterated text of his thought', took place in over thirty school exercise books whose content was composed with the few resources available, written cryptically so as to evade the fascist censors, and smuggled out of prison by his sister-in-law.[4] Central to these notebooks is the question of why the Bolshevik Revolution was not reproduced in economically advanced societies and why, instead of choosing the road to freedom and redemption offered by socialism, the masses had taken to fascist barbarism.

After the revolutionary years of 1919 and 1920, during which Gramsci spoke of the factory councils in Turin and Milan as the Italian equivalent to Russian soviets, preparing 'the whole class for the aims of conquest and government', the reaction was swift and brutal. The beneficiaries of those factories, the bosses and the owners, allied themselves with fascism, and the Blackshirts enforced violent repression.[5] Unlike in Russia, Gramsci argued, in the more advanced capitalist societies 'there was a proper relationship between State and civil society, and when the State trembled a sturdy structure of civil society was at once revealed. The State was only an outer ditch, behind which there stood a powerful system of fortresses and earthworks'.[6] In this view, the task of revolution is not just to seize the state or its governance, but to occupy the fortresses and earthworks of civil society, building revolutionary power by enacting what one of Gramsci's best-known followers, the German radical Rudi Dutschke, would famously describe as 'the long march through the institutions'.[7]

For the imprisoned communist, this theory of revolution was also a doctrine of war. According to Gramsci, every political struggle, even if only analogically, contains a military substratum:

> In military war, when the strategic aim – destruction of the enemy's army and occupation of his territory – is achieved, peace comes. It should also be observed that for war to come to an end, it is enough that the strategic aim should simply be achieved potentially: it is enough in other words that there should be no doubt that an army is no longer able to fight, and that the victorious army 'could' occupy the enemy's territory. Political struggle is enormously more complex: in a certain sense, it can be compared to colonial wars or to old wars of conquest – in which the victorious army occupies, or proposes to occupy, permanently all or a part of the conquered territory. Then the defeated army is disarmed and dispersed, but the struggle continues on the terrain of politics and of military 'preparation'.[8]

Revolution resembles colonial warfare insofar as military victory is only one part of the conflict and is necessarily conjoined to the wholesale transformation of civil society. Gramsci theorizes different forms of social antagonism, differentiating between how they enter the political plane: war of movement, war of position, and underground warfare.

Movement is the phase of open conflict between classes, where the outcome is decided by direct clashes between insurgents and the state. Position, on the other hand, is where forces seek to gain influence and power. And the underground is a slow, hidden conflict, often preparatory in character. He explains the three with well-known tactics: 'Boycotts are a form of war of position, strikes of war of movement, the secret preparation of weapons and combat troops belongs to underground warfare'.[9] While these three modes are fundamentally inseparable, with the success of each depending on the others, Gramsci emphasizes the war of position, because 'in wars among the more industrially and socially advanced States, the war of maneuver must be considered as reduced to more of a tactical than a strategic function', comparable to the function of the siege within military science.[10]

* * *

Gramsci's theory holds true for the fight against fascism, in which comrades need to not only topple the political leadership but also militate against fascism at the level of state institutions and civil society. While historical anti-fascist action, with the French resistance and the Italian partisans, has tended to target the former while leaving the latter intact, revolutionaries have disagreed whether the fight against fascism is an act of social transformation. There is, however, general agreement among militants that such a fight is relative to the mobilization of classes. For Trotsky, anti-fascism is socially necessary but fails to approach politics from a class standpoint. 'It suffices for liberal journalists but not for the oppressed workers and peasants. They have nothing to defend except slavery and poverty. They will direct all their forces to smashing fascism only if, at the same time, they are able to realize new and better conditions of existence'. In other words, social revolution can only be a precondition for, but not a result of, the fight against fascism. 'In consequence', he says, 'the struggle of the proletariat and the poorest peasants against fascism cannot in the social sense be defensive, only offensive'.[11] For Georgi Dimitrov, Bulgarian communist and leader of the Comintern during the fateful years from 1935 to 1943, fascism constituted 'the open terrorist dictatorship of the most reactionary, most chauvinistic and most imperialist elements of finance capital'. For Dimitrov, fascism has its origins in bourgeois society, and so 'whoever does not fight the reactionary measures of the bourgeoisie and the growth of fascism at these preparatory stages is not in a position to prevent the victory of fascism, but, on the contrary, facilitates that victory'.[12] If this is true, that fascism is both a state regime and a civil society, then it might also be true that, in Italy, fascism outlived the fascists.

'That fascism lives on', Theodor W. Adorno would reflect in 1959, 'is due to the fact that the objective conditions of society that engendered fascism continue to exist'.[13] While Adorno was thinking primarily about Germany, where the attempted assassination of Dutschke in 1968 would catalyze the Red Army Faction into action, his description also concerns postwar Italy, where the interests of an extant bourgeoisie and of British and American imperialism directly contradicted any anti-fascist espousals. According to the Belgian economist and Holocaust survivor Ernest Mandel, this led to a military underestimation on behalf of the Allies about the forces of reaction:

> Underlying the miscalculation was a deeper social cause for the new war of attrition into which they inadvertently blundered in Southern Europe. Their class interest was confronted with a real dilemma: how to liquidate fascism whilst preserving the foundations of the bourgeois state, i.e. their political class rule, indispensable for neutralising or, if necessary, confronting mass mobilisations and the threat of revolution.[14]

The result is that Italy's reconstruction preserved fascism within its civil society if not its political governance, and so any resistance would find itself conjoined with revolution.

Italy's postwar economic boom took place, as it had for England in the middle of the nineteenth century and the United States at the start of the twentieth, through large-scale industry, primarily in sectors bound up with the development of new infra-structure: electricity, petrochemicals, ferrous metals, and automo-tive manufacture. 'Industrial production had already matched prewar levels by the end of the 1940s', explains the historian of social movements Steve Wright. 'By 1953 it had jumped another 64 per cent, and had almost doubled again by 1961'.[15] And here, within the nation, uneven development once more prevails. This expansion displaced the concentration of labour from the coun-tryside to the city, from the south to the north, and into the indus-trial triangle formed by Genoa, Turin, and Milan. While much of Italy's fixed capital remained undamaged or was even enlarged by the war effort, the remaining obstacle before accumulation was the newly expanded urban working class, for whom labour disci-pline had become synonymous with fascist rule.

In 1960, against a backdrop of anti-fascist organizing, a survey conducted in Rome asked young workers who had not lived under Mussolini or were not old enough to recall the resistance why they opposed fascism. 'For many such young people', the survey discovered, 'fascism evoked the spectre of class domination in its purest form'.[16] In addition, there remained a live political current of former partisans who opposed the social outcomes of the wartime resistance, insisting that the overturning of fascism should be followed by the fight against capital and the establishment of a socialist state. 'As such', write Nanni Balestrini and Primo Moroni in their history of Italian social movements, 'there were many partisans who had never handed over their guns at the end of Fascism, and, over the course of the 1950s the carabinieri and police (above all, in the mountains but also in some underground spaces beneath the factories) uncovered hundreds of rifles, mortars and revolvers'.[17] If, during postwar reconstruction, the questions of class and fascism overlapped in such a way as to create the conditions for renewed warfare, during the 1970s anti-fascism would become a source of solidarity as well as a cause to wage war as a class against both society and the state.

* * *

Operaismo, or workerism, was an object lesson in what it means to fight as a class under historical conditions when fascism fused with the state and society. According to its principal theorist, Antonio Negri, *operaismo* was 'an attempt to reply politically to the crisis of the labor movement during the 1950s'.[18] In Negri's estimation, such a reply would necessitate drawing on the lessons of anti-fascist resistance to mobilize mass workers as a revolutionary class:

In Italy, between 1943 and 1945, there was an extremely powerful war of resistance. Twentyfive years later, in 1968, the memory was still alive, because antifascism had been linked to the class struggle. The poor in Italy, at least in the north, remained antifascist. By the 1960s the extraparliamentary Left had penetrated all social classes, particularly in the factories. The break with the official Communist party occurred at that level, which was very harmful to the party – precisely because the opposition to it came from the workers. It's hard to imagine such a thing happening today. Moreover, since the PCI was particularly open to Western values and inclined to take issue with the Soviet line, repressing the extreme Left meant entering straight away into the official system of the parties of the "free world." At this point people reacted. Imagine what would have happened if, in France, there had been an extreme Left majority at Renault or Citroën. In France, during the events of May 1968, it was the intellectuals who led the movement of revolt, not the workers. In Italy the opposite occurred: the workers who rejected the historic compromise led the struggles, not the intellectuals. The members of the Red Brigades with whom I was in prison during the 1980s and after my return, in 1997, came from working-class backgrounds. They really believed they could bring about a revolution.[19]

When asked if the militants with whom he fought had considered peaceful ways of ending fascism and improving society – or, to use Gramsci's terms, if the war of movement might have been more successful if it contained the war of position – Negri responds in a way that recalls Castro in Cuba, for whom more gradualist methods had reached deadlock. 'No one thought so at the time', says Negri, 'myself included. Still today I believe that state-sponsored violence exists; and that the response can be nonviolent, though surely not peaceful – in any case, nonviolent resistance is still resistance. Capitalism itself isn't peaceful! It cannot survive without violence'.[20] Though it is possible to detect an echo of Gramsci's thought within Negri's account, to look at the movement in question reveals that it is through such violence that resistance approaches revolution, or that here warfare once again provides the grounds for class solidarity.

The transformative moment through which *operaismo* announced its militancy was the 'hot autumn' of 1969, when the Fiat factories in Turin, especially the flagship plant Mirafiori, were rocked by a wave of militant strikes. Factory workers, encouraged by university students, demanded wage increases across the board, access to the same conditions as those of the white-collar workers within the company, and a more powerful voice when dealing with management. As strikes spread across the city, hitting all sectors of the working population, the politics of incrementalism, according to which increased productivity through disciplined labour would mean better lives for all, gave way to a politics of insurrection, triggering a decade-long war, the 'Years of Lead'. The transition from incrementalism to insurrection alongside the escalation of violence to the point of war is narrated in Nanni Balestrini's 1971 novel *We Want Everything*, the fictionalized autobiography of a southern 'mass worker' who presents as an everyman figure for immigrant labour. 'Because it's us, the proletariat of the south', he tells us,

> an enormous mass of workers, the one-hundred-and-fifty-thousand workers of Fiat who have developed capital and its State. It is us who created all the wealth that exists, of which they leave us only the crumbs. We created all this wealth by dying of work at Fiat or dying of hunger in the south. And it is us, the great majority of the proletariat, who don't want to work and die any more for the development of capital and its State.[21]

Crucially, the narrator knows that for workers to engage in incrementalism is to labour against their own interests, and that any reforms won by the unions would only be conceded on the state's terms; even with better wages and work conditions, these reforms are still mechanisms of productivity through which the worker inadvertently collaborates with the bosses. 'Never, with these strikes, with these reforms', he says. 'Things always had to be taken, by force. Because they'd had it up to here with the State that always fucked them up and they wanted to attack it, because that was the real enemy, the one to destroy'. Insurrection, then, is the only means to truly do right by working people. 'Because they knew that they could have somewhere to live, that their needs could be satisfied, only if they swept away the State, that republic founded on forced labor, once and for all. That's how the great battle can be explained, not because people were pissed off by the heat on July 3'.[22]

Balestrini's novel has the feel of a revolutionary dispatch, a communiqué sent back from the frontlines. It reads like a letter from the war of manoeuvre to fuel the war of position. On this level, it resembles the author's visual art, textual collages of cut-up newspaper, like the anonymous ransom note or list of demands. The book's narrative also inverts the standard passage of revolutionary commitment. The unnamed worker does not fall in with the militants because of class consciousness; instead, class consciousness is the result of channelling an almost instinctive militancy back against its social source, the exploitation and immiseration of workers, culminating in this declaration of all-out war:

Are we all going mad? The bosses who make us work like dogs destroy the wealth we've produced. But it's time to be done with these people. It's time for us to fuck these pigs off once and for all, to get rid of them all and free ourselves forever. Listen, State and bosses, it's war, it's a struggle to the end. Forward, comrades, forward like at Battipaglia, let's burn everything here, let's sweep this lowlife away, let's sweep this republic away.[23]

This is the language of class war: with collective pronouns arrayed in direct opposition and with a blunt insolence that countersigns for solidarity. This prose, the novelist Rachel Kushner argues in a preface to the English translation, is both collectivist and combative: it is 'a kind of vernacular poetry that gets into the mind and stays there'.[24] Over several chapters and culminating with this declaration, the evolving grammar registers the cadence of political awakening, modulating from an individual's complaint to emulate a militant broadcast. It is, as Kushner demonstrates, the language of a revolutionary class:

> The 'I' partly dissolves, and the book becomes something like pirate radio news bulletins of the war on the factory, the war in the streets. The struggle expands. The narrator, wherever he is now, is part of a new collective desire, calling not for higher base pay but for the abolition of capitalism, for the bosses' economy to collapse.[25]

This is a narrative told not through the worker or the militant but, as we reach the warlike climax with its gunshots and its explosions, a class that has remade itself into the agent of social transformation.

In giving expression to a desire for class autonomy from both bosses and the state, the novel's voice corresponds to autonomia, one of several *operaismo* factions active during the 1960s and 1970s, which came to mean that (in Balestrini and Moroni's formulation) 'proletarian sociality would define its own laws and practices across territory under bourgeois military occupation'.[26] Against a backdrop of riots and street fights, of sabotage and kidnappings, of bombings and bank robberies, this movement sought to create spaces anterior to capitalist exploitation and state domination. Its goal was the self-valorization of working people at a time when increasing urbanization coincided with expanding circuits of informal labour. Autonomia thus came into being as a decentralized network of various types of localized social movements and organizations united by pirate radio stations whose content comprised a 'mix between a

classical medium of militant information and a sort of art experiment in media sabotage'.[27] As a broad movement, autonomia
took on the appearance of 'a galaxy within which one could
also recognize various constellations, networks characterized by
different political histories, different cultural backgrounds and
different visions as well as distinct newspapers, means of
communication and headquarters'.[28] It was the emergence of a
new sociality beyond the laws of capitalist exchange, of selling
time and labour, and of private property: it was the mobilization
of class solidarity against the class system.

* * *

The prime example of this thinking can be found at the conclusion of contract negotiations at Mirafiori in 1973, when striking
workers occupied the buildings, refusing to engage the kinds of
economic benefits so often won by strike action. Recalling the
conditions leading up to Gramsci's arrest, when the people of
Turin established workers' councils amid the factory strikes, the
occupation would provide the grounds for autonomous activity.
As the poet and singer Alfredo Bandelli describes it in his 'Ballad
of Fiat', after threats of gunfire against scabs, no concession
would be enough:

> Dear bosses, this time
> It isn't going to go well for you
> From now on you'll have to understand
> We're not going to do any deal
> And this time you won't buy us
> With a measly five-lire pay rise
> If you offer us ten we'll ask for a hundred
> If you offer us a hundred, we want a thousand![29]

'In the days of the occupation', write Balestrini and Moroni,
'Mirafiori became an impregnable fortress, and the state was
wary of intervening in any way. But it was now, all of a sudden,
a useless fortress. The bosses gave in but the workers reaffirmed
their rejection of any deal whatsoever'.[30] That is what we

encounter in Bandelli's poem, an insurrectionary auxesis in which every demand is only a precondition for refusal, an on-ramp to revolution. Emerging into this milieu from the industrially underdeveloped south, militants recognized that the refusal to work, the establishment of autonomy, was in itself a declaration of war. 'The refusal of a coerced peace blossoms on the axis of the refusal of work', wrote the autonomists Fiora Pirri and Lanfranco Caminiti. 'Let's steal war! Let's steal it back from alienation and separation. Revolutionary theory now means a full critique of politics, the theory of war itself. The concrete activity of the subjectivity of war has to be mounted against the labour abstraction'.[31] Like Fanon's 'programme of complete disorder', the autonomist vision of insurrection combines a totalizing concept of war with the social totality of class. 'Unification is a qualitative leap', says Negri, 'the working class in arms and communism in action. That is what we are fighting for: the extinction of the state and the destruction of work – the complete subversion of the present state of things'.[32]

In its commitment to war, autonomia was also responding to the demilitarization of the official communist parties, which during the reconstruction period advocated against class struggle and for a resumption of economic growth within the framework of private ownership, culminating in the ignominious 'historic compromise' first proposed in 1973. The Italian Communist Party, made fearful by the overthrow of Allende's socialist government in Chile, sought a 'democratic alliance' with the centre-right Christian Democratic Party that resulted in a paramilitary crackdown against the non-aligned left movements in the name of anti-terrorism. In direct opposition to this approach, the essence of autonomia was a refusal to compromise. Its exponents instead theorized that all struggles confined within the sphere of work or the processes of state would only ever be part of capital's dialectic, and that those struggles were therefore doomed to provide little more than refinement to the methods of accumulation.

As Mario Tronti, one of autonomia's leading theorists, described it, 'the pressure of labour-power is able to force capital to modify its own internal composition; it intervenes *within* capital as an essential component of capitalist development', ultimately recomposing the forces of production to enable further exploitation.[33] Because those struggles are mediated by wages, any positive change they bring about is tantamount to collaboration with capital, and so the only available passage to social transformation is insurrection. Here he departs from the realm of theory, offering instead a call to arms. 'Big industry and its science', he says, 'are not the prize for whoever wins the class struggle. They are the battlefield itself. And so long as the enemy occupies that field, we must spray it with bullets, without crying over the roses that get destroyed along the way'.[34] In theoretical terms, Tronti reconfigures Gramsci's theory of hegemony so that war is no longer a metaphor or analogy. Rather than incrementally changing civil society and social institutions, the revolutionary task is to destroy them absolutely and to simultaneously build class solidarity outside the stable structures of anything like union management or political process.

* * *

The conceptual apparatus of autonomia, which described its thought as the 'science of class hatred', would become increasingly warlike through the 1970s. This militancy proceeded from the analysis of class composition as understood via worker inquiry. As Negri would write in 1973:

> Only armed struggle as the mass, dialectical complement to the struggle over the immediate interest of the proletariat, as expression of the political need of the working class, corresponds to the workers' demand. Only armed struggle is powerful on the plane of the relations of force between the two classes. Only the riposte, the counterattack, the armed offensive represents the distinctiveness of the worker in contrast to the capitalist transfiguration of the consciousness of the disaster of the rate of profit into a rule of command.[35]

Autonomia is predicated on a reading of class composition at a time of transformation, when the industrial proletariat of the nineteenth and early twentieth century had given way to new forms of social being which had not cohered into a revolutionary class. To use autonomia's own vocabulary, by this time in history the technically skilled 'professional worker' had been replaced by two new social forms: the unskilled but collectively disciplined 'mass worker', the itinerant labour migrants populating the factories; and the 'socialized worker', the decentralized worker defined by communication and sociability but also freed of both the technical structure of workplace discipline and the political organization that articulates collective demands. The rise of the mass and the socialized worker corresponds to the advent of what some autonomists describe as the 'social factory', wherein the command of the factory extends beyond the sites of industrial production and into society and the state at large. It represents a world in which all social relations are mediated by the wage. 'To mobilize all mass workers against the factory system', says Negri, 'and to unleash the whole of abstract labor against the form of exchange value – both struggles are against the factory'.[36]

Central to any understanding of the social factory is gendered labour. For fellow activist Mariarosa Dalla Costa, who provides a feminist clarification of this term from within the discourse of autonomia, the possibility of class solidarity and revolutionary movements begins with recognition of women's work in the home. Her argument is that the 'objective character of capitalist organization' is 'co-operative labor in the factory and isolated labor in the home'. What this means is that community serves as the other zone of hidden exploitation. This social hierarchy is 'mirrored subjectively by the way workers in industry organize separately from the community'. Women are relegated to a support role as 'appendages to men in the home and in the struggle', ultimately subdividing any class along lines of sex and gender. 'This division', she clarifies, 'and this kind of division are the history of the class'.[37] Not just the sites of industry, then, but also the kitchen and the nursery, the neighbourhood and the school, all being extensions of the home and the gendered exploitation it conceals. To go to war against the social factory is to fight on these multiple battlefronts. And this process, for the autonomists, is what constitutes class power outside the formal institutions of redress, building collective identities and class solidarities that encircle the factory and the kitchen, the classroom and the prison.

Other affiliated movements adopted military strategies but without as strong an emphasis on solidarity. With increasing reference to Latin America and the Red Army Faction in Germany, the urban guerrilla was popularized with the Italian militants, most infamously in the form of the Brigate Rosse, or the Red Brigades. As one of these groups, the Metropolitan Political Collective, described their ambitions in 1969, the city would be remade as a war zone:

> The city today is the heart of the system, the organizing centre of economic-political exploitation, the shop window that displays the 'highest peaks', the model meant to motivate the proletariat's integration. But it is also the weakest point in the system, the place where the contradictions appear sharper, when the organized chaos of late-capitalist society is more apparent than usual.
>
> And it is here, in the heart, that the system has to be struck.
>
> For our enemies, for those who would exercise power maliciously and beyond the interests of the masses, the city must now become a treacherous battlefield.[38]

Other groups that committed to this program include Gruppi di Azione Partigiana, who described themselves, after Mao, as a people's army, and Nuclei Armati Proletari, whose name echoes the atomic metaphors of Latin America. These Red Brigades, who announced themselves not 'as the armed wing of an unarmed mass movement, but its greatest moment of unification', commenced their activities in autumn 1970 and gained notoriety just a few months later, after the burning of the Pirelli runway, used for testing tires, in the suburbs of Milan in January 1971. The following year, they carried out what is often regarded as the first political kidnapping in Italian history, taking hostage the engineer Idalgo Macchiarini, known to be one of the most contemptuous bosses of the Sit-Siemens factory in Milan. Macchiarini was kidnapped at gunpoint by a small van in which he was subject to a 'political trial' for twenty minutes before being set free. His assailants communicated their action with the same language used by the repressive state apparatus: 'trial', 'arrest', 'temporarily released'.[39] For Balestrini and Moroni, this would point to an increasingly apparent irony within armed praxis, an authoritarian tendency that aligned militants with the state. Others would denounce the Red Brigades on similar terms, insisting that 'the proletarian masses have no need to further understand what violence is', and that 'the military organization of the masses will not be constructed because a few groups begin military activities' – exceptional given the history of fascism – advocating instead for armed struggle by way of stable and autonomous mass political organizations.[40] The criticism levelled at the Red Brigades was not that they were militarily violent, but that their military violence displaced class solidarity, becoming something like a fetish. As one editorial criticized them, 'the problem of militarization therefore is completely subordinate to the development of mass struggle and must be directed, even in its technical aspects, by the current form of the part (the mass organisms under working-class direction)'. To overextend militarization, to convert an armed people into a fully organized army, is politically anathema to the common material interests of the mass movement – it is, that editorial concludes, a thought 'worthy of fascists'.[41]

While the autonomia movement and many of its theorists maintained their distance from the militaristic program of the Red Brigades, events proceeding from the historic compromise effectively ended this revolutionary phase in postwar Italian history. On 16 March 1978 – and less than a year after the German Autumn, when the Red Army Faction were enacting their campaign of terror – militants blocked the two-car convoy in Rome that was carrying Aldo Moro, the leader of the Christian

Democrats, kidnapping him and murdering five of his body-guards. Offering Moro's release, the militants proposed an exchange for the freedom of several prisoners. When the government took a hard-line position and refused to negotiate, the militants held a 'people's trial', in which Moro was found responsible for the 'villainous complicity of the regime' in 'the conspiracy that covered the murders committed by the state', and of serving within an 'intricate web of personal interests and of corruption'. Their communiqué made the position clear, affirming that 'the duty of all revolutionaries is to organize the proletariat and to build up the forces that will carry out in a definitive way the verdict against the bourgeoisie and its servants'.[42] On 9 May, Moro was directed to a car and told to cover himself with a blanket for transport. He was then shot ten times. His body was left in the trunk of a red Renault 4 in the centre of Rome, in an area between the Pantheon and the Tiber River, only several hundred yards from the separate headquarter buildings of both the Christian Democrats and the Communist Party. While the response to Moro's fate was varied, it neither inspired revolution nor engendered solidarity. The state retaliated with mass arrests, executions, and exiles, rounding up militants of all tendencies irrespective of their involvement, effectively repeating the circumstances of Gramsci's arrest in the late 1920s.

* * *

The state repression of militants is dramatized in another of Balestrini's novels, *The Unseen*, which, similarly to *We Want Everything*, adopts the form of the revolutionary dispatch. If *We Want Everything* documents the emergence of autonomia through the hot autumn, equipping it with voice and personality, *The Unseen* recreates the claustrophobia of repression. With a narrative that cuts between youthful rebellion and the consequent incarceration, presented in blocks of unpunctuated, breathless prose that read as the textual imprint of either solidarity and excitement or isolation and imprisonment, this novel is testimony to the affective capacities of autonomia, its power to mobilize a class despite the injunctions of the state. Its narrative shuttles between the materialization of class solidarity by way of direct action and autonomous constellations:

> to generalize the offensive means to radicalize disaffection with whichever hierarchy you choose to exercise our destructive creativity against the society of the spectacle to sabotage the machines and goods that sabotage our lives to promote indefinite wildcat general strikes always to have mass meetings in all the separate factories to elect delegates who can be recalled by the base to keep continuous links between all the places of struggle to overlook no useful technical means of free communication to give a direct use value to everything that has an exchange value to occupy permanently the factories and the public buildings to organize self-defence of the conquered territories and on with the music[43]

The experience of repression alongside the emergent ideology of militarization:

> we tried to spend the nights at the houses of comrades who considered themselves less known less exposed or better still staying with friends who weren't involved at all or staying with friends of friends the demonstrations and festivals in the square were a thing of the past the movement was like a great ghost absent withdrawn sheltering in its ghettoes the stage was now held by the trickle of clandestine armed actions where responsibility was claimed by dozens of signatures of combat organizations in competition the life of the movement was over but for the comrades it wasn't over it wasn't as if they could stand on the sidelines saying let's wait and see because the repression involved everyone there weren't too many distinctions made[44]

To arrive, ultimately, at the prison:

> my role is to be someone who's going to gaol now I was thinking about the comrades and this consoled me because I was thinking that now they would all be rallying round busy making efforts

on my behalf they wouldn't leave me to fend for myself and I was proud of the fact that I had all these comrades this big family that was taking responsibility for my situation and my problems that would think of everything a lawyer money all the other things that for now I couldn't imagine I felt that I wasn't on my own I was part of a collective strength and this made me feel very strong I would bravely bear everything that lay ahead of me and I was thinking that now I had to behave as if the comrades could see me I wasn't on my own they were with me always there whatever happened[45]

Emblematic of defeat, these passages reverse the narrative tendency of the previous novel, devolving from the collective 'we' and 'our' to the atomized 'I' and 'my' – from the class back to the individual. Nevertheless, the narrative holds together not only in its overwhelming sense of foreclosure but also in a dogged insistence on class solidarity, from which the narrator continues to draw strength until the bitter end, even when the movement is all but completely out of sight. This is legible in the unpunctuated prose form as well as in deference to comrades both real and hypothetical. The sentences may be claustrophobic, blocked out like the prison cell in which the narrative begins and ends, but they are also highly communicative, belonging not to any one individual but instead to a collective, a class; their energy is not that of the radio dispatch but could instead be that of the clandestine missive, the letter folded into a prison text or concealed between cracks in the wall. Theirs is a story whispered fast into the ear of a comrade: they are desperate to convey their tale, to narrate the highs and the lows of the movement, before it disappears forever.

* * *

Autonomia, as a movement-driven realization of class war, did not survive the factionalization and repression of the 1970s. And yet, perhaps its most significant contribution to the militant thinking of class would emerge from one of its practical deficiencies: namely, the myopic focus on the productive process, the factory, at the expense of those excluded from the wage altogether, and especially those engaged in the gendered labour of social reproduction. Rachel Kushner, one of Balestini's most sensitive readers and the author of a feminist retelling of autonomia in her novel *The Flamethrowers*, has noted the gendered exclusions that befall this movement. 'The women would not have their say quite yet', she says. 'This struggle was about men and their exploitation. Women – exploited doubly in Italy, in the piece work they did at kitchen tables for the factories in the north, and by their families for their domestic labor – would have to mark out their own path, and did'.[46] While this is a perennial problem within movements committed to revolution on the social terrain provided by a system that thrives on subdivision, autonomist feminism sought to correct this deficiency. 'At the end of every people's revolution', wrote the feminist theorist Carla Lonzi in 1970, 'woman, who fought alongside everyone else, finds herself pushed aside with all her problems. Are we going to let history repeat itself?' The exclusion not just of women but, more specifically, of gendered labour from autonomia's thinking is a practical problem as much as it is a matter of ideology because it determines why the battles are fought no less than how they are fought. 'War', Lonzi adds, 'has always been an activity that belongs to the male and his model of virility'.[47]

This contradiction, between the interests of primarily male workers and the exploitation of women in the home, also animates the political conflicts in Elena Ferrante's celebrated Neapolitan tetralogy, a set of novels that dramatize the private and interpersonal struggles of women during Italy's postwar reconstruction and through the Years of Lead. Contemplating whether to join the revolt – to 'face the brutality of the police, plunge with my whole personal history into the most incandescent magma of these months' – the narrator, Elena, reckons with the gendering of struggle:

> There were no women who stood out in that chaos. The young
> heroes who faced the violence of the reactions at their own peril

were called Rudi Dutschke, Daniel Cohn-Bendit, and, as in war films where there were only men, it was hard to feel part of it; you could only love them, adapt their thoughts to your brain, feel pity for their fate.[48]

For Elena, encounters with autonomist feminism supercharge an already glowing admiration for her autodidact friend Lila, an 'organic intellectual' in Gramsci's phrase, only to culminate in a vision of generalized warfare:

I imagined a capricious Lila who provoked hatred deliberately and in the end found herself more deeply involved in violent acts. Certainly she had had the courage to push ahead, to take the lead with the crystalline determination, the generous cruelty of one who is spurred by just reasons. But with what purpose? To start a civil war? Transform the neighborhood, Naples, Italy into a battlefield, a Vietnam in the Mediterranean? Hurl us all into a pitiless, interminable conflict, squeezed between the Eastern bloc and the Western? Encourage its fiery spread throughout Europe, throughout the entire planet? Until victory, always? What victory? Cities destroyed, fire, the dead in the streets, the shame of violent clashes not only with the class enemy but also within the front itself, among the revolutionary groups of various regions and with various motivations, all in the name of the proletariat and its dictatorship. Maybe even nuclear war.[49]

If this echoes Che Guevara – whose 1967 address to the Tricontinental famously called for 'two, three, or many Vietnams' in the face of imperialism – we should also pause on the polysemy of 'nuclear', that term now familiar from Guevara's theory of guerrilla warfare.[50] While autonomist feminism developed the movement's thinking in new directions, turning both autonomism and feminism into a practical struggle against patriarchy in particular and against capital as a whole, such thinking begins with recognition that the nuclear family is the atomic core of capitalist social organization. This is why, for Dalla Costa, the nuclear family is central to both class and war, as both a target and battleground: 'To the extent that the exploitation of women through domestic work has had its own specific history, tied to the survival of the nuclear family, the specific course of this struggle which must pass through the destruction of the nuclear family as established by the capitalist social order, adds a new dimension to the class struggle'.[51] Inscribed in the revolution against capitalist work, autonomous feminism seeks to end the exploitation of women through domestic servitude, and so adds the nuclear family as an institute against which to wage war. The task of autonomous feminism is to insist on, and fight for, a practical realization of autonomy. So writes Dalla Costa, affirming another kind of revolution in the revolution: 'The working class organizes as a class to transcend itself as a class; within that class we organize autonomously to create the basis to transcend autonomy'.[52]

10

Army of the Wronged

For W. E. B. Du Bois, the most pressing social issue of the twentieth century was what he called 'the problem of the color-line', and this problem was clarified in relation to both class and war when, in 1951, Du Bois was arrested and tried as 'the agent of a foreign principal'.[1] Since the 1935 publication of *Black Reconstruction in America*, his reframing of the Civil War's aftermath as a period that promised but failed to achieve workers' democracy in the abolition of the plantation economy, Du Bois worked as an academic sociologist, as a campaigner for world peace and nuclear disarmament, and as a diplomat for relations between China, Africa, and the United States. In 1959, he and his wife toured the Soviet Union and the People's Republic of China, where he was hosted in Wuhan by Mao Zedong, who gifted the American a book of his poems. During this time, Du Bois was under investigation from the FBI, who had begun compiling a file on him in 1942. While that original investigation was terminated the following year owing to insufficient evidence of subversive activity, it was resumed in 1949, under J. Edgar Hoover's suspicion that Du Bois was among a group of 'concealed communists'. When, in 1950, Du Bois was appointed as chair of the newly created Peace Information Center – an anti-war organization that worked to publicize the Stockholm Peace Appeal in the United States, ultimately advocating for nuclear disarmament – the Justice Department alleged that he and the other leaders were acting on behalf of the Soviet Union and were thus required to register with the federal government under the Foreign Agents Registration Act. Having refused registration, Du Bois and several others were indicted, but their case was dismissed before the jury could render a verdict, due in no small part to the support offered by distinguished friends and comrades, including the scientist Albert Einstein, who offered to do 'whatever he could', and the poet Langston Hughes, for whom Du Bois's arrest could only mean 'the banner of American democracy will be lowered another notch, particularly in the eyes of the darker peoples of the earth'.[2]

In 1952, reflecting on the successful campaign for his acquittal, Du Bois highlighted the differences between the experience of a celebrity intellectual and the collective life of the anonymously imprisoned, describing this demographic in terms that call forth the militancy that has mobilized successive generations of revolutionaries the world over:

> What turns me cold in all this experience is the certainty that thousands of innocent victims are in jail today because they had neither money, experience, nor friends to help them. The eyes of the world were on our trial despite the desperate effort of press and radio to suppress the facts and cloud the real issues; the courage and money of friends and of strangers who dared stand for a principle freed me; but God only knows how many who were as innocent as I and my colleagues are today in hell. They daily stagger out of prison doors embittered, vengeful, hopeless, ruined. And of this army of the wronged, the proportion of Negroes is frightful. We protect and defend sensational cases where Negroes are involved. But the great mass of arrested or accused black folk have no defense. There is desperate need of nation-wide organizations to oppose this national racket of railroading to jails and chain-gangs the poor, friendless and black.[3]

Such thinking, which is attuned to the mediations between race and class under capital, implies via the language of war that this system of domination and exploitation contains the source of its own reckoning: an 'army of the wronged', a racialized underclass of the imprisoned, around whom revolution should reorient itself.

On this point, Du Bois's writing is exemplary of the Black Radical Tradition, a body of thought with 'social bases predominately made up of peasants and farmers in the West Indies, or sharecroppers and peons in North America, or forced laborers on colonial plantations in Africa', and, increasingly with time, the incarcerated.[4] This tradition had been advanced by Du Bois as well as C. L. R. James, Richard Wright, and, contemporaneous with Du Bois's reflection, Malcolm X. Each of these thinkers demonstrated that central to the functioning of capitalism, to the flow of capital, is race – that race is, in the political scientist Cedric Robinson's words, 'its epistemology, its ordering principle, its organizing structure, its moral authority, its economy of justice, commerce, and power'. Distilled from the overlay of racial and class antagonism, this tradition is one of revolutionary militancy, on whose horizon is war against capital. 'Inevitably', notes Robinson, 'the tradition was transformed into a radical force. And in its most militant manifestation, no longer accustomed to the resolution that flight and withdrawal were sufficient, the purpose of the struggles informed by the tradition became the overthrow of the whole race-based structure'.[5] An army of the wronged, however desperate, could be the agent of that overthrow, a radical force of social transformation.

* * *

Almost two decades later, in 1970, Angela Davis was arrested for supplying Jonathan P. Jackson with guns that were used in an armed assault on the Marin County courthouse. In an essay written during her incarceration, Davis recalled Du Bois's imprisonment and his militant coinage 'army of the wronged', arguing that, in the two decades since his arrest, 'a number of factors have combined to transform the penal system into a prominent terrain of struggle, both for the captives inside and the masses outside'.[6] Davis also suggested that these factors were and continue to be indexed to the centrality of the prison-industrial complex to the maintenance of capital. While increased unemployment is the inevitable by-product of techno-logical development under capitalism, the carceral system is how states manage capital's inability to provide sufficient welfare provision to an ever-expanding surplus population. As Davis notes, 'crime is inevitable in a society in which wealth is unequally distributed, as one of the constant reminders that society's productive forces are being channeled in the wrong direction', and crimes against property – comprising the major-ity of all offenses – 'are profound but suppressed social needs which express themselves in anti-social modes of action'. While it might be tempting to think of property crime as an individual-ized form of protest – or what some anarchists have described as the affirmative 'illegalism' of 'individual reclamation' – at a collective level and 'in the context of class exploitation and national oppression it should be clear that numerous individu-als are compelled to resort to criminal acts, not as a result of conscious choice – implying other alternatives – but because society has objectively reduced their possibilities of subsistence and survival to this level'.[7]

This is why, for Davis, racialized discipline is necessarily rela-tive to class structure. It is a way of maintaining social hierar-chies and policing access to resources: 'While cloaking itself with the bourgeois aura of universality – imprisonment was supposed to cut across all class lines, as crimes were to be defined by the act, not the perpetrator – the prison has actually operated as an instrument of class domination, a means of prohibiting the have-nots from encroaching upon the haves'.[8] Whereas Du Bois described this population of 'the have-nots' or 'the wronged' as an army and suggested their organization, Davis closes the loop, insisting that 'the Black masses are growing conscious of their responsibility to defend those who are being persecuted for attempting to bring about the alleviation of the most injurious immediate problems facing Black communities and ultimately to bring about total liberation through armed revolution, if it must come to this'.[9] The difference between the two perspec-tives is the difference between class struggle and civil war. To be sure: both advocate for defensive protection, organizing for the liberation of the 'the Black masses'. But with Davis the army of the wronged has become synonymous with insurrection and liberation has become total. The peculiar grammar of her final clause, 'if it must come to this', suggests that this kind of movement is no longer some future probability, an unrealized potential, but the active threat of a revolutionary class.

While the militancy of Du Bois and Davis has precedent in older actions – the latter described Nat Turner, the leader of a rebellion by enslaved Virginians in 1831, as a revolutionary who had been delegitimated as a criminal – the immediate historical context of their thinking contained the kinds of social movements implied by 'army of the wronged' and 'armed revolution'. If there is one group that embodies Du Bois's claim and Davis's theory, organizing armed revolt in opposition to racial domination as well as carceral subjugation, that group is the Black Panthers. Founded in 1966 by Huey P. Newton and Bobby Seale, and inspired by Malcolm X and Robert F. Williams, the Panthers set out to win autonomy for Black communities within the United States: their '10-Point Program' included demands for freedom, employment, housing, and an end to police brutality. Far from desiring integration with the capitalist state, the Panthers' aim was total communist revolution in American society, waged in the name of class.

As Fred Hampton, leader of the Chicago Panthers, put it, 'we say primarily that the priority of this struggle is class'. On this point he speaks from within a revolutionary tradition:

Marx, and Lenin, and Che Guevara and Mao Tse-Tung and anybody else that has ever said or knew or practiced anything about revolution, always said that revolution is a class struggle. It was one class—the oppressed—those other class—the oppressor. And it's got to be a universal fact. Those that don't admit to that are those that don't want to get involved in a revolution, because they know that as long as they're dealing with a race thing, they'll never be involved in a revolution. They can talk about numbers; they can hang you up in many, many ways, but as soon as you start talking about class, then you got to start talking about some guns. And that's what the Party had to do.[10]

It was this insurrectionary tendency that endeared the Panthers to the decolonial fighters in Africa, the guerrillas in Latin America, and the autonomists in Italy. The group's earliest iteration was an armed citizens' patrol that monitored police racism in Oakland, California. Newton and Seale raised money to purchase shotguns by selling copies of Mao's Little Red Book. In Seale's recollection, 'sell the books, make the money, buy the guns, and go on the streets with the guns. We'll protect a mother, protect a brother, and protect the community from the racist cops'.[11] The Panthers' notoriety intensified through the late 1960s by way of armed propaganda and open conflict. In May 1967, twenty-six Panthers entered the California State Capitol carrying loaded weapons. And in October, Newton killed a police officer; he was imprisoned for murder, convicted of manslaughter, released on bond, and eventually his convictions were overturned in appeals court. In April of the following year, in a shootout with the Oakland police, the national treasurer Bobby Hutton was killed, and Eldridge Cleaver, minister of information, was wounded. All this led to their being labelled by J. Edgar Hoover as 'the greatest threat to the internal security of the country'.[12]

If these conflicts localize the antagonisms that Davis would soon describe, 1969 saw the Panthers move from a political program of Black nationalism to one of revolutionary internationalism, pledging solidarity to struggles taking place outside of the United States. They devoted pages of their newspaper to covering liberation struggles throughout the third world. Their leaders visited Africa, China, and Cuba. 'In 1970', notes Max Elbaum in his history of radicalism during the period, 'Huey Newton publicly offered to bring the entire Panther Party membership to Vietnam to fight on the side of the NLF; the offer was graciously declined'.[13] While the Panthers had effectively disaggregated by the end of 1974 – in response to ongoing infiltration and sabotage from the police and FBI, factional infighting, and lengthy prison sentences – their legacy would outlive this moment of revolutionary activity. In Elbaum's summary, they successfully 'politicized thousands of African American youth, put forward a program that forced every other organization in the African American community to respond, and more than any other single group spurred young activists of every race and nationality to start down a revolutionary path'.[14] Before several of the remaining Panthers went underground and resurrected the movement as the Black Liberation Army, in the peak years of its existence this group embodied class war as indigenous to the United States.

* * *

Alongside their paramilitary operations, the most prominent spokespersons of both the Black Panthers and the Black Liberation Army were prolific readers and writers, and it is in their autobiographical prose that we encounter another of class war's distinct literary forms: the prison or carceral narrative, with its episodic emphasis on the radicalizing force of literature, when the written word becomes the epiphanic catalyst for liberatory action. If, as Stuart Hall famously insisted, race is, 'also, the modality in which class is "lived", the medium through which class relations are experienced, the form in which it is appropriated and "fought through"', then autobiography, with its emphasis on lived experience, is the literary mode that bears witness to the formation of class from the standpoint of race.[15] A reassertion of humanity in the face of systemic dehumanization, such writing is a form in which to effect what James Baldwin once described in militaristic terms as 'some kind of truce with this reality', a narrative mode in which to assess the things that hurt and the things that helped one's person, connecting individual experience to a broader social situation. 'One writes out of one thing only', he says, 'one's own experience. Everything depends on how relentlessly one forces from this experience the last drop, sweet or bitter, it can possibly give'.[16] This autobiographical tendency is central to the aesthetics of Black radicalism – which, in the incandescent prose of the cultural theorist Fred Moten, belongs to an expressive mode defined not by any 'originary configuration of attributes' but instead by 'an ongoing shiftiness, a living labor of engendering to be organized in its relation to a politico-aesthesis', a narrative form that 'cannot be understood within the particular context of its genesis' but which also 'cannot be understood outside that context either'.[17] Unsurprisingly, this is a type of writing with origins in racial subjugation.

For Frederick Douglass, in whose slave narrative this genre undergoes something like its primal scene, learning to read would double as a formative moment of political education. 'The more I read', he recalled, 'the more I was led to abhor and detest my enslavers', and from this realization comes the combative rhetoric of class identity and collective antipathy: 'I could regard them in no other light than a band of successful robbers, who had left their homes, and gone to Africa, and stolen us from our homes, and in a strange land reduced us to slavery. I loathed them as being the meanest as well as the most wicked of men'. While Douglass met this realization with despairing nihilism – 'It had given me a view of my wretched condition, without the remedy. It opened my eyes to the horrible pit, but to no ladder upon which to get out' – similar episodes abound in the writings of militants from the twentieth century, though with vastly different political energy.[18] As Moten would argue, these subsequent writings 'move with but also out and outside of Douglass's repressive, annular attunement to the secret', determined by but turning against their own conditions of becoming.[19] We encounter a militant version of that turn in Angela Davis's autobiography, written at the age of twenty-eight, which she explains only came to exist through serious deliberation about her hesitancy to personalize or individualize history. The book she envisioned was not the affirmation of a sovereign self but, instead, 'a political autobiography that emphasized the people, the events and the forces in my life that propelled me to my present commitment'. And only this kind of book, she reckoned, might serve a revolutionary purpose, as a conduit for solidarity. 'There was the possibility that, having read it, more people would understand why so many of us have no alternative but to offer our lives – our bodies, our knowledge, our will – to the cause of our oppressed people', and would then 'be inspired to join our growing community of struggle'.[20] Similarly, in the autobiographies of Huey P. Newton and Assata Shakur, as we are going to see, reading is a means of connecting to a greater revolutionary tradition, a way of learning strategies and tactics from movements the world over. For these leaders, however, that there is no ladder out of the horrible pit is a cause for revolution, fuelling a desire not to climb out but to destroy the pit. Their politics is not class mobility within racial capitalism but a revolutionary class against capital as a whole – which, as Ruth Wilson Gilmore reminds us, 'is never not racial'.[21]

* * *

Newton was born in Louisiana in 1942 to a family of sharecroppers who, in 1945, migrated to Oakland. He taught himself to read, later attributing the development of his worldview to this experience. 'When I began to read', he recalls, 'a whole new world opened to me. I became interested in books. I still could not read very well, but each new book made it easier. I did not mind spending many hours, because reading was enjoyment, rather than work'.[22] After high school, Newton attended college and then law school, and read widely in revolutionary thought. 'The literature of oppressed people and their struggle for liberation in other countries is very large', he says of his and Seale's reading, 'and we pored over these books to see how their experiences might help us to understand our plight'.[23] Assessing how to adapt from international revolutionaries, 'transforming what we learned to principles and methods acceptable to brothers on the block', Newton and Seale were drawn to a conceptualization of defensive warfare:

Mao and Fanon and Guevara all saw clearly that the people had been stripped of their birthright and their dignity, not by any philosophy or mere words, but at gunpoint. They had suffered a holdup by gangsters, and rape; for them, the only way to win freedom was to meet force with force. At bottom, this is a form of self-defence. Although that defence might at times take on characteristics of aggression, in the final analysis the people do not initiate; they simply respond to what has been inflicted upon them. People respect the expression of strength and dignity displayed by men who refuse to bow to the weapons of oppression. Though it may mean death, these men will fight, because death with dignity is preferable to ignominy. Then, too, there is always the chance that the oppressor will be overwhelmed.[24]

For Newton, the phrase that best encapsulates militancy of this sort is 'revolutionary suicide', which pledges to fight to the death against oppression and on behalf of community. It is a slogan for class solidarity in opposition to a designated enemy. 'Revolutionary suicide does not mean that I and my comrades have a death wish', Newton clarifies; 'it means just the opposite. We have such a strong desire to live with hope and human dignity that existence without them is impossible. When reactionary forces crush us, we must move against these forces, even at the risk of death. We will have to be driven out with a stick'.[25] Key to this concept is that the revolutionary agent is not singular but collective, and that revolutionary suicide is not the self-sacrificial act of any one person but instead belongs to a movement of persons. And that movement, for Newton, owes itself to an extant class structure but also to a racialized cultural inheritance, having emerged through slavery into capitalism. 'This is a class society', he argued while imprisoned in 1968, 'it always has been. This reactionary class society places its limitations on individuals, not just in terms of occupation, but also regarding self-expression, being mobile, and being free to be creative and do anything they want to do'. Newton recognized, like Douglass before him, that race limited, if not removed, the already minimal possibility of individual mobility within capitalism's class structure. 'In America', he writes 'we have not only a class society, we also have a caste system, and Black people are fitted into the lowest caste. They have no mobility to move up the class ladder'.[26]

Newton developed a race-based political rhetoric with which to inspire potential comrades to wage war as a class. In one of the most potent examples of this, Newton explains the intellectual labour that went into developing insults to use against the police. 'A good descriptive word' was needed, 'one the community would accept and use, would not only advance Black consciousness, but in effect control the police by making them see themselves in a new light'.[27] Like Toussaint Louverture and the Haitian revolutionaries, verbally tying combat strategy to the depredations of slavery and the cultures of voodoo, Newton spoke in a rhetoric of antagonism that owed its affective force to the intergenerational misery of subjugation:

> The pig in reality is an ugly and offensive animal. It likes to root around in the mud; it makes hideous noises; it does not seem to relate to humans as other animals do. Further, anyone in the Black community can relate to the true characteristics of the pig because most of us come from rural backgrounds and have observed the nature of pigs. Many of the police, too, are hired right out of the South and are familiar with the behavior of pigs. They know exactly what the word implies. To call a policeman a pig conveys the idea of someone who is brutal, gross, and uncaring.[28]

If police, as the enforcers of racial capitalism and the wardens of its carceral system, are the negative referent against which the Panthers would define themselves, cultural inheritance also supplied affirmative conceptualization in the form of a language used to inspire solidarity. As with the nucleus and the cell, those scientific metaphors that suggest communal interdependence, and like the traditional practice of oath-taking, Newton envisaged the revolutionary as one with their class, and developed the rhetoric for this kind of solidarity from racial traditions. 'There is an old African saying', he writes. '"I am we". If you met an African in ancient times and asked him who he was, he would reply, "I am we". This is revolutionary suicide: I, we, all of us are the one and the multitude'.[29] Not just antagonism, then, but opposition *en masse*: the multitude versus the pigs. This is the language of class war.

In order to make good on the promise of that rhetoric, the Panthers developed a militancy that went beyond militarism without disavowing it. 'We sought to provide a counter-force', recalls Newton, 'a positive image of strong and unafraid Black men in the community. The emphasis on weapons was a necessary phase in our evolution, based on Frantz Fanon's conception that the people have to be shown that the colonizers and their agents – the police – are not bulletproof'.[30] Vanguardism, adventurism, or propaganda of the deed was, however, strategically limited. Carrying shotguns was effectively anti-police but it did not build class solidarity. It was, the Panthers realized, insufficient to the task of revolutionary suicide.

In the jungles of Latin America, the guerrilla might operate autonomously from the civilian community, but this would be well-nigh impossible in densely populated cities like Oakland. Militarism ultimately obstructed solidarity: 'We soon discovered that weapons and uniforms set us apart from the community. We were looked upon as an ad hoc military group, acting outside the community fabric and too radical to be part of it ... We saw ourselves as the revolutionary "vanguard" and did not fully understand that only the people can create the revolution'.[31] To redress this practically, the Panthers developed the 'survival programs', providing the community with the means for both political education and human flourishing. They offered free breakfast for children, community schooling, clothing distribution, classes on politics and economics, free medical clinics, lessons on self-defence and first aid, transportation to prisons for family members of inmates, an emergency-response ambulance program, drug and alcohol rehabilitation, and testing for blood disease. The survival programs set out to provide autonomy from capitalism, allowing the people to live together with hope and human dignity, thus making good on promises set forth in the language of warfare. The pressure of militarized antagonism between militants and the police generated the conditions for a new social order founded in opposition to and autonomous from the depredations of the state and its economy.

* * *

Assata Shakur, whose autobiography shares historical overlaps with Newton's, provides a sympathetic if critical perspective on the Black Panthers. She joined the Panthers in the late 1960s, working as a medic and in the breakfast program. This was at a time when, faced with infighting and what was revealed only later as state counterintelligence, the group was entering a period of disarray, in which, she recalls, 'friendly openness had been replaced by fear and paranoia', and 'beautiful revolutionary creativity' by 'dogmatic stagnation'.[32] This is not a critique of the Panthers' militancy. It is, instead, a criticism of the insuperable distance between the party and the people, and between theory and practice, which for Shakur would always be the decisive factor in political commitment. 'Before going back to college', she reflected, 'i knew i didn't want to be an intellectual, spending my life in books and libraries without knowing what the hell was going on in the streets. Theory without practice is just as incomplete as practice without theory. The two have to go together. I was determined to do both'.[33] This determination guides the form of her own autobiography, which alternates between an account of her arrest, trial, and imprisonment, on the one hand, and the story of her lifelong political education, on the other. It alternates between the two in such a way that generates a theory of revolution that incorporates personal experience without losing any of its theoretical expansiveness.

The narrative, which resembles the structure of Nanni Balestrini's novel of incarceration, offers practical formulations for warfare that begin to cohere after the warrant for her arrest is issued and she is forced into hiding. 'I didn't have many fixed ideas at first about what i thought armed struggle within the confines of amerika should be like', she confesses. 'I had done a lot of reading about it in other places, but i had no concrete idea how to apply the lessons from those struggles to the struggle of

Black people within the United States'.[34] It is from this perspective, of a committed militant willing and wanting to learn, that we are presented with a racialized vision of class war that culminates with an account of the Black Liberation Army, which is best viewed as a successor to the Panthers and a belated realization of Du Bois's army of the wronged, taking the form of a decentralized, underground network of revolutionary activity.

On 4 July 1973, while detained in the Garden State Youth Correctional Facility, before her transfer to Rikers Island, Shakur composed an open letter addressed 'to my people' that expounds a revolutionary program. It begins with a declaration of war, addressed not to the enemy but to her comrades, poised between love and fury:

> Black brothers, Black sisters, i want you to know that i love you and i hope that somewhere in your hearts you have love for me. My name is Assata Shakur (slave name joanne chesimard), and i am a revolutionary. A Black revolutionary. By that i mean that i have declared war on all forces that have raped our women, castrated our men, and kept our babies empty-bellied.[35]

The antagonism posited here is not anything so simple as the poor against the rich or one race against others. It is, instead, a racialized group assuming its historic role of destroying a system that perpetuates both race and class hierarchies. And it is the beneficiaries of this system whom she names as enemy. 'I have declared war', she clarifies, 'on the rich who prosper on our poverty, the politicians who lie to us with smiling faces, and all the mindless, heartless robots who protect them and their property'. Shakur's identity as a revolutionary is defined in strict opposition, the result of mutual antipathy, and is likewise indexed to the experience of her race. 'I am a Black revolutionary, and, as such, i am a victim of all the wrath, hatred, and slander that amerika is capable of. Like all other Black revolutionaries, amerika is trying to lynch me'. We sense in this a consonance with Newton's vision of revolutionary suicide, with the expression of collective identities – always plural and never singular – indexed to a history of racialized violence and now facing off against the powers of reaction. If the violence is racialized, recalling a history of lynching in the United States, then so too are the means of resistance, now hearkening back to Africa. 'We must create shields that protect us and spears that penetrate our enemies', she adds. 'Black people must learn how to struggle by struggling. We must learn by our mistakes'.[36]

The collective form of this antagonism, the practical organization of its warfare, is the Black Liberation Army – an entity that emerges as the organic extension of her social being. 'I am a Black revolutionary', Shakur announces, 'and, by definition, that makes me a part of the Black Liberation Army'.[37] Unlike the Panthers, this mobilization eschews the party form. It is not an attempt at revolutionary leadership or direct organization; it is a collective name for separate revolutionary actions comprising various collectives working independently out of different cities, and in many cases doing so while hiding from police repression. As an active military force, this army is a primarily underground formation whose actions do not belong to any centralized committee or common leadership and do not cohere within stable chains of command. Its warfare represents a tradition of decentralized and clandestine insurgency familiar from rural struggles in China and Latin America, as well as from decolonial activity in Africa and armed autonomia in Italy.

But rather than depending on anything like an armed nucleus to model a new society, the Black Liberation Army is synonymous with the racialized masses, an outcome of their lived conditions. In Shakur's words, 'pigs also try to give the impression that five or ten guerrillas are responsible for every revolutionary action carried out in amerika', whereas theirs is the aggregate form of all actions waged by the dispossessed and incarcerated. 'We are created by our conditions', she says. 'Shaped by our oppression. We are being manufactured in droves in the ghetto streets, places like attica, san quentin, bedford hills, leavenworth, and sing sing. They are turning out thousands of us. Many jobless Black veterans and welfare mothers are joining our ranks'. As it was in England and America during the nineteenth century, here the army is an implied threat, the promised outcome of sustained immiseration: a war that obtains in the absence of justice. 'There is, and always will be, until every Black man, woman, and child is free, a Black Liberation Army'.[38] This statement appears early in the autobiography, and will be revisited near the end. Composed as a revolutionary bildungsroman, a form usually reserved for moral and spiritual education, the overall narrative dramatizes how she arrived at this perspective, and in so doing doubles as an explication of how class war morphed into new forms in the wake of the Panthers.

* * *

Shakur's autobiography is, then, a story of militancy as well as a critique of racial capitalism, against which that militancy reads as a material necessity. Rather than arrive at the revolutionary imperative via individualized epiphany, her politics come about organically, often through conversations with community organizers, here turning on the limits of social-democratic reform:

'We'll take control of the political institutions in our community. Then we'll take control of the congressional seats, the senate seats, the city council seats, the mayor's office, and every other office that we can take control of. We'll take control of the political offices so we can allocate money to the people who need it'.

'Y'all just wishing and hoping', someone said. 'You can control the social institutions and the political institutions, but unless you control the economic and military institutions, you can only go but so far'.

Everybody just sort of got quiet, thinking.

'Well, what are we supposed to do, then? Just sit back and do nothing?'

'Fighting for community control is just the first step. It can only go so far. What you need is a revolution'.

Everybody started talking about what the brother had said. We were all confused, but we were all enthused. That was the one thing I dug about those days. We were alive and we were excited and we believed that we were going to be free someday. For us, it wasn't a matter of whether or not. It was a question of how.[39]

The answer to that final question proceeds from a critical engagement with both class and race as coeval sources of social debilitation under capitalism and as potential rallying points for insurrection. 'The rich have always used racism to maintain power', we are told. For Shakur, 'it didn't take too much brains to figure out that Black people are oppressed because of class as well as race, because we are poor and because we are Black'.[40] She thus identifies the cornerstone to the entire property system and capitalist accumulation in the United States, with its economy built from slavery, as the carceral system. Prisons are 'profitable business' and 'a way of legally perpetuating slavery', insofar as 'in prison, there are plenty of jobs, and, if you don't want to work, they beat you up and throw you in the hole'. They are, in other words, a place to contain surplus populations at a time when 'so many Black people can't find a job on the streets and are forced to survive the best way they know how', and to ensure profitability, for 'if every state had to pay workers to do the jobs prisoners are forced to do, the salaries would amount to billions'.[41] Rejecting class mobility or the ladder of success – because if 'you're talking about a ladder, you're talking about a top and a bottom, an upper class and a lower class, a rich class and a poor class' – Shakur advocates against fighting within the system, and only for fighting against it.[42]

That race is imbricated with class and that liberation therefore depends on the unmaking of capitalism as a system is a lesson taken from decolonial and liberation movements in Africa, and she outlines this argument in words that recall those of Fanon: 'Revolutionaries in Africa understood that the question of African liberation was not just a question of race, that even if they managed to get rid of the white colonialists, if they didn't rid themselves of the capitalistic economic structure, the white colonialists would simply be replaced by Black neocolonialists'.[43] C. L. R. James makes a similar point in relation to Haiti.

'The race question', he claims, 'is subsidiary to the class question in politics, and to think of imperialism in terms of race is disastrous. But to neglect the racial factor as merely incidental is an error only less grave than to make it fundamental'.[44] Black liberation in the United States is, like the Haitian Revolution as well as decolonization in Africa, a program for complete disorder. And so, alongside all the practical experience in the movement and direct exposure to the machinery of racial capitalism, the forms taken by revolutionary activity still borrow from Asian and Latin American guerrilla warfare. 'There were books and pamphlets in the San Francisco and Berkeley bookstores i had never seen in New York', Shakur recalls from her visit to the West Coast, 'and for the first time i read the theory of urban guerrilla warfare as outlined by Che Guevara, Carlos Mariguella, and the Tupamaros'. Recognizing the practical value of guerrilla warfare for fighting imperialism in the rural periphery, in Vietnam and Cambodia as well as in South and Central America, she notes that one location is not the other. 'Reading about guerrilla warfare in South America and Vietnam was one thing, but thinking in terms of guerrilla war inside the u.s. was another'.[45] Her sense is to affirm 'the common, fundamental laws of armed revolutionary struggle', in particular how these laws had been advanced by Mao, for whom revolution would succeed as a protracted people's war. 'Revolutionary war is protracted warfare. It is impossible for us to win quickly. To win we have got to wear down our oppressors, little by little, and, at the same time, strengthen our forces, slowly but surely'.[46] In the United States, this kind of warfare has a well-defined and historically unique enemy: the police state. 'As far as i was concerned, the police in the Black communities were nothing but a foreign, occupying army, beating, torturing, and murdering people at whim and without restraint. I despise violence, but i despise it even more when it's one-sided and used to oppress and repress poor people'.[47]

After Shakur's arrest on the New Jersey Turnpike, the brutality with which she is treated by the police, and the political sympathies they profess, have her recall one of the Panthers' staple insults. 'When i was in the Black Panther Party', she says, 'we used to call the police "fascist pigs", but i had called them fascists not because i believed they were nazis but because of the way they acted in our communities. As many times as i had referred to police as fascists, these shocked me by the truth of my own rhetoric'.[48] To be shocked by the truth of what might be called theoretical knowledge, to feel affectively its clarification of the real, is a condition of autobiography. And here, warfare presents itself, as it has for so many other militants, not as an outcome to this or that theory but as a necessary response to the kinds of immiseration that cannot be fixed by anything less than systemic unmaking: 'There were sisters and brothers who had been so victimized by amerika that they were willing to fight to the death against their oppressors. They were intelligent, courageous and dedicated, willing to make any sacrifice'. But feeling is not the same as strategy. Impulse falls short of action. 'We were', she concedes, 'to find out quickly that courage and dedication were not enough. To win any struggle for liberation, you have to have the way as well as the will, an overall ideology and strategy that stem from a scientific analysis of history and present conditions'. For all this energy and aspiration, the Black Liberation Army never became a force of social transformation capable of destroying the forms of racial capitalism. 'On the whole, we were weak, inexperienced, disorganized, and seriously lacking in training'.[49] Even while coordination was out of the question, not least because it posed massive security risks, the major problem remained one of class solidarity.

And so, when it comes to class solidarity, Shakur cautions impatient comrades who would substitute military for political struggle, knowing instead that each is required and in relation to the other, especially when subject to state violence. Rather than overstate the transformative potential of either military or political work at the expense of the other, whatever 'armed acts of resistance' might take place should, she insists, be 'actions that Black people would clearly understand and support and actions that were well publicized in the Black community'.[50] Yet this was not to be the case. Her assessment of what instead took place here resembles the autonomist critique of 'armed struggle ideology', which makes a fetish of combat at the expense of solidarity, pinpointing exactly why the Panthers had evolved their program into something more expansive than armed propaganda:

> Some of the groups thought they could just pick up arms and struggle and that, somehow, people would see what they were doing and begin to struggle themselves. They wanted to engage in a do-or-die battle with the power structure in amerika, even though they were weak and ill prepared for such a fight. But the most important factor is that armed struggle, by itself, can never bring about a revolution. Revolutionary war is a people's war. And no people's war can be won without the support of the masses of people. Armed struggle can never be successful by itself; it must be part of an overall strategy for winning, and the strategy must be political as well as military.[51]

The Black Liberation Army is, ultimately, an idea of class solidarity, the name of a common cause, for it does less to describe the particulars of fighting, the strategies and tactics or even an organizational identity, and more to rally militants against a shared enemy. 'The concept of the BLA arose', Shakur reminds us, 'because of the political, social, and economic oppression of Black people in this country. And where there is oppression, there will be resistance. The BLA is part of that resistance movement. The Black Liberation Army stands for freedom and justice for all people'.[52] It is, in the final reckoning, not an army in any technical sense of the term but an expression of class war, a metaphor that wants to be literal, a platform on which to transform struggle into revolution.

***

Bringing our story back to the historical present, there are ongoing debates about the influence of the Black Panthers on the Black Lives Matter movement of the twenty-first century, some of whose members have adopted the language and aesthetic of their militant forebears. In a polemic against this tendency, the political scientist Cedric Johnson, writing in *The Panthers Won't Save Us Now*, has claimed that Black Lives Matter separates its anti-racism from what he describes as a 'meaningful class analysis of black political life', which would involve the work of understanding historical processes from the standpoint of political economy. In this view, Black Lives Matter is not revolutionary but is instead 'essentially a militant expression of racial liberalism', seeking 'full recognition within the established terms of liberal democratic capitalism' as opposed to complete disorder. Unlike the revolutionaries and movements we have encountered elsewhere throughout history, the principal limitation for such a movement is, according to Johnson, that it is so amorphous as to be embraced by 'different class layers', whereby 'the facile expressions of unity in endless memes and viral videos of police-civilian line dances conceal substantive political differences among protestors and within broader US publics'.[53] Any return to the language and aesthetic of the Black Panthers within this frame reads as a kind of formal nostalgia, preserving elements of a bygone revolutionary moment and consuming them in ways that neglect both their strengths and their limitations.

If that critique overestimates the liberalism within a genuinely heterogenous movement, others have offered perspectives that might better enable us to approach Black Lives Matter as an expression of class war, with its desire for revolution. In discussing the necessity of Black Lives Matter, while also disagreeing with those who would dismiss its agenda as one of identity decoupled from anything like material common interest, social historian Nikhil Pal Singh offers the urgent clarification that, in the United States, 'we continue to live in a society structured in dominance in which racism and class exploitation constitute overlapping, coeval dynamics'. Here, different forms of militancy combine into a vision of revolutionary social transformation. 'Race and racism remains a major pivot on which US capitalism turns', he asserts, for both the waged and wageless, who are subject in different ways to diminishing health, life chances and crushing market dependency. We should not be surprised should we find ourselves truly capable of broaching questions of economic justice under the aegis of renewed labor and class struggles that it occurs in tight, if at times tense, rapprochement with a resurgence of militant anti-racist struggles.[54]

Broadly in agreement with this interpretation, the political theorist Asad Haider views Black Lives Matter as a movement that 'carried forward a fundamental revolutionary legacy', one that is inherited from Malcolm X, opposing both liberal compromise and the promotion of a select few elite subjects from an oppressed social group, and one that has thus become increasingly militant in both ideology and tactics. 'But', he cautions, 'this nascent class content was not always easy to maintain and develop. In fact, a reactionary tendency emerged, nourished by the corporate media and the black elite, which tried to introduce a rigid barrier between the Black Lives Matter movement and ongoing anticapitalist struggles, since they supposedly corresponded to different and unrelated identities'.[55]

Looking beyond the movement's self-appointed leadership and the political and corporate co-option of its aesthetic, we can suggest that the specifically radical aspects of Black Lives Matter share more with the Black Liberation Army than the Black Panthers. Both are decentralized forces that, rather than provide vanguard leadership, seek to mobilize in the name of freedom and justice for all people. Likewise, it will be worth remembering that, even if Black Lives Matter has not been a movement of armed insurrection or militant vanguards, surely this is in no small part because today's revolutionaries realize that one of the state's containment strategies is to polarize tensions along ethnic lines and incite armed conflict therein. And yet, in the summer of 2020, when police in Minneapolis murdered a man named George Floyd, Black Lives Matter became a movement of urban revolt. Hundreds of thousands, if not millions, of comrades and their fellow travellers took to the streets in a potent expression of collective rage and systemic unmaking: fighting under clouds of tear gas, reclaiming cities on foot and horseback, smashing and looting, vandalizing squad cars, setting fire to precincts, and establishing autonomous zones. In solidarity with the exploited and immiserated, the dispossessed and the dominated, this movement went to war against the material forms of racism, but not against racism alone. If, as Ruth Wilson Gilmore has argued, 'mass criminalization, and the policing it depends on, is class war' for the age of racial capitalism, then Black Lives Matter – like its predecessor movements – is only the current name for a movement in which the oppressed and exploited have banded together in solidarity to fight back.[56]

Postscript

No War But Class War

On 24 February 2022, Russia invaded Ukraine. Cities were bombarded with heavy artillery; vast columns of tanks and transports clogged the highways; within days, ground forces swarmed the city of Mariupol in the south and pushed deep from the north to the outskirts of Kyiv. While the invasion is undoubtedly an expression of regional dynamics that have placed Ukraine at the centre of rival geopolitical and geo-economic projects – with the interests of the EU and NATO on one side and those of Russia under the leadership of Vladimir Putin on the other – it is worth pausing here to register that this conflict is only one of several wars happening simultaneously and oftentimes with silent complicity, if not material support, from the West. Unlike the actions of the Ethiopian military in Tigray, the Saudi-UAE coalition in Yemen, or Israel in its occupation of Palestine, Russian aggression has been met with almost universal condemnation, an imbalance abetted by the global media narrative.

'Few in the West', writes Susan Watkins in the *New Left Review*, 'can summon up the image, engraved in local memory, of an Afghan wedding blasted to carnage by US bombs, or picture the gruesome reprisals by Anglo-American troops in their siege and subjugation of Fallujah. The bodies on Bucha's streets remain imprinted on the screen'.[1] Such a reminder is made not to diminish the political fact or affective singularity that Russia, acting as an imperialist and capitalist power, has launched a fratricidal war of extermination against another sovereign state, for which millions of civilians and soldiers are destined to suffer. Instead, these comparisons are made to highlight the inverse proportionality of scale and response that regional interstate warfare receives from the wider world.

While the official response from many nations in the global north has focused on providing military aid to the besieged state and imposing economic sanctions on the aggressor, the mainstream narratives of international solidarity have tended towards escalationist calls for military intervention: to hasten the stream of drones and missiles into a torrent of fighter jets or, ultimately, to bombard Russian airfields and police a no-fly zone. Considering this response, the historian Tony Wood has compared our moment to the twilight of the Belle Époque, when inter-imperial tensions fuelled a headlong arms race and public opinion rallied behind national governments. Wood notes that, in 1914, even the parliamentary parties of the left found themselves contributing to this catastrophically belligerent nationalism, 'voting for war credits in their national legislatures and thus enabling the bloodbath they had pledged to avert two years earlier'.[2] If, in Ukraine, a bloodbath is already underway, there remains potential for greater catastrophe still. While the media's demands might accord with the sentiments of the Ukrainian leadership, with President Volodymyr Zelensky campaigning for external military intervention, Putin has reminded the world that Russia is a nuclear power and that any such intervention would have dire consequences. 'Rumours have it', writes the sociologist Wolfgang Streeck, 'that the numerous wargames commissioned in recent years from military thinktanks by the American government involving Ukraine, NATO and Russia have one way or other all ended in nuclear Armageddon, at least in Europe'.[3]

Across the left's various non-parliamentary movements and tendencies, including many of those within both Ukraine and

Russia, one of the more prominent responses to these events has been to refuse critical models based on preferred states altogether. A communist writer known only as Andrew from Kharkiv, in northeast Ukraine, was interviewed during the first month of the invasion. For him, thinking about the war in terms of innocence and guilt only serves to justify xenophobia and genocide, whereas a revolutionary politics meaningfully opposed to imperialism 'should instead seek to expand the islands of civilian resistance and construct universalist communities', building solidarity networks along internationalist class lines rather than the ideology of patriotism. 'Only a mass movement', he says, 'on both sides of the frontline and in the armies themselves, originating from a spark we might not be able to expect right now, will be able to put a stop to the world which has brought war so close to the imperial core for the first time in years'.[4]

Here we should sense the clarification of over two centuries of revolutionary practice – of the various ways that, from the plantations, jungles, and mountains of Haiti through the Paris Commune to the streets of Oakland, and everywhere in between, militants have sought to provide the spark with which to light the waypoints out of interminable darkness. Or, as Wood concludes his reflection on the conflict, it is in the face of disaster that 'the old tools – internationalism, class solidarity, a fierce and uncompromising analytical clarity – will be needed to rearm the left against this new round of inter-imperial contention: against the powerful, against both their wars and their peace'.[5] If this position accords with what we have encountered elsewhere in history, it also condenses into the well-known slogan 'no war but class war', which has been in high circulation in the first half of 2022. As a response to social declension that carries on the tradition of class militancy against imperial militarism, it allows for a distillation of what class war means today and of how it might orient our future struggles.

In this phrase, as ever, class war occupies the space between political action and literary art. Like so many invocations of class war, it is both description and proscription, a critical response to wars of extermination, which it forthrightly rejects, and a call to arms in the name of collective human flourishing: class war against wars of extermination; international solidarity versus ethno-nationalism. While the oppositional grammar harmonizes with revolutionary sloganeering – 'liberty or death', 'socialism or barbarism', 'communism or extinction' – the referential content has its origin in popular storytelling.

The formulation is said to derive from an episode of *Days of Hope*, the 1975 television series written by Jim Allen and directed by Ken Loach, mostly set in the northern counties of England between World War One and the General Strike of 1926. The series follows Ben Hargreaves, an enlisted soldier who becomes a socialist and deserts after witnessing the transposition of military atrocity from the imperial and colonial battlefields of France and Northern Ireland to labour disputes in the Durham coalfields. 'I'm no pacifist', he says when explaining his desertion from the British Army. 'I'll fight in a war, but I'll fight in the only war that counts, and that's the class war, and it'll come when all this lot's over'. It was only later that the self-enclosed phrase 'no war but class war' was taken up, first as a group name and rallying cry for anti-war movements in London associated with the anarchist group Class War as they remobilized in opposition to the 1990–91 Gulf War, the 1999 Kosovo War, and the 2001 Afghanistan War. In the first half of 2022, this phrase has undergone a resurgence in renewed social movements, popular and critical writing, and across the internet, and has been painted in red and black on banners and on walls, in Latin and in Cyrillic.

Regardless of its origins, 'no war but class war' cannot be separated from what Rosa Luxemburg described as the world-historic problem of 1914: the challenge of knowing what kind of action will finally make good on the old cliché of 'war against war', converting political alarm into social revolution. This, she insisted, is 'the actual problem that the world war has posed to the socialist parties, upon the solution of which the destiny of the workers' movement depends'.[6] If the global conjuncture of

1914 elicited such imperatives from one of the world's greatest revolutionaries, Luxemburg's question has been answered in myriad ways throughout history – by Louise Michel and Louis Auguste Blanqui, by Vladimir Lenin and Leon Trotsky, by Mao Zedong, Frantz Fanon, and Che Guevara, by Huey P. Newton and Assata Shakur, and many others besides. Their lives and their actions, as we have read, are part of a shared story that began in Haiti with Toussaint Louverture and made its way through England after the First Industrial Revolution, France at the end of the Second Empire, the American Gilded Age, revolutionary Russia and China, decolonial Africa, the guerrilla movements of Latin America, to erupt in urban revolt against fascism and racial capitalism in Italy and the United States. That is the story we can sense behind the entreaties of 'no war but class war', a story about slaves and peasants and workers, about proletarianization and industrial disputes, about the struggle for decolonization, about guerrilla insurgency, about terrorism, vandalism, and sabotage, and about large-scale combat operations waged against the state and its military and paramilitary forces.

It goes without saying that 'no war but class war' is itself a literary form: five monosyllables, like the first or final line of a haiku, here arranged into a sonic chiasmus in which every part of the first and last feet, each a spondaic stomp, demands vocal emphasis. While repetition, as we encounter it with the repeated 'war', is the very definition of poetic language, here it is also doing political work. Philosophers, from Kierkegaard and Nietzsche to Deleuze and Derrida, have emphasized that repetition is as much about the production of difference as it is about similitude, that it opens up an ideological fracture within the space of language: our war, not theirs, against which we fight. As sound and syntax transform these words from statement into something like a poem, let us re-emphasize that, within the story of class war, the relationship between politics and literature has always been mutually reciprocal. From the standpoint of politics, literature enables the transmission of revolutionary thought, military strategy, and ideological messaging across time and space; and from the standpoint of literature, a politics of class war serves as catalyst for aesthetic transformation, infusing literary forms and modes and genres.

It is in this way that class war belongs to those revolutionaries – so many of whom produced literature of their own – no less than it does to the likes of Émeric Bergeaud, Elizabeth Gaskell, William Morris, Émile Zola, Jack London, Vladimir Mayakovsky, Victor Serge, Zhou Libo, Ding Ling, Ngũgĩ wa Thiong'o, Gabriel García Márquez, Nanni Balestrini, and Elena Ferrante. Class war also abounds in contemporary literature. We read it as our own antiquity in the historical novels of Joseph Andras, C. A. Davids, Rachel Kushner, David Peace, Thomas Pynchon, Jordy Rosenberg, and Éric Vuillard. It animates the speculative imaginings of R. F. Kuang, China Miéville, David Mitchell, Kim Stanley Robinson, and the recently deceased Ursula K. Le Guin. And it absolutely thrives in the poetry of the present, especially in poems composed amid struggle. 'This is how the misanthropocene ends', write Joshua Clover and Juliana Spahr in their eco-apocalyptic georgic from 2014. 'We go to war against it. My friends go to war against it. They run howling with joy and terror against it. I go with them'.[7] Here commitment is alive in the grammar. The merging of 'we', 'they', 'I', and 'them' within a shared present-simple tense epitomizes the tonality of class war. It reads as revolutionary becoming, a new social synthesis made in the affective force of antagonism. And, in its reformulation of what we have encountered at so many other times and in so many other places, this is just one instance of how revolutionary memory – the intergenerational and multi-regional story of class war, its strategies and its tactics, its heroes and its martyrs – is mediated into the contemporary political conjuncture. Class war is carried by literary form, in the substance of its diction and the shape of its grammar, out of the revolutionary past and into the historical present, a moment defined by the death of liberal progress and the proliferation of new crises and new antagonisms.

These postulations refuse left melancholia, an affective condition first described by Walter Benjamin as 'the fatalism of those who are most remote from the process of production and whose obscure courting of the state of the market is comparable to the attitude of a man who yields himself up entirely to the inscrutable accidents of his digestion'.[8] Left melancholia has been analysed more recently by the intellectual historian Enzo Traverso, for whom capitalist individualism has displaced traditional forms of sociability and solidarity – shattering 'the social frameworks of the left's memory, whose continuity was irremediably broken'.[9] While this disarticulation of memory has not stopped revolutionary action, some of the most notable mass movements of the past decade – from Occupy Wall Street through Black Lives Matter to the 15-M in Spain, Gezi Park in Istanbul, the *gilets jaunes* in France, and the insurgent youth in Chile, as well as similar political agitations from Hong Kong to Minsk – are said to be miraculous, because they have 'invented new organizational forms and alliances' while removed from the ideologically enabling and strategically edifying history of revolutionary practice. 'Being orphans', Traverso claims, 'they must reinvent themselves'.[10] Unlike these movements, the familiar practice of armed insurrection – the terrain on which revolutionaries 'had, over the last century, accumulated considerable experience and recorded numerous successes' – seems to have fallen into the domain of reactionary extremism. The practices that could have once or otherwise been revolutionary reappear 'now entirely occupied by Islamic fundamentalism, which, through an impressive historical regression, has substituted sharia for anticolonialism and national liberation'.[11]

Here we approach a conclusion by maintaining that any such reinvention has as much to do with shifting class composition on the terrain of capital, and the new kinds of solidarity that shift inspires, as with anything like revolutionary memory or regressive fundamentalisms. The kinds of revolutionary antagonism we are seeing today are relative to a moment in which the working class must subsist without work and in which dispossession prevails but without institutions to rally the dispossessed. Ours is a world that requires us to know class as something other than cultural identity bound up in the reliable structures of formal labour. This is why so many of today's actions have been described as undertaken by movements for which class remains the inconspicuous undercurrent adjoined to the differently prominent variables of age, gender, geography, race, and religion. Of course, the absence of ready-made class formations is nothing new, even if the social conditions have altered, for that is precisely what we have seen revolutionaries confront throughout the history of capital, and what they have sought to combat using the rhetorical forms and military actions of class war. In every setting we have encountered, the collective agents of revolutionary social transformation have been made and remade, collectively and as individuals, by the nature of their actions.

Finally, then, let us reaffirm that class war has never just been about taking up arms. It is not limited to the practice of warfare, which lends itself the kind of fetish that revolutionaries from England in the 1830s to Italy and the United States in the 1970s would come to characterize as 'the delirium of military ideology'. Instead, and in the discovery of commonality through antagonism, class war has always had just as much to do with international solidarity, with embodied diversity, and with a commitment to collective betterment as it has with bullets, bombs, and barricades. And that is what unites our struggles today with a revolutionary past, linking our orphaned movements to the history and practice of class war. Now, as ever, we are engaged in the assembly of collective actions and mobilizations based in the shared conditions for living that have been forced upon us by capital. But we are also finding new connections, new ways of being together, through the lived experience of antagonism, and on a global scale. All of which brings us full circle, back to Ukraine where, from blast-blackened ruins and with thousands of civilian deaths so far, scores of men, women, and children have joined those millions of Syrian, Sudanese, and Afghan refugees displaced across a planetary landscape. These are the human embodiments of a global underclass, a people dispossessed of all property and only punished by the state.

Their number will multiply exponentially as we advance further into the era of climate refugees, a reality which the inundation of the coasts and the burning of forests will only quicken. In a world where the immiserated subsistence of millions upon millions of humans urgently demands a politics of universal care without borders, the avowal of class war means to arm the people against the powerful in common purpose and common prosperity.

Marx once arrived at a similar thought. Looking at Europe in 1851, after the defeat of the 1848 revolution in France and Louis-Napoleon Bonaparte's subsequent coup, he explained the need for revolutionary reinvention. His chosen metaphor will serve as one last clarification of what we mean when we talk about class war as a protean form that exists between politics and literature:

> The social revolution of the nineteenth century cannot take its poetry from the past but only from the future. It cannot begin with itself before it has stripped away all superstition about the past. The former revolutions required recollections of past world history in order to smother their own content. The revolution of the nineteenth century must let the dead bury their dead in order to arrive at its own content. There the phrase went beyond the content – here the content goes beyond the phrase.[12]

Likewise, class war derives its vitality from the way its two constituent terms constantly revise and redefine one another. As an exhortation that finds form in both word and deed – from the revolutionary slogan painted on banners or shouted through a megaphone, with comrades standing together on the picket line or having one another's backs in a riot, right down to the smouldering wreckage of armed propaganda – class war has always sought to synthesize new collective identities, and with them realize effective strategies for attack. Just as the admonition 'let the dead bury the dead' echoes another of Marx's well-known metaphors, in which the proletariat stands forth as the gravedigger of capital, class war contains within itself an obligation to constantly renew our understandings of the collective revolutionary subject and of how that subject fights, of our class belonging and of how we go to war – because that is the only way we are going to win.

May 2022

Notes

Introduction

1 Serge Halimi and Pierre Rimbert, 'France's Class Wars', *Le Monde diplomatique*, February 2019.
2 'Elite Gathering Reveals Anxiety over "Class War" and "Revolution"', *Financial Times*, 2 May 2019.
3 Chris Talgo, 'America Is in a Class War, Not a Race War,' *The Hill*, 27 August 2020.
4 'Colombia Protests Sharpen Cali's Class War,' *Al Jazeera*, 22 June 2021, aljazeera.com; 'Chile Protests: Cost of Living Protests Take Deadly Toll', *BBC News*, 21 October 2019; Amy Wilentz, 'Haiti Is in the Streets,' *The Nation*, 24 October 2019.
5 Sarah Jones, 'The Coronavirus Puts the Class War into Stark Relief', *New York Magazine*, 10 March 2020.
6 Grace Blakely, 'No, the Tories Aren't "Moving Left" on the Economy', *Tribune*, 13 May 2021.
7 Yanis Varoufakis, 'The COVID Class War', *Project Syndicate*, 30 June 2020.
8 Chandana Mathur, 'COVID-19 and India's Trail of Tears', *Dialectical Anthropology* 44 (2020), 240.
9 Andreas Malm, *Corona, Climate, Chronic Emergency: War Communism in the Twenty-First Century* (Verso, 2020), 25.
10 Matthew T. Huber, *Climate Change as Class War: Building Socialism on a Warming Planet* (Verso, 2022), 3.
11 Jodi Dean, 'Climate Change Is Class War', *Liberation*, 31 July 2019.
12 Dharna Noor, 'Capybaras Are Waging Class War in Argentina', *Gizmodo*, 24 August 2021.
13 Bertolt Brecht, 'The Mother' (1957), in *Collected Plays: Three*, ed. John Willett (Bloomsbury, 2015), 119.

14 Ibid., 120.

15 Karl Marx and Friedrich Engels, 'Manifesto of the Communist Party' (1848), in *The Marx-Engels Reader*, ed. Robert C. Tucker, 2nd ed. (Norton, 1978), 474.

16 Ibid., 483.

17 Étienne Balibar, 'Marxism and War', *Radical Philosophy* 160 (March/April 2010), radicalphilosophy.com. Here it will be worth clarifying the heterogeneity between civil war and open revolution, and that, while emphatically non-synonymous, one potentially opens onto the other. This idea is present in Marx, and especially so in the emphasis on 'phases', but it also has ancient precedent. According to philosopher Giorgio Agamben's writings on ancient Greece, 'civil war marks the threshold through which the unpolitical is politicised and the political is "economized"', an inward turn of conflict that 'assimilates and makes undecidable brother and enemy, inside and outside, household and city.' In other words, civil war reconstitutes social being around violent antagonism. Giorgio Agamben, *Stasis: Civil War as a Political Paradigm*, trans. Nicholas Heron (Stanford University Press, 2015), 15–16.

18 Vladimir Lenin, 'Lessons of the Commune' (23 March 1908), in *Collected Works*, vol. 13 (Progress, 1974), 478.

19 Mao, 'On Contradiction' (August 1937), in *Selected Works of Mao Tse-Tung*, vol. 1 (Foreign Languages Press, 1965), 343.

20 Leon Trotsky, *Terrorism and Communism: A Reply to Karl Kautsky* (1920; repr., Verso, 2007), 133.

21 The Invisible Committee, *To Our Friends*, trans. Robert Hurley (Semiotext(e), 2015), 138.

22 Georg Lukács, *History and Class Consciousness: Studies in Marxist Dialectics* (1923), trans. Rodney Livingstone (MIT Press, 1971), 80.

23 China Miéville, *A Spectre, Haunting: On the Communist Manifesto* (Head of Zeus, 2022), 11.

24 Mark Fisher, 'Choose Your Weapons' (2007), in *K-Punk: The Collected and Unpublished Writings of Mark Fisher (2004–2016)*, ed. Darren Ambrose (Repeater, 2018), 356.

25 Here Clover is responding to E. P. Thompson's argument that the riot emerged, in England, as a response to market dominance rather than solely being an expression of political emotion and actual hunger, which led Thompson to conclude that the marketplace, so often the site of rioting, is 'as much the arena of class war as the factory and mine became in the industrial revolution'.

Joshua Clover, *Riot. Strike. Riot: The New Era of Uprisings* (Verso, 2016), 44.

26 Ruth Wilson Gilmore, 'Fatal Couplings of Power and Difference: Notes on Racism and Geography', *Professional Geographer* 54 (2002), 16.

27 Clara Zetkin, 'German Socialist Women's Movement', *Justice*, 9 October 1909.

28 Selma James, 'Sex, Race, and Class' (1973), in *Sex, Race, and Class: The Perspective of Winning; A Selection of Writings, 1952–2011* (PM Press, 2012), 14.

29 'Onward Barbarians', *Endnotes*, 26 May 2020.

30 Erik Olin Wright, *Classes* (Verso, 1997), 10.

31 E. P. Thompson, *The Making of the English Working Class* (1963; repr., Vintage, 1966), 11.

32 Ibid., 9.

33 This term has recently resurfaced within social thought, finding its most forceful articulation in the work of the sociologist Vivek Chibber, especially in his book *The Class Matrix: Social Theory after the Cultural Turn* (Harvard University Press, 2022). While parts of my argument differ from Chibber's conceptualization, rather than summarize these differences at length here, it will be worth saying that my thinking on common interest is more indebted to the work of the political scientist William Clare Roberts. 'The immediate unity of class interest', he writes in his critique of C. L. R. James, 'was a myth that obscured the hard work of forging a common interest'. William Clare Roberts, 'Centralism Is a Dangerous Tool: Leadership in C. L. R. James's History of Principles', *CLR James Journal* 26:1/2 (January 2021), 233. A useful summary of this concept and its place within political praxis can also be found in Jasper Bernes, 'Revolutionary Motives', *Endnotes* 5 (2020), 195–6.

34 Rosa Luxemburg, 'The Junius Pamphlet: The Crisis of German Social Democracy' (1915), in *Socialism or Barbarism: Selected Writings*, ed. Paul Le Blanc and Helen C. Scott (Left Book Club, 2021), 209.

35 Ellen Meiksins Wood, *The Retreat from Class: A New 'True' Socialism* (Verso, 1998), 189.

36 Ibid., 199.

37 Mike Davis, *Old Gods, New Enigmas: Marx's Lost Theory* (Verso, 2018), 2.

38 Karl Marx, *Capital: A Critique of Political Economy*, vol. 3 (1894), trans. David Fernbach (Penguin, 1981), 1025, 1026.

39 David Peace, *GB84* (Faber, 2004), 68.

40 Franco 'Bifo' Berardi, 'A Coup in Greece: Four Difficult Questions from Franco 'Bifo' Berardi', *Verso Blog*, 29 June 2015, verso-books.com.

41 Lenin, 'Outline of Speech at the Tenth All-Russia Congress of Soviets' (December 1922), in *Collected Works*, vol. 36 (Progress, 1971), 588. Italics in original.

42 Régis Debray, *Revolution in the Revolution? Armed Struggle and Political Struggle in Latin America* (1967), trans. Bobbye Ortiz (Verso, 2017), 109.

43 James and Grace Lee Boggs, *Revolution and Evolution in the Twentieth Century* (Monthly Review Press, 1974), 16.

44 C. L. R. James, *The Black Jacobins: Toussaint L'Ouverture and the San Domingo Revolution* (1967; repr., Penguin, 2001), 248.

45 Frantz Fanon, *The Wretched of the Earth*, trans. Constance Farrington (Grove Press, 1963), 36.

46 Michael Hardt and Antonio Negri, *Multitude: War and Democracy in the Age of Empire* (Penguin, 2004), 70, 74.

47 Fredric Jameson, *An American Utopia: Dual Power and the Universal Army* (Verso, 2016), 61.

48 Silvia Federici, *Re-enchanting the World: Feminism and the Politics of the Commons* (PM Press, 2019), 32.

49 Louise Michel, *Red Virgin: Memoirs of Louise Michel*, trans. Bullitt Lowry and Elizabeth Ellington Gunter (University of Alabama Press, 1981), 51.

50 Leon Trotsky, *History of the Russian Revolution* (1930), trans. Max Eastman (Victor Gollancz, 1965), 508.

51 Fanon, *Wretched of the Earth*, 240.

52 Assata Shakur, *Assata: An Autobiography* (1987; repr., Zed Books, 2001), 17.

53 Ernesto Che Guevara, *Guerrilla Warfare* (1961; repr., BN Publishing, 2007), 41.

54 Friedrich Engels, *The Peasant War in Germany* (1870), trans. Moissaye J. Olgin (International Publishers, 1926), marxists.org.

55 Christopher Hill, *The English Revolution, 1640: An Essay* (Lawrence and Wishart, 1940), 11.

56 Ibid., 59.

57 Gerrard Winstanley, 'A New Year's Gift for the Parliament and Army' (1649), in *Selected Writings*, ed. Andrew Hopton (Aporia, 2008), 67.

58 Claude-Henri de Saint-Simon, 'Letters from an Inhabitant of Geneva to His Contemporaries' (1803), in *The Political Thought of Saint-Simon*, ed. Ghita Ionescu (Oxford University Press, 1976), 73.

1 The Burning South

1 Toussaint L'Ouverture, 'Letter to Dessalines' (8 February 1802), in *The Haitian Revolution*, ed. Nick Nesbitt (Verso, 2008), 76.

2 Henri Christophe, *Haytian Papers: A Collection of the Very Interesting Proclamations and Other Documents* (W. Reed, 1816), 7.

3 Émeric Bergeaud, *Stella: A Novel of the Haitian Revolution* (1859), trans. and ed. Lesley S. Curtis and Christen Mucher (New York University Press, 2015), 104.

4 Quoted in Victor Hugo, *Bug-Jargal* (1826), trans. and ed. Chris Bongie (Broadview, 2004), 202n28.

5 Marlene L. Daut, 'All the Devils Are Here: How the Visual History of the Haitian Revolution Misrepresents Black Suffering and Death', *Lapham's Quarterly*, 14 October 2020.

6 L'Ouverture, 'Letter to Dessalines' (8 February 1802), 76.

7 Jean Jacques Dessalines, 'Liberty or Death! A Proclamation' (1804), in Marcus Rainsford, *An Historical Account of the Black Empire of Hayti: Comprehending a View of the Principal Transactions in the Revolution of Saint Domingo with Its Ancient and Modern State* (Albion Press, 1805), 448.

8 Christophe, *Haytian Papers*, 154.

9 Peter Hallward, 'Haitian Inspiration: On the Bicentenary of Haiti's Independence', *Radical Philosophy* 123 (January/February 2004).

10 Jean-Jacques Rousseau, *Discourse on Political Economy and The Social Contract* (1755), trans. Christopher Betts (Oxford University Press, 1994), 52, 53.

11 Jean-Jacques Rousseau, *Discourse on the Origin and Foundations of Inequality among Men* (1755), trans. and ed. Helena Rosenblatt (Bedford, 2011), 82–3.

12 Rousseau, *Discourse on Political Economy and The Social Contract*, 53.

13 Susan Buck-Morss, *Hegel, Haiti, and Universal History* (University of Pittsburgh Press, 2009), 21.

14 Aimé Césaire quoted in Nick Nesbitt, *Universal Emancipation: The Haitian Revolution and the Radical Enlightenment* (University of Virginia Press, 2008), 223n25.

15 Denis Diderot, *Les Éleuthéromanes* (1772; repr., Ghio, 1884), 96; George Jacques Danton, 'Unity and Strength' (10 March 1793), in *Voices of Revolt: Speeches of George Jacques Danton* (International, 1928), 44; Maximillian Robespierre, *Report upon the Principles of Political Morality Which Are to Form the Basis*

of the Administration of the Interior Concerns of the Republic (1794); while the quotation about the vessel of revolution on the sea of blood is frequently attributed to Saint-Just, as in Stanley Loomis, *Paris in the Terror: June 1793–July 1794* (Jonathan Cape, 1964), 284, it more likely originated with the revolutionary journalist Bertrand Barère. In the memoirs of Joachim Vilate, he recalls a gathering at which the journalist, 'impatient de montrer son ardeur pour les principes', utters the phrase 'le vaisseau de la Révolution ne peut arriver à bon port que sur une mer rougie des flots de sang', to which Saint Just replies with the equally sanguinary, 'une nation ne se régénère que sur des monceaux de cadavres', or 'a nation is only regenerated on heaps of cadavers'. Joachim Vilate, *Causes secrètes de la révolution du 9 au 10 thermidor* (Paris, 1794), 14.

16 Robin Blackburn, *The Overthrow of Colonial Slavery, 1776–1848* (Verso, 1988), 163.

17 Ibid., 169.

18 Adam Hochschild, *Bury the Chains: Prophets and Rebels in the Fight to Free an Empire's Slaves* (Houghton Mifflin, 2005), 256.

19 Blackburn, *Overthrow of Colonial Slavery*, 54.

20 C. L. R. James, *The Black Jacobins: Toussaint L'Ouverture and the San Domingo Revolution* (1967; repr., Penguin, 2001), 306.

21 Julius S. Scott, *The Common Wind: Afro-American Currents in the Age of the Haitian Revolution* (Verso, 2018), 157.

22 Ibid., xv.

23 James, *The Black Jacobins*, 120.

24 Lenin, 'On Slogans' (1917), in *Collected Works*, vol. 25 (Progress, 1974), 185.

25 J. V. Stalin, 'The Party's Three Fundamental Slogans on the Peasant Question', *Bolshevik* 7–8, 15 April, 1927.

26 L'Ouverture, 'Letter to Biassou' (15 October 1791), in *The Haitian Revolution*, 2.

27 James, *The Black Jacobins*, 95.

28 Zora Neale Hurston, *Tell My Horse: Voodoo and Life in Haiti and Jamaica* (Harper Perennial, 2009), 113.

29 Deborah Jenson, 'Jean-Jacques Dessalines and the African Character of the Haitian Revolution', *William and Mary Quarterly* 69:3 (July 2012), 615.

30 Peter Linebaugh and Marcus Rediker, *The Many-Headed Hydra: Sailors, Slaves, Commoners, and the Hidden History of the Revolutionary Atlantic* (Beacon Press, 2000), 330.

31 Hugo, *Bug-Jargal*, 123.

32 L'Ouverture, 'Letter to Biassou' (15 October 1791), 1.

33 Thomas O. Ott, *The Haitian Revolution, 1789–1804* (University of Tennessee Press, 1973), 171.

34 Priyamvada Gopal, *Insurgent Empire: Anticolonial Resistance and British Dissent* (Verso, 2018), 5.

35 Dessalines, 'Liberty or Death!', 448.

36 Eric Williams, *Capitalism and Slavery* (University of North Carolina Press, 1944), 210.

37 Christophe, *Haytian Papers*, 222.

38 William Wordsworth, 'To Toussaint L'Ouverture' (1803), in *The Poetical Works of Wordsworth*, ed. Henry Reed (Troutman & Hayes, 1854), 225.

39 Ernest Jones, 'The New World, a Democratic Poem' (1851), in *Notes to the People*, vol. 1 (Merlin Press, 1967), 6.

2 Army of Redressers

1 Robert William Reid, *The Peterloo Massacre* (Random House, 1989), 115.

2 'Manchester Political Meeting', *Manchester Observer*, 21 August 1819.

3 E. P. Thompson, *The Making of the English Working Class* (1963; repr., Vintage, 1966), 441–2.

4 Ibid., 682.

5 Robert Sayre and Michael Löwy, 'Figures of Romantic Anti-capitalism', *New German Critique* 32 (Spring/Summer 1984), 54.

6 Ibid., 61.

7 Anahid Nersessian, *Utopia, Limited: Romanticism and Adjustment* (Harvard University Press, 2015), 16.

8 Percy Bysshe Shelley, 'The Masque of Anarchy' (1819), in *Poetical Works*, ed. Thomas Hutchinson (Oxford University Press, 1970), 344.

9 Peter Linebaugh, *Stop, Thief! The Commons, Enclosures, and Resistance* (PM Press, 2014), 81.

10 Charlotte Brontë, *Shirley* (1849), ed. Andrew and Judith Hook (Penguin, 1974), 62.

11 Ibid.

12 Ibid., 335.

13 Gavin Mueller, *Breaking Things at Work: The Luddites Are Right about Why You Hate Your Job* (Verso, 2020), 10.

14 Brontë, *Shirley*, 337.

15 Eric Hobsbawm, *Uncommon People: Resistance, Rebellion and Jazz* (Abacus, 1999), 13.

16 'To All Croppers, Weavers &c & Public at Large' (March 1812), in *Writings of the Luddites*, ed. Kevin Binfield (Johns Hopkins University Press, 2004), 208.

17 'To Mr Smith Shearing Frame Holder at Hill End Yorkshire' (March 1812), in ibid., 209, 210.

18 Lord Byron, 'Debate on the Framework Bill in the House of Lords' (27 February 1812), in *The Complete Works of Lord Byron* (Galignani and Co., 1837), 811.

19 Byron, 'Song for Luddites' (1816), in ibid., 331.

20 Byron, 'Debate on the Framework Bill,' 812.

21 Friedrich Engels, *The Condition of the Working Class in England* (1845; repr., Oxford University Press, 1993), 310.

22 Ibid.

23 Ibid., xvi.

24 Dorothy Thompson, *The Dignity of Chartism* (Verso, 2015), 154.

25 Karl Marx and Friedrich Engels, 'Manifesto of the Communist Party', in *The Marx-Engels Reader*, ed. Robert C. Tucker, 2nd ed. (Norton, 1978), 483.

26 Tom Hazeldine, *The Northern Question: A History of a Divided Country* (Verso, 2020), 45.

27 Feargus O'Connor, 'Physical Force', *Northern Star*, 15 December 1838, 8.

28 Francis Maceroni, *Defensive Instructions for the People: Containing the New and Improved Combination of Arms, Foot Lancers; Miscellaneous Instructions of the Subject of Small Arms and Ammunition, Street and House Fighting, and Field Fortification* (J. Smith, 1832), 67.

29 Charles Davlin, 'Questions from the Loom' (28 July 1838), in Mike Sanders, *The Poetry of Chartism: Aesthetics, Politics, History* (Cambridge University Press, 2009), 226–8.

30 'The Sacred Month: The Crisis, the Warning', *Northern Star*, 3 August 1839, 4.

31 'To the Working Millions', *Northern Star*, 3 August 1839, 4.

32 'Where Are We? How Are We? What Do We Want? And How Do We Get It?', *Northern Star*, 25 January 1840, 4.

33 Benjamin Disraeli, *Sybil: or The Two Nations* (1845; repr., Oxford, 2017), 58–9.

34 Ibid., 60.

35 Ibid., 90.

36 Engels, *Condition of the Working Class*, 302.

37 'The People's Charter', *Northern Star*, 15 January 1848, 2.

38 'The War of Classes', *Northern Star*, 19 February 1848, 4.

39 Ibid.
40 Thompson, *Dignity of Chartism*, 165.
41 'The War of Classes', 4.
42 See Simon Rennie, *The Poetry of Ernest Jones Myth, Song, and the 'Mighty Mind'* (Legenda, 2015), 98.
43 Terry Eagleton, *The English Novel: An Introduction* (Wiley, 2013), 19.
44 Elizabeth Gaskell, *North and South* (1854; repr., Penguin, 2000), 84.
45 William Morris, 'How We Live and How We Might Live' (1885), in *How I Became a Socialist*, ed. Owen Holland (Verso, 2020), 58.
46 Ibid., 58.
47 E. Belfort Bax, Victor Dave, and William Morris, *A Short Account of the Commune of Paris* (Socialist League, 1886), 65.
48 William Morris, *News from Nowhere and Other Writings* (1890), ed. Clive Wilmer (Penguin, 2004), 155.

3 Defend the City

1   Jules Vallès, *The Insurrectionist* (1885), trans. Sandy Petrey (Prentice Hall, 1971), 96.
2   Ibid., 91.
3   Ibid., 97.
4   Peter Kropotkin, *The Conquest of Bread and Other Writings* (1892), ed. Marshall Shatz (Cambridge University Press, 1995), 19.
5   Ibid., 52.
6   David Harvey, *Rebel Cities: From the Right to the City to the Urban Revolution* (Verso, 2012), 5.
7   Prosper-Olivier Lissagaray, *History of the Paris Commune of 1871* (1876), trans. Eleanor Marx (Verso, 2012), 254.
8   Kristin Ross, *Communal Luxury: The Political Imaginary of the Paris Commune* (Verso, 2015), 56.
9   Ibid., 112.
10 Édith Thomas, *The Women Incendiaries: English Translation from the French* (Secker & Warburg, 1967), 58.
11 Victor Hugo, *Les Misérables* (1862), trans. Norman Denny (Penguin, 1982), 1054–5.
12 Louise Michel, *Red Virgin: Memoirs of Louise Michel*, trans. Bullitt Lowry and Elizabeth Ellington Gunter (University of Alabama Press, 1981), 53.
13 Victor Hugo, 'La Commune' (1871), in *Oeuvres complètes*, vol. 42 (La Librairie Ollendorff, 1913), 188. My translation.

14 Émile Zola, *The Fortune of the Rougons* (1871), trans. Brian Nelson (Oxford University Press, 2012), 293.

15 Fredric Jameson, *The Antinomies of Realism* (Verso, 2013), 114.

16 Émile Zola, *Germinal* (1885), trans. Peter Collier (Oxford University Press, 2008), 522.

17 Émile Zola, *Money* (1891), trans. Valerie Minogue (Oxford University Press, 2014), 336.

18 Émile Zola, *La Débâcle* (1892), trans. Elinor Dorday (Oxford University Press, 2017), 476.

19 Ibid.

20 Friedrich Engels, '1891 Introduction', in Karl Marx, *The Civil War in France* (1871; repr., Foreign Languages Press, 1966), 6.

21 Lissagaray, *History of the Paris Commune*, 130.

22 Walter Benjamin, *The Arcades Project*, trans. Howard Eiland and Kevin McLaughlin (1982; repr., Harvard University Press, 2002), 793.

23 Lissagaray, *History of the Paris Commune*, 130.

24 Engels, '1891 Introduction', 7.

25 Marx, *Civil War in France*, 46, 50.

26 Michel, *Red Virgin*, 64.

27 Gavin Bowd, *The Last Communard: Adrien Lejeune, the Unexpected Life of a Revolutionary* (Verso, 2012), 24.

28 Marx, *Civil War in France*, 72–3.

29 Ross, *Communal Luxury*, 100.

30 Lissagaray, *History of the Paris Commune*, 161.

31 Marx, *Civil War in France*, 24.

32 Gustave Courbet quoted in Laura Franchetti, 'When the Communards Tore Down the Vendôme', *Tribune*, 16 May 2021, tribune.co.uk.

33 Central Committee of the National Guard, 'The National Guard Opposes Prussian Entry into Paris' (1871), in *Communards: The Story of the Paris Commune of 1871, As Told by Those Who Fought For It*, ed. and trans. Mitchell Abidor (Marxist Internet Archive, 2010), 17.

34 Louis Auguste Blanqui, '7 February 1856', in *The Blanqui Reader: Political Writings, 1830–1880*, ed. Philippe Le Goff and Peter Hallward, trans. Philippe Le Goff, Peter Hallward, and Mitchell Abidor (Verso, 2018), 161.

35 Blanqui, 'Instructions for an Armed Uprising' (1868), in ibid., 228–9.

36 Blanqui, 'La Situation' (June 1876), in ibid., 163.

37 Blanqui, 'Instructions for an Armed Uprising', 204–6.

38 Ibid., 207.
39 Michel, *Red Virgin*, 47.
40 Michel, 'The Black Marseillaise' (1865), trans. Charles J. Stivale, in Stivale, 'Louise Michel's Poetry of Existence and Revolt', *Tulsa Studies in Women's Literature* 5:1 (Spring 1986), 46.
41 Michel, *Red Virgin*, 53.
42 Edith Thomas, *Louise Michel: Rebel Lives*, trans. Penelope Williams (Black Rose Books, 1980), 80.
43 Ibid., 88.
44 Michel, *Red Virgin*, 66.
45 Ibid., 125.
46 Lissagaray, *History of the Paris Commune*, 311–14.
47 Ibid., 382.
48 Ibid., 385.
49 Marx, *Civil War in France*, 20.
50 Ibid., 24–5.
51 Ibid., 67.
52 Benjamin, *The Arcades Project*, 24.
53 Walt Whitman, *Leaves of Grass: A Textual Variorum of the Printed Poems*, ed. Sculley Bradley, Harold W. Blodgett, Arthur Golden, and William White, vol. 3 (New York University Press, 1980), 632.
54 Lenin, 'In Memory of the Commune' (15 April 1911), in *Collected Works*, vol. 17 (Progress, 1974), 143.

4 School of War

1 C. L. R. James, *The Black Jacobins: Toussaint L'Ouverture and the San Domingo Revolution* (Penguin, 2001), 69, 197.
2 W. E. B. Du Bois, *Black Reconstruction in America* (Harcourt, 1935), 358.
3 Ibid., 66.
4 Ibid., 64–5.
5 Elizabeth Gaskell, *North and South* (1854; repr., Penguin, 2000), 132.
6 Émile Zola, *Germinal* (1885), trans. Peter Collier (Oxford University Press, 2008), 199.
7 Friedrich Engels, *The Condition of the Working Class in England* (1845; repr., Oxford University Press, 1993), 332.
8 Karl Marx, 'Chartism' (1853), in *Marx and Engels on the Trade Unions*, ed. Kenneth Lapides (International Publishers, 1989), 43.
9 Ibid.

10 Marx, letter to Engels (11 January 1860), in *An Unfinished Revolution: Karl Marx and Abraham Lincoln*, ed. Robin Blackburn (Verso, 2011), 189.

11 Lenin, 'On Strikes' (1899), in *Collected Works*, vol. 4 (Progress, 1974), 315.

12 Ibid., 317.

13 Giovanni Arrighi and Beverly J. Silver, *Chaos and Governance in the Modern World System* (University of Minnesota Press, 1999), 78.

14 Matthew Josephson, *The Robber Barons: The Great American Capitalists, 1861–1901* (Harcourt, 1934), 4.

15 Ibid., 80.

16 Frank Norris, *The Octopus: A California Story* (1901; repr., Penguin, 1986), 40.

17 Ibid., 18.

18 Ibid., 357.

19 Paul A. Gilje, *Rioting in America* (Indiana University Press, 1999), 3.

20 Louis Adamic, *Dynamite: The Story of Class Violence in America* (Viking Press, 1931), 26.

21 Robert Bruce *1877: Year of Violence* (Ivan R. Dee, 1987), 59.

22 Philip Sheldon Foner, *The Great Labor Uprising of 1877* (Monad, 1977), 44.

23 Robert Ovetz, *When Workers Shot Back: Class Conflict from 1877 to 1921* (Brill, 2018), 87–8.

24 Ibid., 36.

25 Adamic, *Dynamite*, 36.

26 Chris Carlsson, 'The Workingmen's Party & the Denis Kearney Agitation', *Found San Francisco* (1995), foundsf.org.

27 Du Bois, *Black Reconstruction in America*, 359.

28 United States Strike Commission, *Report on the Chicago Strike of June–July, 1894* (Government Printing Office, 1895), 143.

29 Mary Harris Jones, *Autobiography of Mother Jones* (1925), ed. Mary Field Parton (Dover, 2004), 80.

30 Ibid., 95.

31 Jack London, 'War of the Classes' (1905), in *War of the Classes, Revolution, The Shrinkage of the Planet* (Mondial, 2006), 3.

32 Jack London, *The Iron Heel* (Penguin, 2006), 64.

33 Ibid., 151–2.

34 Ibid., 157–8.

35 Ibid., 166.

36 Ibid., 10.

37 Ibid., 221n1.

38 Ibid., 233.
39 Ibid., 249.
40 Ibid., 166.
41 Lenin, 'Preface to the French and German Editions of Imperialism, the Highest Stage of Capitalism' (6 July 1920), in *Collected Works*, vol. 22 (Progress, 1974), 194.
42 Trotsky, 'Bonapartism, Fascism and War' (October 1940), in *The Writings of Leon Trotsky, 1939–20* (Pathfinder, 1974), 416.
43 Trotsky quoted in Joan London, *Jack London and His Times: An Unconventional Biography* (Doubleday, 1939), 315.
44 Trotsky in ibid., 315.

5 Towards a Red Army

1 Leon Trotsky, *The First Five Years of the Communist International* (1924; repr., Monad, 1972), 49.
2 'The Scheme for a Socialist Army' (15 January 1918), in Erich Wollenberg, *The Red Army: A Study of the Growth of Soviet Imperialism* (Martin Seeker and Warburg, 1940), 365.
3 Leon Trotsky, *Literature and Revolution* (1925), ed. William Keach, trans. Rose Strunsky (Haymarket, 2005), 30.
4 Lenin, 'Leo Tolstoy as the Mirror of the Russian Revolution' (11 September 1908), in *Collected Works*, vol. 15 (Progress, 1977), 208.
5 Leo Tolstoy, *War and Peace* (1867), trans. Louise Maude (Oxford University Press, 2010), 949.
6 Lenin, 'Tolstoy as the Mirror', 208.
7 Viktor Shklovsky, 'Art as Technique' (1917), in *Literary Theory: An Anthology*, ed. Julie Rivkin and Michael Ryan, 3rd ed. (Wiley, 2017), 11.
8 Tolstoy, *War and Peace*, 1292.
9 Lenin, 'Tolstoy as the Mirror', 208–9.
10 Lenin, 'Tolstoy and the Proletarian Struggle' (18 December 1910), in *Collected Works*, vol. 16 (Progress, 1974), 354.
11 Mikhail Tukhachevsky, 'Revolution from Without', trans. Lynette Gill, *New Left Review* 1:55 (May/June 1969), 91–2.
12 Walter Rodney, *The Russian Revolution: A View from the Third World* (Verso, 2018), 87.
13 Vladimir Mayakovsky, 'Vladimir Ilyich Lenin' (1924), in *Poems* (Progress, 1972), 193.
14 Ibid., 194.
15 Ibid., 181.
16 Ibid., 204.

17 Ibid., 215.

18 Leon Trotsky, 'The Sacred Task of the Red Army' (10 March 1920), in *How the Revolution Armed: The Military Writings and Speeches of Leon Trotsky*, vol. 3, marxists.org.

19 NLR Editors, 'Introduction to Tukhachevsky', *New Left Review* 1:55 (May/June 1969), 84.

20 Wollenberg, *The Red Army*, 145–6.

21 Victor Serge, *Memoirs of a Revolutionary* (1951), trans. Peter Sedgwick with George Paizis (NYRB, 2012), 55–6.

22 Ibid., *133*.

23 Victor Serge, *Birth of Our Power*, trans. Richard Greeman (Victor Gollancz, 1968), 22.

24 Ibid., 247–8.

25 Lenin, 'The Proletarian Revolution and the Renegade Kautsky' (1918), in *Collected Works*, vol. 28 (Progress, 1974), 284. For a different translation of this formulation, see Wollenberg, *The Red Army*, 3–4.

26 Susan Buck-Morss, 'The City as Dreamworld and Catastrophe', *October* 73 (Summer 1995), 15.

27 Louis Lozowick, 'Tatlin's Monument to the Third International', *Broom: An International Magazine of the Arts* 3:3 (October 1922), 232.

28 Viktor Shklovsky, *Knight's Move* (1923), trans. Richard Sheldon (Dalkey, 2005), 70; Lenin, 'Karl Marx (A Brief Biographical Sketch with an Exposition of Marxism) (1914), in *Collected Works*, vol. 21 (Progress, 1974), 54.

29 T. J. Clark, 'Reinstall the Footlights', *London Review of Books* 3922 (16 November 2017), lrb.co.uk.

30 Ibid.

31 Serge, *Memoirs of a Revolutionary*, 305.

32 Ibid., 266–7.

33 Tamara Deutscher, 'War and Peace in Stalin's Russia', *New Left Review* 1:163 (May/June 1987), 100.

34 Kliment Voroshilov, 'Order of the USSR Revolutionary Military Council (21 June 1929), in *Field Regulations of the Red Army, 1929* (JRS, 1929), 1.

6 Protracted Peoples' Wars

1 Lin Biao, 'Long Live the Victory of People's War! In Commemoration of the 20th Anniversary of Victory in the Chinese People's War of Resistance against Japan', *Peking Review* 36, 3 September 1965, 36.

2 Ibid., 36.

3 Mao, 'Jinggang Mountain' (1928), in *The Poems of Mao Zedong*, ed. and trans. Willis Barnstone (University of California Press, 2008), 37.

4 Mao, 'Problems of War and Strategy' (6 November 1938), in *Selected Works of Mao Tse-Tung*, vol. 2 (Foreign Languages Press, 1965), 225.

5 Mao, 'Problems of Strategy in China's Revolutionary War' (December 1936), in *Selected Works of Mao Tse-tung*, vol. 1 (Foreign Languages Press, 1965), 180.

6 Mao, 'Report on an Investigation of the Peasant Movement in Hunan' (March 1927), in ibid., 28.

7 Edgar Snow, *Red Star over China: The Classic Account of the Birth of Chinese Communism* (Grove, 1968), 133–4.

8 Mao, 'Analysis of the Classes in Chinese Society' (March 1926), in *Selected Works*, vol. 1, 13.

9 Ibid., 19.

10 Ibid., 13.

11 Ibid., 19.

12 Mao, 'Report on an Investigation of the Peasant Movement', 23–4.

13 Mao, 'A Single Spark Can Start a Prairie Fire' (5 January 1930), in *Selected Works*, vol. 1, 122.

14 Chou Li-po, *The Hurricane*, trans. Hsu Meng-Hsiung (Foreign Language Press, 1955), viii.

15 Ibid., 141.

16 Mao, 'A Single Spark Can Start a Prairie Fire', 117.

17 Ibid., 118.

18 Ibid., 125.

19 Ting Ling, 'Sun over the Sangkan River', *Chinese Literature* 1 (Spring 1953), 54.

20 Ibid., 55.

21 Ibid., 55, 58.

22 'Extracts from the Resolution of the Ninth ECCI Plenum on the Chinese Question' (25 February 1928), in *The Communist International, 1919–1943 Documents*, ed. Jane Degras, vol. 2, *1923–1928* (Routledge, 1971), 439.

23 Rebecca E. Karl, *China's Revolutions in the Modern World: A Brief Interpretive History* (Verso, 2020), 98.

24 Ibid., 99.

25 Chen Yi, 'Climbing Dayu Mountain' (Autumn 1935), in *Poets of the Chinese Revolution*, ed. Gregor Benton and Feng Chongyi, trans. Gregor Benton (Verso, 2019), 211.

26 Chen Yi, 'Bivouacking' (Spring 1935), in ibid., 212.
27 Mao, 'On Contradiction' (August 1937), in *Selected Works*, vol. 1, 331–2.
28 Mao, 'On Tactics against Japanese Imperialism' (27 December 1935), in ibid., 153.
29 Mao, 'Why Is It That Red Political Power Can Exist in China?' (5 October 1928), in ibid.
30 Mao, 'Tactics against Japanese Imperialism', 155.
31 Ibid., 168.
32 Ibid., 170.
33 Mao, 'On Protracted War' (May 1938), in *Selected Works*, vol. 2, 114–15.
34 Ibid., 143.
35 Ibid., 186.
36 Mao, 'The People's Liberation Army Captures Nanjing' (April 1949), in *Poets of the Chinese Revolution*, 249.
37 C. L. R. James, *The Black Jacobins: Toussaint L'Ouverture and the San Domingo Revolution* (Penguin, 2001), 62.
38 Lin Biao, 'Long Live the Victory of People's War!', 36.
39 Lin Biao quoted in Alexander C. Cook, 'Introduction: The Spiritual Atom Bomb and Its Global Fallout', in *Mao's Little Red Book: A Global History*, ed. Alexander C. Cook (Cambridge University Press, 2014), 10.
40 Bobby Seale, *Seize the Time: The Story of the Black Panther Party and Huey P. Newton* (Black Classics Press, 1991), 82.

7 For Complete Disorder

1 Frantz Fanon, 'This Africa to Come' (Summer 1960), in *Toward the African Revolution: Political Essays*, trans. Haakon Chevalier (Grove Press, 1988), 180.
2 Ibid., 180–1.
3 Ibid., 181.
4 Ibid.
5 Mao, 'U.S. Imperialism Is a Paper Tiger' (14 July 1956), in *Selected Works of Mao Tse-tung*, vol. 5 (Foreign Languages Press, 1965), 311.
6 Lenin, 'Imperialism, the Highest Stage of Capitalism' (1917), in *Collected Works*, vol. 22 (Progress, 1974), 266.
7 Walter Rodney, *How Europe Underdeveloped Africa* (1972; repr., Verso, 2018), 27.
8 Ibid., 260.
9 Ibid., 61.

10 This reference to allegory is different to Fredric Jameson's well-known and controversial argument that, in third-world texts, 'the story of the private individual destiny is always an allegory of the embattled situation of the public third-world culture and society'. By contrast, my argument is peculiar to the literature of social antagonism, makes no claim on universalism or necessity, and instead wants to observe that decolonial action and its literatures, however local, tend to take on a more expansive dimension through material relationships to nation, continent, and the world-system. These relationships can be pre-existing and mediated, such as the economic domination of parts of Africa by parts of Europe as documented by Rodney, but also forward reaching and aspirational, such as this or that revolutionary's attempt to rally the people around an idea of nation or continent, as in Fanon's thinking of Algiers and Africa. See Fredric Jameson, 'Third-World Literature in the Era of Multinational Capitalism', *Social Text* 15 (Autumn 1986), 65–88; but also see, for a useful summary of the controversy, and especially of Aijaz Ahmad's rebuttal to Jameson published in the next issue of *Social Text*, Neil Lazarus, *The Postcolonial Unconscious* (Cambridge University Press, 2011), 89–113. Jameson has returned to this debate, publishing a long commentary in *Allegory and Ideology* (Verso, 2020), 187–216.

11 Frantz Fanon, *The Wretched of the Earth*, trans. Constance Farrington (Grove Press, 1963), 132.

12 Geo Maher, *Decolonizing Dialectics* (Duke University Press, 2017), 90.

13 Thomas Sankara, 'Who Are the Enemies of the People?' (26 March 1983), in *Thomas Sankara Speaks: The Burkina Faso Revolution, 1983–1987*, ed. Michael Prairie (Pathfinder Press, 2007), 52.

14 Ibid., 53.

15 Ibid., 52.

16 Ibid., 55.

17 Frantz Fanon, 'Letter to the Resident Minister' (December 1956), in *The Psychiatric Writings from Alienation and Freedom*, ed. Jean Khalfa and Robert J. C. Young, trans. Steven Corcoran (Bloomsbury, 2020), 285–7.

18 Fanon, 'West Indians and Africans' (1955), in *Toward the African Revolution*, 20.

19 Fanon, 'Disappointments and Illusions of French Colonialism', in ibid., 57.

20 Kwame Nkrumah, *Class Struggle in Africa* (International Publishers, 1970), 14.

21 Amilcar Cabral, 'National Liberation and Culture', in *Return to the Source: Selected Speeches of Amilcar Cabral*, ed. Africa Information Service (New York Review Press, 1973), 55.

22 Ibid., 54.

23 Ibid., 55.

24 Jennifer E. Sessions, *By Sword and Plow: France and the Conquest of Algeria* (Cornell University Press, 2017), 3.

25 'Proclamation of the FLN, 1 November 1954', in *Colonial Rule in Africa: Readings from Primary Sources*, ed. Bruce Fetter (University of Wisconsin Press, 1979), 204.

26 Elaine Mokhtefi, *Algiers, Third World Capital: Freedom Fighters, Revolutionaries, Black Panthers* (Verso, 2018), 21.

27 Jean Lartéguy, *The Centurions*, trans. Xen Fielding (Penguin, 1961), xvii.

28 Ibid., 452.

29 Ibid., 514–15.

30 Ibid., 305–6.

31 Zohra Drif, *Inside the Battle of Algiers: Memoir of a Woman Freedom Fighter*, trans. Andrew Farrand (Just World Books, 2017), 128.

32 Ibid., 104.

33 Ibid., 110.

34 Ibid., 116.

35 Ibid., 122.

36 Ibid., 127–8.

37 Ibid., 128.

38 Leon Trotsky, 'Why Marxists Oppose Individual Terrorism', *Der Kampf*, November 1911, marxists.org.

39 Achille Mbembe, *Necropolitics* (Duke University Press, 2019), 33.

40 Ibid., 34.

41 Fanon, *Wretched of the Earth*, 36.

42 Ibid., 61.

43 Ibid., 38.

44 Ibid., 37.

45 Ibid., 41.

46 Ibid., 36.

47 Ibid., 93.

48 James Ngugi, *A Grain of Wheat* (Heinemann, 1967), 13.

49 Caroline Elkins, *Britain's Gulag: The Brutal End of Empire in Kenya* (Pimlico, 2005), 25.

50 Ngugi, *A Grain of Wheat*, 218.

51 Ibid., 110.
52 Fanon, *Wretched of the Earth*, 36–7.
53 Ibid., 42–3.
54 Ibid., 93–4.
55 Ibid., 85.
56 Ibid., 135.
57 Che Guevara, *Congo Diary: Episodes of the Revolutionary War in the Congo*, ed. Che Guevara Studies Center (Seven Stories Press, 2022), 237.

8 The Armed Nucleus

1 José Martí, 'Letter to Manuel Mercado' (18 May 1895), in *Selected Writings*, trans. Esther Allen (Penguin, 2002), 349.
2 Fidel Castro, 'Castro Announces the Revolution' (9 January 1959), in *The Cuba Reader: History, Culture, Politics*, ed. Aviva Chomsky, Barry Carr, Pamela Maria Smorkaloff, and Robin Kirk (Duke University Press, 2003), 342.
3 Richard Gott, *Guerrilla Movements in Latin America* (Doubleday, 1971), 31.
4 Karl Marx, 'Revolutionary Spain', *New-York Daily Tribune*, 30 October 1854.
5 Gott, *Guerrilla Movements*, 29.
6 Ibid., 13.
7 Fidel Castro, 'First Declaration of Havana' (1960), in *The Declarations of Havana* (Verso, 2018), 85.
8 Gabriel García Márquez, *One Hundred Years of Solitude* (1967), trans. Gregory Rabassa (Penguin, 1970), 1.
9 Ibid., 106.
10 Ibid., 98–9.
11 Ibid., 106.
12 Ibid., 133.
13 Fredric Jameson, 'No Magic, No Metaphor', *London Review of Books* 39:12, 15 June 2017.
14 Norberto Fuentes, *The Autobiography of Fidel Castro*, trans. Anna Kushner (Norton, 2010), xv.
15 Ernesto Che Guevara, *Guerrilla Warfare* (1961; repr., BN Publishing, 2007), 8.
16 Michael Löwy, *The Marxism of Che Guevara: Philosophy, Economics, Revolutionary Warfare* (Rowman and Littlefield, 1973), xvii.
17 Guevara, *Guerrilla Warfare*, 7.
18 Ibid., 9.

19 Guevara, 'The Role of a Marxist-Leninist Party' (1963), in *Selected Works of Ernest Guevara*, ed. Rolando Bonachea and Nelson Valdes (MIT Press, 1969), 107.

20 Guevara, *Guerrilla Warfare*, 36.

21 Ibid., 10.

22 Ibid., 32.

23 Ibid., 32–3.

24 Löwy, *The Marxism of Che Guevara*, 89–90.

25 Guevara, *Guerrilla Warfare*, 104–5.

26 Blackburn quoted in Régis Debray, *Strategy for Revolution: Essays on Latin America* (Jonathan Cape, 1970), 7.

27 Sartre quoted in Debray, Régis Debray, *Revolution in the Revolution? Armed Struggle and Political Struggle in Latin America* (1967), trans. Bobbye Ortiz (Verso, 2017), 11.

28 Ibid., 15.

29 Ibid., 20.

30 Ibid., 24–5.

31 Ibid., 26.

32 Ibid., 29.

33 Ibid., 45.

34 Ibid., 38.

35 Ibid., 35.

36 Ibid., 85.

37 Ibid.

38 Ibid., 107–9.

39 Ibid., 110.

40 Ibid., 111.

41 Ibid., 67, 75.

42 Mike Davis, *Planet of Slums* (Verso, 2006), 59.

43 Ibid., 108.

44 Carlos Marighella, 'Declaration by the ALN October Revolutionary Group' (September 1969), in *For the Liberation of Brazil*, trans. John Butt and Rosemary Sheed (Penguin, 1971), 25.

45 Marighella, *Mini-manual of the Urban Guerrilla* (1969; repr., Abraham Guillen Press, 2002), 3.

46 Ibid., 4.

47 Ibid., 36–7.

48 Ibid., 37.

49 Ibid., 7.

50 Ibid.

51 'Final Schleyer Communiqué' (19 October 1977), in *The Red Army Faction: A Documentary History*, vol. 1, *Projectiles for the People*, trans. André Moncourt and J. Smith (PM Press, 2009), 507.

52 'The Urban Guerrilla Concept' (1971), in ibid., 97–8.

53 Ibid.

54 Stephen Aust, *Baader-Meinhof: The Inside Story of the R.A.F.* (Oxford University Press, 2009), 36. This escalationist phrasing – delivered in a speech during a teach-in, in 1968, at the Technical University in Berlin – would inform Meinhof's widely circulated article, 'From Protest to Resistance', published around the same time and republished in Ulrike Meinhof, *Everybody Talks about the Weather ... We Don't: The Writings of Ulrike Meinhof*, ed. Karen Bauer (Seven Stories Press, 2008).

9 Fighting after Fascism

1 Antonio Gramsci, 'Neither Fascism nor Liberalism: Sovietism!', *L'Unità*, 7 October 1924.

2 Editors' introduction to Gramsci, *Selections from the Prison Notebooks of Antonio Gramsci*, ed. and trans. Quintin Hoare and Geoffrey Nowell Smith (International, 1971), lxxxix.

3 Ibid., xcii.

4 Perry Anderson, *The Antinomies of Antonio Gramsci* (Verso, 2020), 34.

5 Gramsci, 'To the Section Commissars of the Fiat-Brevetti Workshops', *L'Ordine Nuovo*, 13 September 1919.

6 Gramsci, *Selections from the Prison Notebooks*, 207.

7 For a clear-eyed discussion of this phrase and its relationship to Gramsci and Dutschke, as well as to Mao, see Boris Buden, 'To Make the Long March Short: A Short Commentary on the Two Long Marches that Have Failed Their Emancipatory Promises', *Crisis & Critique* 5:2 (2018), 128–41.

8 Gramsci, *Selections from the Prison Notebooks*, 229.

9 Ibid., 229–30.

10 Ibid., 235.

11 Leon Trotsky, 'On the Causes for the Defeat of the Spanish Revolution', *Socialist Appeal* 3:17 (21 March 1939).

12 Georgi Dimitrov, 'Working Class Unity – Bulwark against Fascism, Speech to the Seventh World Congress of the Communist International, Moscow, August 13, 1935', in *The US Antifascism Reader*, ed. Bill V. Mullen and Christopher Vials (Verso, 2020), 56–8.

13 Theodor W. Adorno, 'The Meaning of Working Through the Past' (1959), in *Critical Models: Interventions and Catchwords*, trans. H. W. Pickford (Columbia University Press, 1998), 98–9.

14 Ernest Mandel, *The Meaning of the Second World War* (Verso, 1986), 133.

15 Steve Wright, *Storming Heaven: Class Composition and Struggle in Italian Autonomist Marxism* (Pluto Press, 2002), 7.

16 Ibid., 35.

17 Nanni Balestrini and Primo Moroni, *The Golden Horde: Revolutionary Italy, 1960–1977*, trans. Richard Braude (Seagull Books, 2021), 412.

18 Wright, *Storming Heaven*, 6.

19 Antonio Negri and Anne Dufourmantelle, *Negri on Negri: In Conversation with Anne Dufourmentelle*, trans. M. B. DeBevoise (Routledge, 2004), 34–5.

20 Ibid., 35–6.

21 Nanni Balestrini, *We Want Everything: The Novel of Italy's Hot Autumn* (1971), trans. Matt Holden, intro. Rachel Kushner (Verso, 2016), 171.

22 Ibid., 131.

23 Ibid., 172.

24 Kushner, introduction to *We Want Everything*, xi.

25 Ibid., xvi.

26 Balestrini and Moroni, *The Golden Horde*, 446.

27 Franco 'Bifo' Berardi, 'RADIOACTIVITY #1 Radio Alice', *Ràdio Web MACBA*, rwm.macba.cat.

28 Balestrini and Moroni, *The Golden Horde*, 453–4.

29 Alfredo Bandelli, 'The Ballad of Fiat" (1970), in Balestrini and Moroni, *The Golden Horde*, 453–4.

30 Balestrini and Moroni, *The Golden Horde*, 445.

31 Fiora Pirri and Lanfranco Caminiti, 'Diritto alla Guerra (1981), in Balestrini and Moroni, *The Golden Horde*, 573.

32 Negri, 'Workers' Party against Work' (1973), in *Books for Burning: Between Civil War and Democracy in 1970s Italy*, ed. Timothy S. Murphy, trans. Arianna Bove, Ed Emery, Timothy S. Murphy, and Francesca Novello (Verso, 2005), 113.

33 Mario Tronti, *Workers and Capital*, trans. David Broder (Verso, 2019), 21-22.

34 Ibid., xvii.

35 Negri, 'Workers' Party against Work', 87–8.

36 Negri, 'Crisis of the Planner-State: Communism and Revolutionary Organization' (1971), in *Books for Burning*, 26.

37 Mariarosa Dalla Costa, 'Women and the Subversion of the Community' (1972), in *Women and the Subversion of the Community: A Mariarosa Dalla Costa Reader*, ed. Camille Barbagallo (PM Press, 2019), 39.

38 Collettivo Politico Metropolitano, 'Lotta sociale e organizzazione nella metropoli' (1970), in Balestrini and Moroni, *The Golden Horde*, 406.

39 Balestrini and Moroni, *The Golden Horde*, 425.

40 Ibid., 411.

41 Wright, *Storming Heaven*, 151.

42 Henry Tanner, 'Terrorists in Italy Say Morro Will Die," *New York Times*, 16 April 1978, 1.

43 Nanni Balestrini, *The Unseen* (1987), trans. Liz Heron (Verso, 2011), 133.

44 Ibid., 19.

45 Ibid., 123.

46 Kushner, introduction to *We Want Everything*, xv.

47 Carla Lonzi, 'Manifesto di Rivolta femminile' (1970), in Balestrini and Moroni, *The Golden Horde*, 483.

48 Elena Ferrante, *Those Who Leave and Those Who Stay*, trans. Ann Goldstein (Europa, 2014), 63.

49 Ibid., 314.

50 Guevara, 'Message to the Tricontinental' (April 1967), in *Selected Works of Ernest Guevara*, ed. Rolando Bonachea and Nelson Valdes (MIT Press, 1969), 182.

51 Dalla Costa, 'Women and the Subversion of the Community', 35.

52 Ibid., 36.

10 Army of the Wronged

1 W. E. B. Du Bois, *In Battle for Peace: The Story of My 83rd Birthday* (1952; repr., Oxford University Press, 2007), 34.

2 Ibid., 74.

3 Ibid., 106.

4 Cedric J. Robinson, *Black Marxism: The Making of the Black Radical Tradition* (University of North Carolina Press, 1983), xxx–xxxi.

5 Ibid.

6 Angela Y. Davis, 'Political Prisoners, Prisons, and Black Liberation' (May 1971), in *If They Come in the Morning: Voices of Resistance*, ed. Angela Y. Davis (Verso, 2016), 34.

7 Ibid., 35–6.

8 Ibid., 34.

9 Ibid., 41.

10 Fred Hampton, 'It's a Class Struggle, Godamnit!', speech delivered at Northern Illinois University, November 1969, marxists. org.

11 Bobby Seale, *Seize the Time: The Story of the Black Panther Party and Huey P. Newton* (Black Classics Press, 1991), 83.

12 Mumia Abu-Jamal, *We Want Freedom: A Life in the Black Panther Party* (South End Press, 2004), 118. This ubiquitous statement first appeared on 15 June 1969, when it ran as part of a United Press International story reproduced in multiple regional newspapers and on *CBS Evening News*. It then reappeared in the *Wall Street Journal* on 29 August 1969. For a detailed account of the attribution and promotion of Hoover's statement, see Waldo E. Martin and Joshua Bloom, *Black against Empire: The History and Politics of the Black Panther Party* (University of California Press, 2013), 244n45.

13 Max Elbaum, *Revolution in the Air: Sixties Radicals Turn to Lenin, Mao and Che* (2002; repr., Verso, 2018), 67.

14 Ibid., 69.

15 Stuart Hall, 'Race, Articulation, and Societies Structured in Dominance' (1980), in *Essential Essays*, vol. 1, ed. David Morley (Duke University Press, 2018), 216.

16 James Baldwin, *Notes of a Native Son* (1955; repr., Beacon Press, 2012), 7.

17 Fred Moten, *In the Break: The Aesthetics of the Black Radical Tradition* (University of Minnesota Press, 2003), 24.

18 Frederick Douglass, *Narrative of the Life of Frederick Douglass, An American Slave, Written By Himself* (1845), ed. William L. Andrews and William S. McFeely (Norton, 1997), 33.

19 Moten, *In the Break*, 24.

20 Angela Davis, *An Autobiography* (International, 1974), xvi.

21 Ruth Wilson Gilmore, *Abolition Geography: Essays Towards Liberation* (Verso, 2022), 471.

22 Huey P. Newton, *Revolutionary Suicide* (1973; repr., Penguin, 2009), 55.

23 Ibid., 116.

24 Ibid., 117.

25 Ibid., 3.

26 Huey P. Newton, 'In Defense of Self-Defense', *The Black Panther* 2, 16 November 1968, 12.

27 Newton, *Revolutionary Suicide*, 175.

28 Ibid., 176.

29 Ibid., 359.

30 Ibid., 355.

31 Ibid.

32 Assata Shakur, *Assata: An Autobiography* (1987; repr., Zed Books, 2001), 231.

33 Ibid., 180.
34 Ibid., 241.
35 Ibid., 49–50.
36 Ibid., 50–2.
37 Ibid., 50.
38 Ibid., 52.
39 Ibid., 183.
40 Ibid., 190.
41 Ibid., 64–5.
42 Ibid., 190.
43 Ibid., 190.
44 C. L. R. James, *The Black Jacobins: Toussaint L'Ouverture and the San Domingo Revolution* (1967; repr., Penguin, 2001), 230.
45 Shakur, *Assata*, 197.
46 Ibid., 243.
47 Ibid., 235–6.
48 Ibid., 10.
49 Ibid., 242.
50 Ibid., 243.
51 Ibid., 242.
52 Ibid., 169.
53 Cedric Johnson, *The Panthers Can't Save Us Now: Debating Left Politics and Black Lives Matter* (Verso, 2022), ix–x, 141.
54 Nikhil Pal Singh, 'Race and America's Long War: An Interview with Nikhil Pal Singh', *Salvage*, 11 March 2020, salvage.zone.
55 Asad Haider, *Mistaken Identity: Mass Movements and Racial Ideology* (Verso, 2022), 30.
56 In Gilmore's *Abolition Geography*, this phrase appears and reappears, with only slight variation, on pages 290, 451, and 479.

Postscript: No War But Class War

1 Susan Watkins, 'An Avoidable War?', *New Left Review* 133/34 (January/April 2022), 6.
2 Tony Wood, 'Matrix of War', *New Left Review* 133/34 (January/April 2022), 64.
3 Wolfgang Streek, 'Return of the King', *Sidecar*, 4 May 2022.
4 Andrew, 'Letters from Ukraine Pt 1', *Endnotes*, 18 March 2022.
5 Wood, 'Matrix of War', 64.
6 Luxemburg, 'The Junius Pamphlet', 209.
7 Joshua Clover and Juliana Spahr, *#Misanthropocene: 24 Theses* (Commune Editions, 2014), 8.

8 Walter Benjamin, *Selected Writings: 1931–1934*, ed. Michael W. Jennings, Howard Eiland, and Gary Smith, trans. Rodney Livingstone et al. (Harvard University Press, 1999), 426.

9 Enzo Traverso, *Left-Wing Melancholia: Marxism, History, and Memory* (Columbia University Press, 2016), 9.

10 Enzo Traverso, *Revolution: An Intellectual History* (Verso, 2021), 29. The brief survey of mass movements reproduced here is a condensation of Traverso's more expansive catalogue.

11 Ibid.

12 Marx, 'The Eighteenth Brumaire of Louis Bonaparte', in *The Marx-Engels Reader*, ed. Robert C. Tucker, 2nd ed. (Norton, 1978), 597.

Index

A Grain of Wheat (Ngũgĩ. wa Thiong'o) 168–9
A Manual for Manuel (Cortázar) 179
Ação Libertadora Nacional 190–1
Adamic, Louis 96–7, 98–9
Adorno, Theodor W. 200
Africa 150–71, 189, 234, 235
   Algerian War of Independence 16, 150–1, 157–8, 159–65, 167
   background 151–4
   class in 155
   class solidarity 156–7
   colonial oppression 151, 161–2
   cultivation of solidarities 150–1
   decolonial insurgency 162–5
   exploitation 153–4
   Fanon on 165–7
   imperial rule 157–8
   lived experience 163
   local context 154–7
   organizational challenge 155
   regional contexts 169–71
   and solidarity 167–71
   underdevelopment 153
Agamben, Giorgio 252n17

Algerian Civil War
Algerian National Liberation Front 157, 159–65
Algerian War of Independence 16, 150–1, 157–8, 159–65, 167
Algiers, battle for 154–5
Allen, Jim 244
Allende, Salvador 106, 175–6, 207
Althusser, Louis 185
American Civil War 88–90, 93
Anderson, Perry 197
Andrew from Kharkiv 243
antagonism 14, 14–18
   class 49, 57-8, 78
   revolutionary 47, 247-8
   social 89–90, 111, 116, 159, 173, 198
anti-fascism 196–201, 202, 245
armed struggle, as development 159
armies, and class 112. *See also* Red Army
army, the 16–18
Arrighi, Giovanni 93
austerity 9
autonomia movement 205–17, 223
   factionalization 214
   feminist 214–17

Mirafiori strikes 206–8
repression of militants
212–14
autonomist feminism 214–17
avant-garde art 122–4

Bakunin, Mikhail 105
Baldwin, James 224
Balestrini, Nanni 201, 206
The Unseen 212–14
We Want Everything 203–5,
212
Balibar, Étienne 7
'Ballad of Fiat' (Bandelli)
206–8
Bandelli, Alfredo, 'Ballad of Fiat'
206–8
Barbados 43
Barcelona uprising, 1917 118
barricades 69
Batista, Fulgencio 172
Bayo, Alberto 173
Beijing 128
Benjamin, Walter 86, 246–7
Berardi, Franco 'Bifo' 15
Bergeaud, Émeric, Stella 26
Beverly Hills, Milken Institute
conference 1
The Birth of Our Power (Serge)
119–22, 124–5
Black Liberation Army 194,
224, 231–7, 239
Black Lives Matter movement
237–40, 247
Black Panthers 148–9, 222–4,
226–30, 230–1, 237, 239
Black Radical Tradition 220
Black radicalism 245
and capitalism 220
class solidarity 236–7
defensive warfare 226–7
lived experience 224
and oppression 234

radicalizing force of literature
224–6, 226–7
revolutionary militancy 220,
220–4
Shakur's revolutionary
program 231–3
slave narrative genre 225
Black Reconstruction in
America (Du Bois) 218
black square (Malevich) 123–4
Blackburn, Robin 33, 34, 185
Blakeley, Grace 3
Blanqui, Louis Auguste 79–82,
245
Instructions for an Armed
Uprising 80–2
Boggs, James and Grace Lee
15–16
Bolivia 187
Bonaparte, Louis 77
Brazil 190–3
bread, as a symbol for freedom
67–8
Brecht, Bertolt 5–6
Brontë, Charlotte 73
Shirley 50
Buck-Morss, Susan 30, 123
Buenos Aires, Nordelta 4–5
Bug-Jargal, Hugo 38–9
Burkina Faso 155–7
The Burning of Cap (Périn) 27
Byron, Lord, 'Song for Luddites'
53–4

Cabral, Amílcar 158–9, 189
Caminiti, Lanfranco 207
Cape Verde 159
Capital (Marx) 13–14, 54
capitalism 6–7, 41
American 92–5
imperial phase 152
and race 220
racial 233, 240

revolutionary dialectic 55
war against 41–4
and warfare 63–4
Capitalism and Slavery
(Williams) 42
Carlsson, Chris 99
Carteau, Felix 26
Cassou, Jean 75–6
Castro, Fidel 172–4, 176, 177,
179–80, 186, 202
The Centurions (Lartéguy)
161–2, 165
Césaire, Aimé 31
Charles I, King 22, 23
Chartism 55–64
aim 62
and condition of England
novels 62–5
general strike 57–8
logic of redress 56
and the use of force 56–7
chauvinism 106
Chen Yi 140–2
Chiang Kai-shek 129
Chibber, Vivek 253n33
Chile 2, 106, 207, 247
Chinese Communist Party
129
Chinese Red Army 130, 137,
139, 140, 143
Chinese Revolution 128–49,
151–3, 189, 245
assault on cities 139–40
Autumn Harvest Uprising
129
capture of Beijing 128
class composition 142
class militancy 134
conception of war 131–3
decolonial warfare and class
struggle 143–5
emphasis on land 130–1,
141–2

foundation of People's
Republic of China 148
the Long March 140–2
Mao Zedong Thought 148–9
Mao's descriptions of
revolution 134–5
metaphors 135–6
'On Contradiction' (Mao
Zedong) 142–5
peasant movement 134
People's Liberation Army
144, 147
principal strategies 130–1
protracted people's war 145,
145–7
red classics 132–3
reprisals 140
strategy 136–8
transitional period 140
Christophe, Henri 25–6, 29,
32–3
Cienfuegos, Camilo 173
civil society, and the State 198
civil war 7, 12, 15, 16–17, 165,
252n17
Clark, T. J. 123–4
class
common interest 12–13
definition 9–11, 11–14, 18
Marx on 13–14
military threat of 47
and race. *see* Black radicalism
and sex 10
Trotsky on 117–18
understanding 247–8
and war 108–12, 118–22,
131–3
class antagonism 49, 57–8, 78
class autonomy 205
class belonging 100, 104–5
class composition 142, 209
class consciousness 8–9, 28,
34–5, 116–17, 121

class formation 11, 14, 36,
    182–3
class hierarchies, demolition of
    47
class mobilization 113, 173
class relations 59–60, 151–2
class solidarity 22, 33, 47, 78–9,
    81, 83, 87, 106, 111, 116,
    133, 156, 182–3, 189,
    191–3, 206, 213, 214,
    236–7
class structure 11, 14
class struggle 6–7, 8, 12, 180
    and decolonial warfare
    143–5
class war, understanding 5–9,
    243–50
class warfare 2
    first recorded utterance of
    term 58–9
class-based militarism 114–18
classless society 8, 69–70
Cleaver, Eldridge 223
climate change 4–5, 249
Clover, Joshua 9, 246,
    252–3n25
Cold War 175, 179
collective beings 26
collective consciousness 15
collective identity 37–9,
    231–2
collective labour 68
collective opposition, language
    of 27–8
Colombia 2, 187
colonial imaginary, the 26
colonialism 153–4, 166
Combination Act of 1799 55
Combinations of Workmen Act
    of 1825 55
common cause 47, 79, 136–7,
    170
common interests 12–13, 80–1

commonality 33, 136, 188, 248
    weaponized 38
communism 65, 77
condition of England novels
    62–5
conflagration 25–8
constructivism 122–4, 126
Cortázar, Julio, *A Manual for
    Manuel* 179
counterinsurgency 161–2
Courbet, Gustave 78–9
COVID-19 pandemic 2–4
crime 221
Cromwell, Oliver 22–3
Cuba 148
Cuban Missile Crisis 179
Cuban Revolution 179, 180,
    185, 189
    guerrilla warfare 172–4
    lessons 175–6
cultural identity 37–9, 248
culture, weaponized 34–6
Cuomo, Andrew 3

Dalla Costa, Mariarosa 209–10,
    216–17
Danton, George Jacques 32, 40
Daut, Marlene L. 27
Davis, Angela 220–2, 223, 225–6
Davis, Mike 13
    Planet of Slums 190
Davlin, Charles, 'Questions of
    the Loom' 57
Days of Hope (TV series) 244
de Saint-Simon, Henri 23–4
Dean, Jodi 4
The Debacle (Zola) 73–4
Debray, Régis 15, 180, 189–90,
    192
    *Revolution in the Revolution?
    Armed Struggle and
    Political Struggle in Latin
    America* 185–9

Debs, Eugene 100
Declaration of the Rights of
    Man 31
decolonial warfare 41–2,
    150–71
  background 151–4
  class solidarity 156–7
  and class struggle 143–5
  cultivation of solidarities
    150–1
  Fanon on 165–7
  nation building 155–7
  regional contexts 169–71
  social dynamics 157–9
  and solidarity 167–71
  the enemy 151
decolonization 14, 16, 21,
    165–7, 235
deep warfare 159
*Defensive Instructions to the
    People* (Maceroni) 56–7
defensive protection 222
defensive warfare 187–8,
    226–7
Delescluze, Louis Charles 84
democracy 62
Dessalines, Jean-Jacques 25,
    28–9, 29, 32–3, 38, 41
Deutscher, Tamara 126
development, armed struggle as
    159
Dickens, Charles 73
dictatorship of the proletariat
    146
dictatorships 175
Diderot, Denis 31–2
Diggers, the 22–3
Dimitrov, Georgi 199–200
Ding Ling, *Sun over the Sangkan
    River* 138–9
Discourse on Inequality,
    (Rousseau) 30
dispossession 59, 110

Disraeli, Benjamin 73
  Sybil: or The Two Nations
    59–60
Dmitrieff, Elisabeth 69
domination 155, 165
Douglass, Frederick 225–6,
    226–7, 228
Drif, Zohra 162–4
Du Bois, W. E. B. 88–90, 99,
    106, 218–20, 220, 221–2
  *Black Reconstruction in
    America* 218
Dutschke, Rudi 198, 200

Eagleton, Terry 62
Einstein, Albert 219
Elbaum, Max 223–4
Elbrick, Charles 190
Elkins, Caroline 168
Endnotes collective 10
Engels, Friedrich 6–7, 8, 9, 15,
    22, 41, 54, 55, 60, 76, 77,
    85–6, 91, 103, 105, 165
English Civil War, 1640–60
    22–3, 144, 188
Enlightenment ideals 31
equality 65
escalation 9
Euro-American perspective 21
Europe 15
European Union, COVID-19
    pandemic 3
exclusion 214–17
exploitation 10, 11–12, 155,
    209–10, 217

Fanon, Frantz 16, 19, 150–1,
    153, 154–5, 157–8, 170,
    173, 229, 234, 245
  The Wretched of the Earth
    165, 165–7
fascism 105–6, 199–200, 201,
    202

FBI 218, 223
Federici, Silvia 18
feminist autonomia movement
  214–17
Ferrante, Elena 215–16
15-M 247
Fildes, Ann 46
First Industrial Revolution 21,
  49, 245
Fisher, Mark 9
force, object of 61–2
Frame Breaking Act of 1812 53
France 114
  Algerian War of Independence
    159–65. see National
    Liberation Front (FLN)
  gilets jaunes 1, 247
  Second Empire 21, 67, 72,
    76–7, 245
  see also French Revolution;
    Paris Commune
Franco-Prussian War 73–4,
  75–6, 86
freedom 29, 30–1, 106
French Revolution 22, 23–4,
  40, 42, 53, 144, 160, 188,
  255–6n15
  revolutionary ideals 30, 31
  revolutionary slogans 36, 37
  slogans 31–2
  the Terror 32
French-Indochina War 160

Gaillard, Napoléon 69
Gallic Wars, 50 BC 27
Gaskell, Elizabeth 73
  North and South 63, 90
gendered exclusions 214–17
gendered labour 209–10, 215
General Council of the
    International Working-
    Men's Association 78
genocide 243

George Floyd, murder of
  239–40
Germinal (Zola) 73, 90–1
Gezi Park protests, Istanbul 247
gilets jaunes 1, 247
Gilje, Paul A. 96
Gilmore, Ruth Wilson 10, 226,
  240
global underclass 248–9
Gold Coast 158
Gopal, Priyamvada 41
Gorky, Maxim, Mother 5–6
Gott, Richard 173
Gramsci, Antonio 196–9, 202,
  203, 208, 216
Grossman, Vasily, Life and Fate
  125–6
group identities 15
Gruppi di Azione Partigiana
  210
guerrilla warfare 21, 56–7,
  169–71, 172–95, 216
  affirmative measures 181
  asymmetry 182
  belligerent forces 181–2
  civilian/combatant
    cooperation 183–4
  class formation 182–3
  class solidarity 182–3, 191–3
  Cuban Revolution 172–4
  Debray on 185–9
  field manuals 179–80,
    180–93
  Guevara on 180–5
  and land rights 183
  Latin America 175–6, 180–93
  literary culture 176–80
  Marx on 174–5
  origins 174–5
  popular support 182
  social character 193
  spread of 194–5
  task 181

tactics 146
urban 189–93, 194–5
Guevara, Ernesto Che 20, 159,
    170–1, 173, 180, 185, 187,
    188, 189, 192, 195, 216,
    235, 245
field manual 180–5
Guinea-Bissau 158–9
Guyana 43

Haider, Asad 239
Haiti and the Haitian
    Revolution 2, 16, 24,
    25–44, 47, 88, 89–90,
    147, 159–60, 228, 234–5,
    245
affinities with revolutionary
    France 29–31
burning of Cap-Français
    25–8
casualties 34
class consciousness 34–5
class solidarity 33
class war 41–4
egalitarian principles 31–3
impact 43–4
intimations of the coming
    catastrophe 34
massacre of remaining white
    occupiers 28–9
racialized caste system 33–4
revolutionary class 27, 41
revolutionary ideals 29–31,
    32–3
revolutionary slogans 36–7
siege of Crête-à-Pierrot fort
    35
slave population 33–4
social contexts 33–5
social transformation 39–41
and sovereignty 29
voodoo 37–9
weaponized culture 34–6

Hall, Stuart 224
Hallward, Peter 29
Hampton, Fred 222–3
Hancock, Matt 3
Hardt, Michael 16–17
Harney, George Julian 61–2
Harvey, David 68
Haywood, Bill 102
hegemony, theory of 208
hidden exploitation 209–10
Hill, Christopher 22
Hobsbawm, Eric 51
Hoover, J. Edgar 218, 223
*How Europe Underdeveloped
    Africa* (Rodney) 153–4
Huber, Matthew T. 4
Hughes, Langston 219
Hugo, Victor 73, 83, 110
    Bug-Jargal 38–9
    Les Misérables 70–2
human rights 32
Hunt, Henry 45–6
The Hurricane (Zhou Libo)
    135–6
Hurston, Zora Neale 38
Hutton, Bobby 223

immiseration 28–9, 50, 232,
    236
imperial warfare 49
imperialism 143, 152, 156, 243
independence 14, 29, 45
India 3, 148
industrialization 49–54
revolutionary dialectic 55
inequality 30, 33
*Instructions for an Armed
    Uprising* (Blanqui) 80–2
The Insurrectionist (Vallès) 66
intergenerational misery 228
international solidarity 244
internationalism 106, 113–14,
    116–18

Invisible Committee, the 8
Ireland 62
The Iron Heel (London)
101–6
Islamic fundamentalism 247
Israel 241
Italian Communist Party (PCI)
196, 207
Italy 196–217
Aldo Moro kidnapping
211–12
anti-fascism 196–201, 245
autonomia movement
205–17, 223
fascist rule 196–9
kidnappings 211–12
Mirafiori strikes 203,
206–8
operaismo 202–5
partisans 201
post-war economic boom
200–1
reconstruction 200
Red Brigades 210–12
repression of militants
212–14
uneven development 201
Years of Lead 203, 215–16
Jackson, Jonathan P. 220
Jamaica 33, 43
James, C. L. R. 16, 34, 37, 88,
247, 220, 234–5, 253n33
James, Selma 10
Jameson, Fredric 17–18, 73,
178, 267n10
Japan 145
jobless growth 13
Johnson, Boris 3
Johnson, Cedric, *The Panthers
Won't Save Us Now* 238
Johnson, Joseph 45
Jones, Ernest 61–2
'New World, A Democratic

Poem' 44
Jones, Mother 100–1
Jones, Sarah 3
Josephson, Matthew 93–4

Kamenev, Lev 107
Karl, Rebecca E. 140
Kautsky, Karl 105
Kenya, Mau Mau uprising
168–9
kidnapping 190–1, 211–12
King Ludd 52
Kropotkin, Peter 67–8
Kushner, Rachel 205, 214

'La Marseillaise' 66–8, 87
labour, militarization of 8
labour aristocracy 105, 106
labour-power 206–8
labour wars 96
land rights 5, 183
language 19, 135
of armed conflict 98
of collective opposition
27–8
of patriotic exhortation 49
Lartéguy, Jean, *The Centurions*
161–2, 165
Latin America 2, 106, 137,
170–1, 223, 245
Debray on 185–9
guerrilla warfare 175–6,
180–93
literary culture 176–80
urbanization 190
Le Monde diplomatique
(journal) 1
Lefebvre, Henri 68
left melancholia 246–7
Lenin, V. I. 7, 8, 15, 20, 36,
86–7, 92, 105, 107–8, 122,
125, 152, 245
military writings 108

reading of Leo Tolstoy
109–12, 125–6
and terrorism 164
Les Misérables (Hugo) 70–2
Les Rougon-Macquart (Zola)
72–3
Levellers, the 22–3
Li Lisan 139
liberal aesthetics 39
Life and Fate (Grossman)
125–6
Lin Biao 128, 136, 148
Linebaugh, Peter 49
Lissagaray, Prosper-Olivier 75,
76, 84, 84–5
Lissitzky, El 124
literary expression 19
literary romance 20
literary thinking 19–20
literature
    radicalizing force 224–6,
    226–7
    understanding 18–21
Liu Bang 147
lived experience 14, 224
Loach, Ken 244
London, and 86
London, Jack
    The Iron Heel 101–6
    War of the Classes 101
Lonzi, Carla 215
Louverture, Toussaint 25, 27–8,
    28, 29, 32–3, 36, 36–7,
    39–40, 40–1, 43–4, 228,
    245
Löwy, Michael 47–8, 180
Lozowick, Louis 123
Luddite crisis 49–54
Lukács, Georg 8–9, 47
lumpenproletariat 166
L'Unità 196
Luxemburg, Rosa 12, 15, 78,
    102, 244–5

Macchiarini, Idalgo 211
Maceroni, Colonel Francis,
    *Defensive Instructions to
    the People* 56–7
McLuhan, Marshall 173
Maher, Geo 155
Malcolm X 220, 222, 239
Malevich, Kazimir 123–4
Malm, Andreas 4
Manchester and Salford
    Yeomanry 45–6
Manchester Observer
    (newspaper) 46
Manchester Patriotic Union 45
Mandel, Ernest 200
*Manifesto of the Communist
    Party* (Marx and Engels)
    55
Mao Zedong 7, 8, 20, 78, 152,
    166–7, 186, 218, 245
    and class solidarity 134
    conception of class war
    131–3, 139
    conception of war 131–3
    on decolonial warfare and
    class struggle 143–5
    descriptions of revolution
    134–5
    emphasis on land 130–1
    foundation of People's
    Republic of China 148
    Little Red Book 148–9
    the Long March 140
    'On Contradiction' 142–3
    poetry 130, 146–7
    principal strategies 130–1
    protracted people's war 145,
    145–7, 235
    reading of red classics 132–3
    revolutionary policy 137
    strategy 136–8
Mao Zedong Thought 148–9
Marighella, Carlos 180, 235

Mini-manual of the Urban Guerrilla 190–3
Márquez, Gabriel García, *One Hundred Years of Solitude* 176–9
Martí, José 172
Marx, Eleanor 75
Marx, Karl 6–7, 8, 9, 15, 20, 41, 42, 76, 77, 85–6, 103, 115
  Capital 13–14, 54
  and civil war 165, 252n17
  on class 13–14
  on guerrilla warfare 174–5
  Manifesto of the Communist Party 55
  and revolutionary reinvention 249–50
  on strikes 91–2
'The Masque of Anarchy' (Shelley) 48–9
material conditions 14
Mau Mau uprising, Kenya 168–9
Mayakovsky, Vladimir 114–16
Mbembe, Achille 165
Meinhof, Ulrike 196, 271n54
memory, disarticulation of 247
metaphors 8, 27, 30, 36, 92, 111, 135–6, 179, 216–7, 249
Metropolitan Political Collective 210
Mexico 176
Michel, Louise 19, 71–2, 76–7, 82–4, 245
Miéville, China 9
Milan 197, 210
militarism 84–5
  class-based 114–18
militarization 122, 125, 184, 212, 213

military discipline, and class consciousness 121
military ideology 52
military intervention 118
military substratum, political struggle 198
Milken Institute conference, Beverly Hills 1
Mini-manual of the Urban Guerrilla (Marighella) 190–3
mobile insurrection 95–9
mobilization 13–14
modernity, *longue durée* 21
Mokhtefi, Elaine 160–1
Money (Zola) 73
Monument to the Third International (Tatlin) 123
moral force 60
Moro, Aldo 211–12
Moroni, Primo 201, 206
Morris, William 63–5, 86
  News from Nowhere 65
Moten, Fred 225
Mother (Gorky) 5–6
Mueller, Gavin 51
Mussolini, Benito 196

Napoleon 39, 113, 118, 174–5
Napoleonic Wars 39, 49, 53, 108–12
nation building 155–7
national chauvinism 12, 49, 75
national destiny 170
naturalism 20, 72, 94
Negri, Antonio 16–17, 202–3, 207, 208
neo-colonialism 156
Nersessian, Anahid 48
New Labour 9
New Left Review 241–2
'New World, A Democratic Poem' (Jones) 44

Newcastle upon Tyne 58
News from Nowhere (Morris) 65
Newton, Huey P. 20, 148–9, 189, 222, 223, 226, 226–30, 231, 245
Ngũgĩ. wa Thiong'o 168–9
Nicaragua 176
Nkrumah, Kwame 158
'no war but class war' 243–6
Nordelta, Buenos Aires 4–5
Norris, Frank, *The Octopus* 94–5
North and South (Gaskell) 63, 90
Northern Star (newspaper) 56, 57–8, 58–9, 61–2
novel, the 62–5
nuclear family, the 216–17
Nuclei Armati Proletar 210

Occupy movement 86, 247
O'Connor, Feargus 56
The Octopus, Norris 94–5
'On Contradiction' (Mao Zedong) 142–3
One Hundred Years of Solitude (Márquez) 176–9
operaismo 202–5
Ovetz, Robert 98

Palestine 165, 241
The Panthers Won't Save Us Now (Johnson) 238
Paris, siege of 75–6, 83, 86
Paris Commune 7, 19, 64–5, 66–87, 98
  as anti-war 78
  arrests 84
  background 74–6
  barricades 69
  canon 76–7
  combatants 68–9

Committee for Public Safety 69
  destruction of the grand Vendôme Column 78–9
  fall of 84–5
  first decree 86
  ideological underpinnings 79–82
  'La Marseillaise' rewritten 67
  legacy 85–7
  Louise Michel 82–4
  Marx and Engels on 85–6, 103
  military strategy 68–9
  Montmartre Women's Vigilance Committee 83
  outbreak 76–8
  place in history 74
  role of women 69–70, 76–7, 82–4
  war declared on 78
  Zola and 72–4
patriotism 49, 106, 243
Peace Information Center 218
peasants, mobilization 131–2
Peasants' War, 1524–5 22
Peng Dehuai 130
Peninsular War 174–5
People's Republic of China 148
Périn, René, *The Burning of Cap* 27
Peru 148
Peterloo Massacre 45–9
Pétion, Alexandre 29
Petrograd Soviet, the 107
Pirri, Fiora 207
Planet of Slums (Davis) 190
poetry 62, 246
police brutality 222, 235–6, 239–40
political allegiances 188
political conflict, exploiting 93–4

political power 24, 137
political solidarity 116–17
political struggle, military
    substratum 198
Polverel, Étienne 40
popular support 22–3, 182
prison-industrial complex
    220–1
proletarianization 55
proletariat, the
    class consciousness 8
    expansion of 118
    mobilization 12
    revolutionary 112
    violent overthrow of the
        bourgeoisie 6–7
propaganda 36, 123, 181
protracted people's war 145,
    145–7, 152, 159, 181, 235
psychological warfare 191–2
Putin, Vladimir 241

'Questions of the Loom', Davlin
57

race and racism 39, 106, 224.
    See also Black radicalism
race question, the 234–5
racial capitalism 233, 240
racial justice 2
racial solidarity 157
racial subjugation 91, 225
racialized discipline 221
racialized violence 231–2
railways 95–9
reactionary distress 2
reading 19
radicalizing force 226–7
rebellion 15–16
recruitment 170
Red Army 107–26, 152
    call for internationalism,
        116–18

class-based militarism
    114–18
class-based political education
    126
and constructivist artwork
    122–4
defence of Stalingrad 126
economic base 124–5
formation of 107–8
model of class war 126–7
principles underlying 111–12
Tukhachevsky and 112–14
uniqueness 117, 122
Red Army Faction 165, 194–5,
    200, 210
Red Brigades 210–12
Reform Act of 1832 56
refugees 248–9
Revolution in the Revolution?
    Armed Struggle and
    Political Struggle in Latin
    America (Debray) 185–9
revolutionary affinities 88
revolutionary antagonism 47,
    247–8
revolutionary class 27, 41
revolutionary commitment 196,
    204
revolutionary discipline 111,
    119
revolutionary discourse 6–9,
    125
revolutionary immanence 43,
    47
revolutionary memory 246,
    247
revolutionary necessity 109
revolutionary policy 137
revolutionary proletariat 112
revolutionary reinvention
    249–50
revolutionary romanticism
    47–8

revolutionary slogans 32, 36–7,
    244
revolutionary suicide 227,
    228–9, 231–2
revolutionary traditions 176
Roberts, William Clare 253n33
Robespierre, Maximillian 32
Robinson, Cedric 220
Rodchenko, Alexander 124
Rodney, Walter 114
    *How Europe Underdeveloped
    Africa* 153–4
romanticism 47–8, 63
Rome 201
Ross, Kristin 69, 77
Rousseau, Jean-Jacques 31, 33,
    36–7
    Discourse on Inequality 30
    The Social Contract 29–30
ruling class power 9–10
Russia, Imperial 21, 92, 112,
    114
Russia, invasion of Ukraine
    241–3, 248
Russian Civil War 116, 124
Russian Revolution 19, 86–7,
    107–8, 114, 128, 151–3,
    245
    and literature 108–9
    revolutionary slogans 36
Russo-Japanese War, 1904
    101

Saint-Domingue. *see* Haiti and
    the Haitian Revolution
Saint-Just, Louis Antoine de 32,
    256n15
St Peter's Field massacre 45–9
Sankara, Thomas 155–7, 157
Santiago de Cuba raid 173
Sartre, Jean-Paul 185
Sayre, Robert 47–8
Schleyer, Hanns Martin 194

Schwartz, Alan 1
scorched earth 25–8, 44
Scott, Julius S. 34–5
Scramble for Africa 152–3
Seale, Bobby 148–9, 222, 223,
    226
Serge, Victor 118–22
    The Birth of Our Power
    119–22, 124–5
Sessions, Jennifer E. 159–60
sex, and class 10
Shakur, Assata 20, 226, 230–7,
    245
Shanghai 129, 134
Shelley, Percy Bysshe, 'The
    Masque of Anarchy' 48–9
Shirley (Brontë) 50
Singh, Nikhil Pal 238–9
Sino-Japanese War 145–7
slave narrative genre 225
slavery 30–1, 33–4, 42, 89–90
social antagonism 89–90, 111,
    116, 159, 173, 198
social cohesion 86
The Social Contract, (Rousseau)
    29–30
social factory, the 209
social hierarchy 2
social inertia 110
social interdependence 166–7
social transformation 19,
    39–41, 110, 132, 248
socialism 64
socialist economy 124–5
solidarity 51–2, 53, 104, 121,
    134, 150–1, 166–7, 201
    Africa 167–71
    international 244
    political 116–17
    racial 157
    tricontinental 152
    See also class solidarity
solidarity networks 243

Somerville, Alexander, *Warnings to the People on Street Warfare* 57
'Song for Luddites', Byron 53–4
Sonthonax, Léger-Félicité 40
Soviet avant-gardes 122–4
Spahr, Juliana 246
Spain 247
Sri Lanka 165
Stalin, Josef 36, 112–13, 119, 126
State, and civil society 198
Stella (Bergeaud) 26
Stenberg Brothers 124
Stockholm Peace Appeal 218
Stockport 58
Stolypin, Pyotr 112
strategic essentialism 38
Streeck, Wolfgang 242
strikes 90–2
    America 95, 95–9, 100–1
    The Iron Heel (London) 101–6
    tactics 97
    value of 92
    as war 100
subaltern radicalism 18
suffrage 56
Sun over the Sangkan River (Ding Ling) 138–9
Sun Tzu 147
suprematism 123–4
survival programs 229
Sybil: or The Two Nations, Disraeli 59–60
Symbionese Liberation Army 194

Tatlin, Vladimir 123
temporality 7–8
terrorism 21, 162–5
Thiers, Adolphe 76, 78
Thompson, Dorothy 55, 62

Thompson, E. P. 11–12, 41, 46–7, 252–3n25
Tigray 241
Tolstoy, Leo 125–6
    War and Peace 109–12
Traverso, Enzo 247
tricontinental solidarity 152
Tronti, Mario 207–8
Trotsky, Leon 8, 19, 78, 105–6, 116–18, 120, 125, 152, 245
    advocacy of permanent revolution 126
    anti-fascism 199
    class-based militarism 116–18
    formation of Red Army 107–8
    military writings 108–9
    scale of revolutionary necessity 109
    and terrorism 164–5
Trump, Donald 3
Tukhachevsky, Mikhail 112–14, 118
Turin 197, 203, 206–8
Turner, Nat 222

Ukraine, Russian invasion of 241–3, 248
underdevelopment 153, 163
unemployment 220–1
uneven development 153, 201
Union des Femmes 69
United Kingdom 245
    class relations 59–60
    COVID-19 pandemic 3
    enclosure 47–8
    Luddite crisis 49–54
    suffrage 56
    see also Chartism; Peterloo Massacre
United States of America 88–106

Index

African American
politicization 224
army of the wronged 218–40
Black Liberation Army 194,
224, 231–7, 239
Black Lives Matter movement
237–40
Black Panthers 148–9,
222–4, 226–30, 230–1,
237, 239
Black radicalism 218–40,
245
capitalism 92–5
capitalist class 93–4
caste system 227
Civil War 88–90, 93
class militancy 89
COVID-19 pandemic 3
Gilded Age 21, 245
global hegemony 93
The Iron Heel (London)
101–6
labour wars 96
Paint Creek-Cabin Creek
strike 100–1
penal system 220–1, 234
police brutality 222, 235–6,
239–40
political disturbance, summer
2020 1–2
racial subjugation 91
racialized violence 2,
231–2
rail strikes of 1877 95–9,
103, 104
revolutionary militancy
220–4
slave rebellion, 1865 89–90,
103, 104
strikes 95
survival programs 229
United States Strike Commission
100

The Unseen (Balestrini)
212–14
urban warfare 70–4, 189–93,
194–5, 235. see also Paris
Commune
urbanization 68, 190

Vallès, Jules, The Insurrectionist
66–87
Varoufakis, Yanis 3
Venezuela 176, 190
Vietnam 148
Vietnam War 194
violence
Fanon on 166–7
and immiseration 28–9
voodoo 37–9, 228

war and warfare
and capitalism 63–4
and class 108–12, 118–22,
131–3
and class solidarity 189
of manoeuvre 199
of movement 202–3, 204
object of 61–2
of position 199, 202–3, 204
War and Peace (Tolstoy)
109–12
War of the Classes (London)
101

Warnings to the People on Street
Warfare (Somerville) 57
Watkins, Susan 241–2
We Want Everything (Balestrini)
203–5, 212
wealth redistribution 1
Weather Underground 165, 194
Whitman, Walt 86
Williams, Eric, Capitalism and
Slavery 42
Williams, Robert F. 222

Winstanley, Gerrard 23
women
  emancipation 69
  exploitation 217
  gendered exclusions 214–17
  Paris Commune role 69–70,
    76–7, 82–4
Wood, Ellen Meiksins 12–13
Wood, Tony 242, 243
Wordsworth, William 43
worker-peasant alliance 189
World War One 107, 118–19
World War Two 126, 157–8,
  199
The Wretched of the Earth
  (Fanon) 165, 165–7
Wright, Erik Olin 11
Wright, Richard 220
Wright, Steve 201

xenophobia 243
Xiang Yu 147

Yemen 241
Yu Xin 147

ZAD movement 86
Zelensky, Volodymyr 242
Zetkin, Clara 10
Zhou Libo, *The Hurricane*
  135–6
Zhu De 130
Zinoviev, Grigory 107
Zola, Émile
  The Debacle 73
  Germinal 73, 90–1
  Les Rougon-Macquart 72–3
  Money 73